OTHER BOOKS BY
D. JAMES KENNEDY

WHAT IF THE BIBLE HAD NEVER BEEN WRITTEN?

D. JAMES KENNEDY
AND JERRY NEWCOMBE

THOMAS NELSON PUBLISHERS
Nashville
Printed in the United States of America

Published in association with the literary agency of Alive Communications, 1465 Kelly Johnson Blvd., Suite #320, Colorado Springs, CO 80920.

Published in Nashville, Tennessee, by Thomas Nelson, Inc., Publishers.

Unless otherwise noted, Scripture quotations are from THE NEW KING JAMES VERSION. Copyright © 1979, 1980, 1982, 1990, Thomas Nelson, Inc., Publishers.

Scripture quotations noted NIV are from the HOLY BIBLE: NEW INTERNATIONAL VERSION®. Copyright © 1973, 1978, 1984 by International Bible Society. Used by permission of Zondervan Publishing House.

Scripture quotations noted KJV are from the KING JAMES VERSION.

Library of Congress Cataloging-in-Publication Data

Kennedy, D. James (Dennis James), 1930–
    What if the Bible had never been written? / D. James Kennedy and Jerry Newcombe.
       p. cm.
    Includes bibliographical references and index.
    ISBN 0-7852-7154-6
    1. Bible—Influence—Western civilization. I. Newcombe, Jerry. II. Title.
BS538.7.K46 1998
220—dc21   98–12298
                                                        CIP

Printed in the United States of America
1 2 3 4 5 6 BVG 02 01 00 99 98 97

To my faithful secretary of many years,

Mrs. Mary Anne Bunker,

*who has enabled me to complete
the manifold tasks that I face each year.*

CONTENTS

ACKNOWLEDGMENTS

There are a few people we need to thank for their involvement in this project. First of all, thanks go to Mary Anne Bunker, Ruth Rohm, and Nancy Britt for their secretarial help. Also, thanks are due to Kirsti Newcombe and Mary Hesson for assisting with a couple of chapters. Another person who deserves much credit is a brilliant young scholar and budding writer, R. Matthew Wray, who came up with outstanding research in the realms of law, literature, discovery, and science.

Thanks are also due once again to Robert Folsom for his editing of the initial manuscript of this book. In addition, thanks are due to Greg Johnson of the literary agency of Alive Communications and Rick Nash, who together helped bring this book to birth in the first place.

PREFACE

We live in a time when the history books have been rewritten; when Christianity is widely held by the intelligentsia to be a repressive force; when the Bible is viewed as a means of oppression, not liberation. But the facts of history tell a different story.

The purpose of this book is to set the record straight: to show that the Bible has been an unmatched force for good. This book is the third in a series on how to address our culture's current backlash against historic Christianity. It supplements two earlier books by the same authors: *What If Jesus Had Never Been Born?* (1994) and *The Gates of Hell Shall Not Prevail* (1996).

What If Jesus Had Never Been Born? documents how Christ has transformed much of the world in a multitude of ways. That book was well received by many different Christian leaders, both in the United States and in other countries. Here's an analysis from *Christian Book Review:*

> The wide range of sources cited, including critics of Christianity, adds
> substantial support to the authors' conclusions. . . . In a day when
> Bible-believing Christians are frequently portrayed as those who
> would destroy freedom, liberty, and education, a clear understanding
> of the positive contributions of Christianity throughout the ages is
> important for all believers. *What If Jesus Had Never Been Born?* is an
> excellent resource that covers a broad range of topics clearly and care-
> fully documents how the followers of Jesus Christ have benefited the
> human societies that they have impacted. This book reminds us that
> although the historical record of the actions of Christ's followers is not
> perfect, it stands up favorably in comparison with the influence of any
> other religion or philosophy on the planet![1]

The next book in this series, *The Gates of Hell Shall Not Prevail*, documents the anti-Christian bigotry held by many in our world today and spells out practical steps to deal with that bias. "But the authors," observes Dr. George Grant in *World* magazine, "have not simply collected another litany of modern woes. They throw the searchlights of history and scripture on our contemporary concerns, offering us a theology of hope and an agenda of action."[2] Dr. Ted Baehr, writing in his publication *Movieguide,* says this about *The Gates of Hell Shall Not Prevail:*

This book is a practical volume that shows Christians how to deal with the culture and become more than conquerors. As soon as you read it, you will want your friends to read it. This book helps us to understand that for two thousand years a battle has raged between the Church and the forces of darkness for the hearts of mankind. However, no matter what tactics or weapons evil has used, the Church has been and always shall be victorious.[3]

What If the Bible Had Never Been Written? is also geared toward equipping and building up Christians at a time when Christianity is "politically incorrect." Like the other two books in this series, the authors trust this book will provide more fodder for those trying to reclaim our world for Christ, more fodder for those engaged on the Christian side in the "culture wars." This new book continues to explore in greater depth the theme of *What If Jesus Had Never Been Born?* It documents numerous ways, not explored in the earlier book, in which Christianity has benefited humanity. As in the two earlier works, the authors have made it their aim to cite a wide variety of sources—including many secular sources—to make their points.

OVERVIEW OF THIS BOOK

Part 1 of *What If the Bible Had Never Been Written?*, titled "The Bible and Civilization," highlights the many ways the Book of books has changed our world. It begins with an introduction to the whole book. After the introduction comes a chapter on the Bible and morality. As Abraham Lincoln put it, "But for [the Bible], we could not know right from wrong."[4] The following chapter looks at how the Bible has changed society by transforming the human heart—where true change always begins.

From there the book moves into a discussion of the Bible and law. For many centuries, Western law has been based on biblical law. Much of what is right in our justice system comes from the influence of the Bible. Then, because many people feel the two don't mix, the next chapter will deal with the issue of the Bible and politics. Some of our strongest, positive social movements have had their origins in the Holy Bible. Following that information, the authors offer a penetrating look at the Bible and its role in shaping the United States, including its founding documents.

The next chapter focuses on the Bible and science. Modern man doesn't realize the incredible contribution the Bible made to the birth of modern science. Many of the early great scientists were influenced by the Bible, a fact documented here in detail. As scientists, they believed that in probing the laws of the universe, they were—in the words of the great astronomer Johannes Kepler—"thinking God's thoughts after him."

Next comes an analysis of the Bible's impact on literature. From Dante to Shakespeare, from Milton to Bunyan, from Dickens to Dostoevsky, the Scriptures have influenced literature like no other book.

The following two chapters tell how the Bible has helped shape various parts of our world, affecting both missionary efforts and exploration. The Word of God often inspired death-defying voyages and arduous travels for the purpose of spreading its message. Those journeys in turn ended up opening remote pockets of the world to the rest of civilization.

Many aspects of our everyday life have their roots in some aspect of the Bible, or began in organizations that are Bible-based, or originated with an individual who was inspired by the Good Book. For example, common phrases such as "brother's keeper" or "the second mile" come right out of the pages of Holy Writ. And the popular game of basketball was invented in a Massachusetts chapter of the Bible-centered YMCA (at a time when that organization was thoroughly Christian). The final chapter of Part 1 focuses on how the Bible has affected such everyday things.

Part 2 of the book, "How I Know the Bible is the Word of God," begins with a chapter on the incredible evidences that authenticate the Bible as the Word of God. Next comes a look at the central message of the Bible—the eternally significant accomplishments of Christ our Savior. Afterward, we'll see how the Book of books is the key to spiritual growth.

The final chapter includes a discussion of the challenges facing the further dissemination of the message of the Bible to the world and a look at the Bible and revival. The only real hope for our world is spiritual revival.

The authors pray that this book will bolster your faith and help you to get a glimpse of just how influential the Scriptures have been and continue to be. May God bless you as you embark on this journey to learn more about the greatest book the world has ever known!

PART 1

THE BIBLE AND CIVILIZATION

CHAPTER 1

THE BOOK
OF BOOKS

"Forever, O LORD,
Your word is settled in heaven."

—Psalm 119:89

The Bible's name actually means "Book of books," for it is not only one book; it is sixty-six books in one, sixty-six love letters from God to us. Their diversity is amazing: these sixty-six books were written by about forty different authors, living on several different continents, in the nations of Palestine, Babylon, Greece, Rome, Asia Minor, and perhaps Arabia. They wrote in different languages—Hebrew, Greek, and Aramaic—and were separated in time by some sixteen centuries! (That's like going from our time all the way back to Mohammed's day!) Yet the Bible tells the same story from beginning to end. There's a golden thread that weaves through it.

THE BIBLE'S INCREDIBLE UNITY

We begin in the book of Genesis in a garden—in paradise. There is the Tree of Knowledge of Good and Evil. We end in the book of Revelation, again in the paradise of God, where there is a tree. In the beginning man is driven out because of his sin and forbidden to eat of the tree. At the end he is invited to come in and partake of the tree that he might live forever. We began in a garden where there was a river. We end in paradise where there is a river that flows from the throne of God. The same doctrines are taught throughout the Bible. The same person, Jesus Christ, is the central theme of the Bible: it is about Him. It builds to His coming, describes it, and interprets what it means. The golden thread is the redemption of sinful man by the grace of God through faith in the shed blood of the Redeemer.

Keep in mind that no human publisher commissioned the writing of such a book. No editor set forth a plan; no editorial committee oversaw its development; no one distributed an outline to the different authors. Despite these facts, there is every sort of literature in the Bible, including prose and poetry; history and law; biography and travel; genealogies, theologies, and philosophies. And somehow, all of these elements combine to provide an incredible unity from Genesis to Revelation.[1]

Suppose that forty different artists were to paint a picture without having any idea what the others might be doing—or that others were doing anything at all. Imagine someone collecting these pieces and arranging them all upon a huge wall, and the result was a perfect picture that displayed all the features of Jesus Christ.

Or suppose that forty different sculptors, without any knowledge of what the others were doing, each decided to create a piece of sculpture. And when the pieces were brought together, they formed an exquisite statue of Christ. These outcomes are incomprehensible, yet the Bible is a greater accomplishment by far.

No other book in all the world has ever been made in this way. Having written a number of books, I know what publishers and editors and editorial committees do. None of this process was involved in writing the Bible. But we see in this book an incredible unity that testifies that the hand that made this book is divine. Writer James C. Hefley says, "The sixty-six books are a perfect whole, a purposeful revelation, a progressive proof that the Bible is more than the work of fallible men."[2]

WHAT IF THE BIBLE HAD NEVER BEEN WRITTEN?

The impact of the Bible on our culture, on our nation, on world history has been enormous. Author and former Yale professor William Lyons Phelps observed, "Our civilization is founded upon the Bible. More of our ideas, our wisdom, our philosophy, our literature, our art, our ideals come from the Bible than from all other books combined."[3]

But what if the Bible had never been written? That's a frightening thought! And yet, with Christian-bashing the only safe form of bigotry in practice today, it seems that many people wish that were the case. The purpose of this book is to show that the overall impact of the Bible on civilization has been overwhelmingly positive.

THE BIBLE HAS INSPIRED PEOPLE FROM ALL WALKS OF LIFE

People from various backgrounds with various positions in life have profited from the Word of God. The great English philosopher John Locke, whose political writings contributed enormously to American democracy, once said, "The Bible is one of the greatest blessings bestowed by God on the children of men. It has God for its author, salvation for its end, and truth without any mixture for its matter. It is all pure, all sincere; nothing too much; nothing wanting."[4]

- General Robert E. Lee, one of the greatest military men America ever produced, said, "In all my perplexities and distresses, the Bible has never failed to give me light and strength."[5]
- Psychologist William James said, "The Bible contains more true sublimity, more exquisite beauty, more morality, more important history, and finer strains of poetry and eloquence than can be collected from all other books, in whatever age or language they may have been written."[6]
- Napoleon Bonaparte, the great conqueror, said, "The Bible is no mere book, but a living power that conquers all that oppose it."[7]
- Sir William Gladstone, among the greatest prime ministers England ever had, said, "I have known ninety-five great men of the world in my time. And of these, eighty-seven were followers of the Bible."[8]
- President John Quincy Adams said, "The Bible is the book of all others to read at all ages and in all conditions of human life; not to be read once, or twice, or thrice through, and then laid aside; but to be read in small portions of one or two chapters a day."[9]
- Immanuel Kant, philosopher not known for orthodox religion, said, "The existence of the Bible as a book for the people is the greatest benefit which the human race has ever experienced."[10]
- Ruth Bell Graham said, "If our children have the background of a godly, happy home and this unshakable faith that the Bible is indeed the Word of God, they will have a foundation that the forces of hell cannot shake."[11]
- Reid Buckley, who trains professional speakers and who is the brother of William F. Buckley Jr., said, "Any born English-speaking son or daughter of the Christian West, who has not savored, indeed, soaked him- or herself in the King James Version of the Holy Bible is irreparably ignorant and culturally deprived."[12]

And on and on it goes.

In fact, read what the late professor Allan Bloom wrote in his block-buster book *The Closing of the American Mind* about his Jewish grandparents who were "ignorant people by our standards" and yet were very well educated in the Bible compared to people of today:

> I do not believe that my generation, my cousins who have been educated in the American way, all of whom are M.D.s or Ph.D.s, have any comparable learning. When they talk about heaven and earth, the relations between men and women, parents and children, the human condition, I hear nothing but cliches, superficialities, the material of satire. . . . A life based on the Book is closer to the truth. . . . The Bible is not the only means to furnish a mind, but without a book of similar gravity, read with the gravity of the potential believer, it will remain unfurnished.[13]

CHRIST IS THE KEY

Let us not forget the reason the Bible was written and preserved: "that you may know that you have eternal life" (1 John 5:13). Christ is the key to the inspiration of the Bible. This is why the books of the Old and New Testament fit together so well into one cohesive whole. Taken together, they present the progressive unfolding of Christ:

> The Law gives the *foundation* for Christ.
> History shows the *preparation* for Christ.
> Poetry expresses *aspiration* for Christ.
> Prophecy proclaims an *expectation* of Christ.
> The Gospels record the historical *manifestation* of Christ.
> Acts relates the *propagation* of Christ.
> The Epistles give the *interpretation* of Christ.
> Revelation describes the *consummation* of all things in Christ.[14]

Christ is indeed the key to the Bible, and it is His salvation message that we are commanded to proclaim to the world. No other means than the global distribution of the Bible has been more effective at spreading the good news.

THE WORLD'S NUMBER ONE BEST-SELLER

To speak of the Bible is to speak in superlatives. It is the most published and most widely read book in the world. It is the number one

best-seller in the world and has been for centuries. It is the most widely
translated book on the planet. Even as you read these words, there are
missionaries around the world studying various languages in order to
translate the Bible, or portions of it, into that tongue. Those missionaries may even be the first to put that language in writing! Such work has
gone on for centuries. Hundreds of the world's languages first appeared
in writing thanks to the Bible.[15] In the past five hundred years, since the
time of Johannes Gutenberg, the Bible has been published in 2,123 different languages and dialects.[16]

Even in those places where the Bible has been forbidden, there is a
great hunger for the Word of God. Just recently in Cuba, the Communist dictatorship has allowed the sale of the Bible. The United Bible
Societies reports:

> Since 1993, we have been allowed to put Bibles in every library in the
> country, also under the Ministry of Culture, and this year [1996], as in
> '92 and '94, we were able to distribute the Bible at the International
> Book Fair, where once again, it was the best-selling book. For us, it is
> very interesting that people who do not belong to a church buy this
> Bible in the Book Fair. . . . There is something like an explosion in
> Cuba because everyone wants to have a Bible.[17]

How important is the Bible to those who don't have a copy but would
like one? We in America often take the Scriptures for granted. We usually have more than one copy, and we don't realize how precious a copy
of the Bible is for those who don't have one. For example, I read recently
about a remote village in Indonesia named Seko Rongkong, where many
Christians had to share just one Bible among all the church members.
Then they heard about free Bibles available to them in their language;
the only catch was they had to walk all the way to Sapah to get them.
Yet Sapah was far away—a seven-day walk! So a delegate of seven
hearty souls walked all the way, picked up the fifteen heavy boxes and
carried them all the way back to their village! The United Bible Societies reports that this loving act brought much joy to the villagers: "There
was great excitement in Seko Rongkong when the travelers returned
with three hundred Indonesian Bibles—enough for everyone in the village!"[18] No other book inspires this kind of incredible excitement and
commitment. The Bible is indeed the Book of books.

In their *World Annual Report 1995*, the United Bible Societies describes
their worldwide distribution of the Bible, or portions of it, for that year
(November 1, 1994, to October 31, 1995). They distributed 17.7 million copies of the whole Bible, 11 million copies of "Testaments," 27
million copies of portions of the Bible, 17 million copies of "New Reader

Portions" and 452 million copies of "Selections" from the Bible![19] Their work goes on in more than two hundred countries around the world.[20] What other book can come anywhere near to such worldwide distribution? The chart reporting this distribution states that these figures "do not include distribution by other publishers."[21] The Bible is *far and away* the world's best-seller.

In America we see a huge number of consumer dollars spent on the Scriptures. The average annual sales of Bibles in the United States is roughly $200 million![22] The United Bible Societies laments, "It is thought that nine out of ten Americans own a Bible, but fewer than half read it."[23] But wait a minute. The population of the United States is about 270 million; that means the Bible has slightly more than 120 million readers in this country alone! What book could even come anywhere close in readership?

Recently, a report on network TV sneered that the Bible was the most widely distributed book, but the least read. The report was wrong. The Princeton Religious Research Center, associated with the Gallup poll organization, has found that 11 percent of the American population read the Bible *every day*. They found that 22 percent read the Bible weekly; 14 percent monthly; and 26 percent less than monthly.[24] Granted, those numbers could be higher, but even so, we see that nearly half of Americans (126,900,000 people) read the Bible sometime during the month. Certainly no other book is read as often. The Bible is the world's best-seller.

THE COLLEGE QUESTIONS

Why do so many people read the Bible? Of course, it is because it is the Word of God. People also read the Bible because it answers life's deepest questions. Perhaps you've heard of "the college questions"— so called because they're often asked on college campuses. Perhaps you've asked them yourself:

Who am I?
Why am I here?
Where did I come from?
What is my purpose?
What is the significance of my life?
Where am I going?
What is my destiny?
What should I do?
How should I live?

The Bible answers all these questions. It has answers that are found nowhere else in the world. And it contains about eight thousand promises that we can count on. In Joshua 1:8, we read that if we rely on the Bible as a source of wisdom and seek to follow it, then it will make us prosperous and successful in everything we do. In Philippians 4:19, God promises to meet the believer's needs through Christ Jesus. In James 1:5, we're promised that if we ask for wisdom from God, He will grant it. A promise is only as good as the one who makes the promise. When God promises us something, it's as good as done. Our job is to learn those promises and apply them to our lives.

"NO MAN IS POOR OR DESOLATE WHO HAS THIS TREASURE FOR HIS OWN"

Henry Van Dyke, a Presbyterian clergyman and author who lived around the turn of the century, once wrote a profound short essay on the Bible and its influence in the world, including its usefulness in life and in death. I close this chapter with his beautiful prose:

The Bible
Henry Van Dyke
Born in the East and clothed in Oriental form and imagery, the Bible walks the ways of all the world with familiar feet and enters land after land to find its own everywhere. It comes to the palace to tell the monarch that he is a servant of the Most High, and into the cottage to assure the peasant that he can be a son of God. Children listen to its stories with wonder and delight, and wise men ponder them as parables of life.

It has a word of peace for the time of peril, a word of comfort for the time of calamity, a word of light for the hope of darkness. Its oracles are repeated in the assembly of the people, and its counsels whispered in the ear of the lonely. The wicked and the proud tremble at its warnings, but to the wounded and penitent it has a mother's voice.

No man is poor or desolate who has this treasure for his own. When the landscape darkens and the trembling pilgrim comes to the valley named of the shadow, he is not afraid to enter; he takes the rod and staff of Scripture in his hand, he says to his friend and comrade, "Goodbye, we shall meet again"; and comforted by that support, he goes toward the lonely pass as one who walks through darkness into light.[25]

CHAPTER 2

THE BIBLE AND MORALITY

"Do not be deceived, God is not mocked; for whatever a man sows, that he will also reap."

—Galatians 6:7

Abraham Lincoln once received a cherished gift. It was the Holy Bible given to him by a delegation of black Americans. The date was September 7, 1864, and at that time Lincoln made a memorable statement about the Holy Scriptures: "In regard to this great book, I have but to say, it is the best gift God has given to men. All the good the Savior gave to the world was communicated through this book. *But for it we could not know right from wrong.*"[1]

The Bible has given the world the highest code of morality known to man. Had the Bible never been written, we would never have known about the moral perfection of Jesus Christ; we would never have received the most sublime moral code given to man; indeed, man may never have graduated from the time where "every man did that which was right in his *own* eyes" (Judg. 21:25 KJV, emphasis mine). The Bible has undergirded Western civilization's moral code for more than a thousand years. In more recent times, as the Bible has become less important to our cultural elites, as it has been dramatically kicked out of our schools, as it has been denigrated and mocked by our celebrities, we have begun to revert to doing that which is right in our own eyes! Part of the purpose of this chapter, then, will be to expose the myth that we can have morality without the Bible's standards of conduct.

JESUS IS THE MODEL OF MORAL PERFECTION

Have you ever noticed that our noblest heroes suffer by careful examination? Many times I have come to admire a historical figure and have devoted myself to examining the person, only to discover the inevitable feet of clay. One could look at George Washington, a noble and generally wonderful man, and then discover that he not only tolerated slavery, but he owned slaves! The most noble humans all have their foibles and weaknesses.

Yet as we examine the major figure of the Bible, what do we learn? Jesus is the Altogether Lovely One. He has no peer. Whom shall we set alongside of Jesus of Nazareth? Will it be Mohammed, Buddha, Laotse, Kung Fu-tse (Confucius), Gandhi, the Dalai Lama? There is no one like Him. Which of the religious leaders, for example, died for the sins of the people? Which, indeed, rose from the dead? Which have followers who even make such a claim? There are none!

Jesus never confessed a sin. This is astonishing! It is axiomatic in the spiritual realm that the holiest of men have been those who were most conscious of their sin and guilt. Isaiah abhorred himself when he saw the living God and said, "I am a man of unclean lips" (Isa. 6:5). Peter said, "Depart from me, for I am a sinful man" (Luke 5:8). And Paul said, "Christ Jesus came into the world to save sinners, of whom I am chief" (1 Tim. 1:15). But Jesus confessed no sin, for He had none.

Every person who has ever lived has been a sinner—except Jesus. He is the only perfect human being ever to grace the planet. He even said to His enemies, "Which of you convicts Me of sin?" (John 8:46). When they finally did get people to accuse Him of sin, their accusations were all contradictory and such palpably false charges that Jesus didn't even respond to them. He amazed Pilate with His silence:

And the chief priests accused Him of many things, but He answered nothing. Then Pilate asked Him again, saying, "Do You answer nothing? See how many things they testify against You!" But Jesus still answered nothing, so that Pilate marveled. (Mark 15:3–5)

JESUS' MORALITY

Jesus was the first person in history to articulate the golden rule. He said, "And just as you want men to do to you, you also do to them likewise" (Luke 6:31). Through the ages millions have held up the example of Christ's golden rule. Compare it to the world's golden rule—"He who has the gold makes the rules."

Read the words of a few sages on the impact of Christ's morality on humankind. Immanuel E. Fichte said, "Jesus did more than all other philosophers in bringing heavenly morality into the hearts and homes of common men."[2] William Jennings Bryan said of Jesus, "Reared in the home of a carpenter, never having access to the wisdom of the past, never coming in contact with the sages of other lands, and yet, when only thirty years of age He gave to the world a code of morality the like of which the world has never seen."[3]

Thomas Jefferson, who did not believe that Jesus was God, nevertheless had a very high regard for His morality. He even wrote a book, *The Life and Morals of Jesus,* in order to cull out the moral teachings of Christ. Jefferson wanted to separate these teachings from Christ's miracles (a fruitless and misguided task—remove Jesus' divinity and He no longer is Savior). Jefferson described the moral system of ethics that Jesus gave us as "the most sublime and benevolent code of morals which has been offered to man."[4]

Listen to what psychiatrist J. T. Fisher and coauthor L. S. Hawley say in their book *A Few Buttons Missing* about Jesus' morality as expressed in the Sermon on the Mount:

> If you were to take the sum total of all authoritative articles ever written by the most qualified of psychologists and psychiatrists on the subject of mental hygiene—if you were to combine them and refine them and cleave out the excess verbiage—if you were to take the whole of the meat and none of the parsley, and if you were to have these unadulterated bits of pure scientific knowledge concisely expressed by the most capable of living poets, you would have an awkward and incomplete summation of the sermon on the mount. And it would suffer immeasurably through comparison. For nearly two thousand years, the Christian world has been holding in its hands the complete answer to its restless and fruitless yearnings. Here . . . rest the blueprints for successful human life with optimum mental health and contentment.[5]

Jesus constructed His moral system on the Old Testament base and expanded it. The moral code that God revealed to Israel, Jesus took and treated more thoroughly. Because of Jesus, the divine revelation that God gave the Jews spread throughout the world. Had Jesus never come and the New Testament never been written, the vast majority of humankind would know nothing of the Old Testament. It would just be the sacred writings of a wandering and obscure nation. Instead, because of Christianity, both the Old and New Testaments, with their higher codes of morality, have now gone out into all the world! Benjamin Disraeli, one of the great British prime ministers of the last century, said:

> The pupil of Moses may ask himself whether all the princes of the House of David have done so much for Jews as that Prince who was crucified. . . .
>
> Had it not been for [Jesus], the Jews would have been comparatively unknown, or known only as a high Oriental Caste which had lost its country. Has not He made their history the most famous history in the world?
>
> The wildest dreams of their Rabbis have been far exceeded. Has not Jesus conquered Europe and changed its name to Christendom? All countries that refuse the cross wilt, and the time will come when the countless myriads of America and Australia will find music in the Songs of Zion, and solace in the parables of Galilee.[6]

As Christianity spread into various nations on the earth, the message of the Bible spread the most transforming code of ethics man has ever known. We documented this in Chapter 11 of our previous book *What If Jesus Had Never Been Born?*

AN EXAMPLE OF THE BIBLE'S IMPACT ON MORALITY

Consider one of the most famous examples of how the Bible has impacted morality. The Bible helped prick the conscience of a nation that had gone astray on a particular issue—slavery! American slavery is an inexcusable chapter of our past. With 20/20 hindsight, we can see how appalling it was for major elements of society to tolerate slavery. While it's true that some slaveholders and even some pastors in the South used the Bible to justify slavery, in truth, the Bible played a major role in the dissolution of "the peculiar institution."

There were always Christians in America opposed to slavery. Just as the Bible was the motivation for William Wilberforce's lifelong crusade against slavery and the slave trade in the British Empire (as we'll see in Chapter 5, "The Bible and Politics"), so the Bible inspired most of America's abolitionists. For example, two-thirds of the members of the abolition society in 1835 were ministers of the gospel.[7] Many of the courageous people who ran the Underground Railroad were Quakers. There was an antipathy toward slavery on the part of some Christians in the South, most notably Robert E. Lee (who fought for the South to protect his "native Virginia"). President Lincoln said in his first Inaugural Address: "Intelligence, patriotism, Christianity, and a firm reliance on Him who has never yet forsaken this favored land, are still competent to adjust, in the best way, all our present difficulty."[8]

The Bible also influenced the moral opposition to American slavery through a book that helped to increase awareness of the situation to millions. I refer to *Uncle Tom's Cabin* by Harriet Beecher Stowe, the daughter of a minister. One encyclopedia writes, "No book has had a more direct and powerful influence on American history than Mrs. Stowe's *Uncle Tom's Cabin*."[9] That claim is probably an overstatement; nonetheless, it's astounding that this historically significant novel is today both maligned and misunderstood — and unread, I might add. Primarily because it's so politically incorrect today, *Uncle Tom's Cabin* is virtually ignored or held up to ridicule. This attitude is just another example of our history being rewritten to conform to the ideas of the politically correct crowd. Revisionist history notwithstanding, when *Uncle Tom's Cabin* was first published in 1852, it had a profound influence on the nation's tolerance of slavery. And the Bible unquestionably influenced both the author and her work. The Bible was even important to the book's protagonist, Uncle Tom. English professor John Adams writes this of Stowe's classic novel:

> Slavery, in its criminal regard of human souls as mere property, was, she thought, a relation different in kind from the woes of ordinary life. Uncle Tom took issue with his creator upon this point, for she showed his basic tragedy to be that he was a true Christian among the heathen; and he himself rightly regarded slavery as only one added indignity. A certain "unfashionable old book," from which he read solely in the New Testament, separated him more completely from his fellow men than either color or servitude.[10]

Near the beginning of the novel one of the minor characters says, "I ain't no Christian like you, Eliza; my heart's full of bitterness; I can't trust in God. Why does he let things be so?" She responds, "O, George, we must have faith. Mistress says that when all things go wrong to us, we must believe that God is doing the very best."[11] This roughly parallels the classic promise of Romans 8:28, "And we know that all things work together for good to those who love God, to those who are the called according to His purpose."

Consider also these poignant closing words of the story by Stowe:

> If this persecuted race, with every discouragement and disadvantage, have done thus much, how much more they might do, if the Christian church would act towards them in the spirit of her Lord. . . . Both

North and South have been guilty before God; and the *Christian church* has a heavy account to answer.[12]

Even more than a hundred years after *Uncle Tom's Cabin* shook the nation, these words are still thought-provoking. Interestingly, there is still slavery in certain regions of the world *today*. I guarantee you it exists in those quarters where the Bible is forbidden, where bounties are placed on the heads of those who open the Judeo-Christian Scriptures. In recent years, Christians from the African country of Sudan have been kidnapped by Muslims and sold into slavery in Northern Sudan, Libya, and Saudi Arabia. The media's silence on this subject has been deafening. Louis Farrakhan, who has denounced slavery with great fervor, has denied that it exists among some of the Arab nations (which, by the way, grant him money); but the existence of slavery today in some Muslim countries has been well documented.[13]

WHY CAN'T WE HAVE MORALITY WITHOUT RELIGION?

We cannot have morality without religion. Yet this premise seems to be virtually alien to many Americans today. "What? You cannot have morality without religion? Absurd!" they say.

Why is it that we can't have morality without religion? Let me make a couple of things clear. There are some people who are irreligious who live reasonably decent sorts of lives, but when they do, they merely borrow Christian ethics. Dr. Erwin Lutzer, pastor of the Moody Memorial Church in Chicago and author of *Exploding the Myths That Could Destroy America*, writes with great lucidity:

> An atheist's logic tells him that he is of no more value than a baboon or a grain of sand, yet his life contradicts such a conclusion. He may provide for his wife and family, and if you were to steal his car he would want you to be punished—all this because he is created in the image of God.
>
> We have not yet seen the full result of humanism in the United States. *We are still coasting on the values derived from our rich Judeo-Christian heritage.*[14]

The Lack of Inclination to Follow Man's Code of Ethics

The first reason you can't have morality without religion is not that you can't draw up a common code of ethics. It is that without an external authority, most people will not follow it. Now, I will grant that the humanists have drawn up a code, and they have gotten *some* people to follow it. Twice in this century, once in the 1930s and later in the 1970s, humanistic luminaries have met together to lay out their vision for society. Their plans have been written up in *The Humanist Manifestos I and II.* For example, they write in their second manifesto: "We affirm that moral values derive their source from human experience. Ethics is autonomous and situational, needing no theological or ideological sanction."[15] Situational ethics means that what's wrong in one situation may be right in another situation. "And every man did that which was right in his own eyes."

Many of the humanists' goals have been realized in America's public schools. They have managed to throw the Bible out of the schools. But the result has not been what they imagined! By every conceivable criterion, our public schools are a mess, and the banishing of our rich Judeo-Christian heritage in the schools has everything to do with it.

What's noteworthy about the *Humanist Manifesto* is that as humanists drew up their set of ethics, what they essentially did was turn Christian ethics upside down. They took everything that has been considered immoral for centuries and declared it to be moral. So their "ethics" condone gambling, divorce, suicide, free love, fornication, adultery, incest, euthanasia, and a number of other things—all of which for centuries have been considered immoral acts. It is undoubtedly a popular move to take a list of immoral acts and call that morality! It has never been difficult to get people to follow the path of immorality. The hard thing is to get them to follow the path of morality.

A few years ago media mogul and humanist Ted Turner said it was time to abandon the Ten Commandments, which he called obsolete. Instead, he pontificated, we needed an updated version. He came up with such a list, which he called the Ten Voluntary Initiatives.[16] Question: Even if you remember that news story, can you name even *one* of these new pseudo-commands? If you could name all ten of them, do you know anyone who keeps them and lives by them—in the way that millions actually hold up the Ten Commandments as a moral guide for their lives? People can come up with all sorts of lists of moral dos and don'ts. But what is morally binding about these lists? Nothing. If there's no God, there's no accountability. As Dostoevsky said, "If God does not exist, everything is permissable."[17]

"Our Morality Can't Be Imposed on Others"

The second reason you can't maintain morality without religion is because you cannot impose your morality on others. This is the very argument the humanists are always making.

I have never in my life attempted to impose my morality on anyone else because, you see, I have no morality that I have created—unlike the humanist and the atheist. They have been extremely successful in imposing their set of ethics and morals (or lack of them) on other people. The only way they succeed at all in doing so is by legal enforcement. Eventually that leads to tyranny—a despot enforcing laws on a people who otherwise have descended completely into anarchy.

I was in the Senate several years ago when the Family Protection Act was introduced as legislation. It was a rather long bill that had quite a few articles in it. It was designed to protect the integrity of the family, which is under great attack in our time from all sorts of different forces. Each of the various articles in this bill was based on some moral view of what the family should be. This bill was viciously attacked by people who were antifamily because it put them in a very difficult position. They promoted legislation that hurt the family, causing the further disintegration of the traditional family. So we see that morality as it concerns the family *is* going to be legislated. As the family goes, so goes society. Therefore, the question always comes down to this: Whose morality, God's or man's? Are we going to have a Christian nation—a nation under God—or a humanist nation—a nation under man?

In the humanist state there is nothing but man. The rights of individual citizens are nothing other than those that the state, at any given time, can extend or withhold as it deems best. The humanist's state inevitably leads to tyranny and despotism.

People have lost sight of the fact that there is a sovereign God who said, "By Me kings reign," and that Jesus Christ has been declared to be the King of kings and Lord of lords. The whole world is His kingdom, and He is sovereign over all.

Examine the historical facts, and you will conclude this nation began its life in a godly Christian home with a loving heavenly Father. But like the prodigal son, this prodigal nation was also enticed by dreams of the far country—a far country that bears the name "secular humanism." Ah, my friends, the travel brochures were beautiful. There was license and liberty without law. All your wildest fantasies could come true. There was nothing to restrain your passions. You might enjoy it all.

Keep in mind that secular humanism is nothing other than atheism with a Madison Avenue makeover. Atheism is negative—no God. Humanism wanted a positive face. Atheism said, "Down with God." Humanism says, "Up with man" because man is going to be seated on God's throne.

Our relativistic morality was brought home very clearly to the president of Yale University in a meeting of university professors and educators. He said that we need a new renaissance of education and morality in American colleges. You would think he would have been applauded. But he was booed! They hissed. They asked, "Whose morality, professor, are you going to impose upon them?" He couldn't answer the question because he, too, had abandoned the revealed ethic. That is why the people listening to him were so astonished.

Thankfully, I was asked to speak at Yale after that incident. I believe that, apart from Billy Graham, I was the first evangelical to speak openly about the gospel at that campus in the twentieth century! My topic was: "Absolutes in a Relativistic Age."[18]

We read in Scripture after Jesus delivered the Sermon on the Mount, "And so it was, when Jesus had ended these sayings, that the people were astonished at His teaching, for He taught them as one having authority" (Matt. 7:28–29). The word for *astonished* in Greek means "knocked out." Here Jesus is declaring an ethical code. Not only is He declaring an ethical code, He is saying that everybody must live by an ethical code, and the day will come for Him to enforce it:

> Many will say to Me in that day [the great Day of Judgment], "Lord, Lord, have we not prophesied in Your name, cast out demons in Your name, and done many wonders in Your name?" And then I will declare to them, "I never knew you; depart from Me, you who practice lawlessness!" (Matt. 7:22–23)

In our schools, children are taught they should simply sit down and rationally, reasonably decide what they value; then those values become their morals. But Dr. Allan Bloom, author of *The Closing of the American Mind*, writes, "Reason cannot establish values, and belief that it can is the stupidest and most pernicious illusion."[19]

Materialism, in the philosophical sense of the word, is man without God, without revelation. Materialism cannot even support reason, much less morality. Without God, rationality (reason) cannot be established. Charles Darwin knew this. He said it was a horrid thought to realize that all of his speech may have no more significance or meaning than the babbling of a monkey. He said, "Would anyone trust the conviction of a monkey's mind, if there are any convictions in such a mind?"[20]

Another materialist, Pierre Cabanis, made a very significant statement when he said, "The brain secretes thought as the liver secretes bile."[21] According to Cabanis, you have no control over the bile that your liver secretes, and you have no control over the thoughts your brain secretes. Materialists and evolutionists believe matter can think. But don't be too astounded at that, because they're not sure those thoughts have any more significance than the babbling of a monkey.

Dr. Lutzer points out, "Consider: If man is only a biological accident that arose by chance chemical reactions of impersonal forces, it is difficult if not impossible to make any distinction between right and wrong."[22] According to the godless worldview, Lutzer writes, "What we call mind is just the product of physical and chemical changes in the brain."[23] Therefore, what you think depends simply upon the chemical reaction of the calcium, phosphate, and sugars currently operating in your brain! This dubious hypothesis reminds me of the legal case in which the defense mounted for a man who had killed someone was the famous "Twinkie" defense. "Why, Your Honor, my—my client here is not guilty of—of any crime because, you see, he couldn't help himself in killing that man. He had eaten too many Twinkies. He had too much sugar in his brain and his brain secreted the thought to kill the man."

Dr. Stephen Jay Gould, Harvard University professor and a leading evolutionist in America today, said, "We're an afterthought—a little accidental twig."[24] Just a little twig—not even a branch or a tree. Man is just a little twig! What is a little twig good for? Nothing but to be picked up and thrown in the garbage can. That a "twig" could create a moral code for the whole world to live by is as silly as it sounds.

God: The Only One Who Can Create a Moral Code

There is no one but God who is righteous enough, who is powerful enough, and who is wise and loving enough to be able to create a moral code by which man must live. But wonder of wonders! God has not only created such a moral code, He has even graciously offered it to those who have broken it, even to those who have despised and rejected it.

He has condescended to send His own Son into the world to be the only One who has ever perfectly lived by His code, and then to send Him to the cross. There upon the cross, all of our transgressions, all of our sins, all of our iniquities, all of our violations of His code were heaped upon Christ. Christ endured in body and soul the infinite wrath of God Almighty, paying the penalty for our sins.

Because so many people don't know the love of Christ, because they don't know the message of the Bible, and because they think that morality is relative, our country is in moral chaos. This is further evidence that you can't have religion without morality. Opines Lutzer:

> Morality and religion can never be divorced. In fact, the basis of morality is the existence of God. Morality and religion are Siamese twins that cannot be separated. If they are, morality will die. . . .
> Let me say with clarity: *God is absolutely necessary for morality.* No moral theory can arise out of atheism. Those who wish to create a secular state where religion has no influence will of necessity bring about meaninglessness, lawlessness, and despair. Such conditions often spawn a totalitarian state, instituted to restore order by brute force.
> . . . Humanists do talk about morality. But when they do, they piggyback on the Judeo-Christian ethic. When they believe in human dignity, freedom, and peace, they are assuming a theistic view of the world.[25]

A variation of this same point was made a hundred years earlier by William Holmes McGuffey.

You probably have heard of the McGuffey Readers. McGuffey was a Presbyterian clergyman and an educator, president of a college, and many other things. But the McGuffey Readers he produced had an enormous impact on this country in the last century. First published in 1836, over 120 million copies of the books were sold, and they strengthened America's moral backbone for almost a century. He said:

> Religion is a social concern; for it operates powerfully on society, contributing, in various ways, to its stability and prosperity. Religion is not merely a private affair; the community is deeply interested in its diffusion; for it is the best support of the virtues and principles on which the social order rests. . . .
> Erase all thought and fear of God from a community, and selfishness and sensuality would absorb the whole man. Appetite, knowing no restraint, and suffering, having no solace or hope, would trample in scorn on the restraints of human laws. Virtue, duty, principle, would be mocked and spurned as unmeaning sounds. A sordid self-interest would supplant every other feeling; and man would become, in fact, what the theory of atheism declares him to be,— *a companion for brutes*.[26]

McGuffey did a great deal to hold in place some of the Christian foundations of this country. So too did Noah Webster, who produced the *Blue-backed Speller*, which was full of Christian teaching, doctrine, and ethics. At that same time, however, there were termites working to totally transform our schools into godless, irreligious institutions where there was no moral standard at all.

ABSOLUTES IN A RELATIVISTIC AGE

Dr. Allan Bloom writes in the first sentence of the introduction of *The Closing of the American Mind*, "There is one thing a professor can be absolutely certain of: almost every student entering the university believes, or says he believes, that truth is relative."[27]

Mark Twain said that the problem with most people is not what they don't know, but what they know for certain that isn't true. I think that statement is applicable to this discussion. Virtually all of our high school students are taught, directly or indirectly, that there are no absolutes.

You probably heard about the teacher who said to his class, "You can know nothing for certain."

One student responded, "Teacher, are you sure?"

He said, "I'm certain."

If you were to ask a high school graduate how he knows that there are no absolutes, how he knows all truth is relative, he might either shrug and say, "Because the teacher said so," or declare with smugness, "Where have you been for the past fifty years? Haven't you heard of the theory of relativity? Don't you know that we live in a relativistic universe and that everything is relative? Einstein said it, and it must be so."

No, Einstein didn't say that. Einstein said that relativity refers only to the realm of physics—not ethics. So how is it that Einstein's theory has been transported into every other discipline? How did America end up with a relativism deduced from Einstein's theory of relativity, which has nothing whatever to do with ethics or morals? The eminent historian Paul Johnson, author of *Modern Times: The World from the Twenties to the Eighties,* writes:

> Mistakenly but perhaps inevitably, relativity became confused with relativism. No one was more distressed than Einstein by this public misapprehension. He was bewildered by the relentless publicity and error which his work seemed to promote. . . . Einstein was not a practising Jew, but he acknowledged a God. He believed passionately in absolute standards of right and wrong. . . . He lived to see moral relativism, to him a disease, become a social pandemic. . . . The public response to relativity was one of the principal formative influences on the course of twentieth-century history. It formed a knife, inadvertently wielded by

its author, to help cut society adrift from its traditional moorings in the faith and morals of Judeo-Christian culture.[28]

Sometimes students don't realize that when a teacher or professor says there are no absolutes, he is also saying there is no God. God is the ultimate absolute. He is absolutely supreme, He is absolutely omnipotent and omniscient. What He says is the ultimate and absolute truth. Therefore, keep in mind that when anyone says there are no absolutes (including moral absolutes), that person is declaring a veiled atheism.

With relativistic morals there also comes subjectivism. Without God, there is no objective standard outside ourselves, and so today, rather than talk about ethics, we talk about "values"—a term that Nietzsche gave us. "Values" are simply anything that anyone chooses to place a value upon. Somehow, we have come to a place of believing that every person has the authority to decide whatever is good or bad for him or her, whatever is right or wrong, whatever is of value and what is not. "Everyone did that which was right in his own eyes."

A corollary of that belief is that a person cannot impose his values upon anyone else. That is true, as long as we are talking about the values that we have simply made up. God's Law, however, applies to all created beings, because He is the Creator, and He applies it to all without exception.

Another corollary is that since our values do not come from God, they must come from some source that influences us, and that source is cultural. Such values are relative, individual, subjective, and culturally induced. Yet when it really matters, that view of life is intolerable.

One of the most interesting examples of how we can't live with moral or cultural relativism is the Nuremberg War Trials after World War II. You may recall that Nazi leaders were brought before that court and charged with genocide and war crimes. What was their defense? The Supreme Court in Germany had declared that Jews were nonpersons. They said in effect, "We have done nothing wrong. We acted according to our own culture, according to our own mores, according to our own laws. We were told that they could be killed. Who are you to come from another culture, another society, and impose your morals on us?"[29]

The notion that one society cannot impose its morals on another had been taught in most of the universities in the world for the previous fifty years, and it absolutely threw the allied attorneys for a loss. They didn't know what to say. If there are no absolutes, if all values are culturally induced, if we cannot impose our culture upon another culture, then how dare we say that the Nazis were grievously wrong in killing millions of people? The lawyers were so taken aback that, after huddling for some time, they finally decided to retreat. Since they apparently were not willing to retreat to the moral law of God, they retreated to "natural law," which has been held through many centuries. Though it is less precise than God's Law, it still has moral content. It was on the basis of natural law that the Nazis were convicted.[30]

TRAGIC RESULTS

For thirty-five years now, children in public schools have been taught there are no moral absolutes. They must choose their own values. Again, in the last verse of the book of Judges, we read, "Every man did that which was right in his own eyes" (Judg. 21:25 KJV). That is the standard that exists today in our country.

Because of the widespread belief of relative morality, because of the widespread ignorance or rejection of the message of the Bible, today we face a rising tide of immorality and unbelief—these two conditions inevitably go together.

Consider the "Graduate School of Unbelief": crime, murder, kidnapping, assault, robbery, burglary, rape, extortion, and a hundred other forms of crime. What is this horror except the fruit of secularism? Who can measure the human misery or even count the cost of our prison system, our courts, our jails, and our police? Did you ever hear of a born-again murderer? extortioner? I haven't and I doubt I ever will. (There is an exception to this, but not in the real world. Many Hollywood movies now feature the phenomenon of what movie critic Michael Medved calls "the evangelical serial killer." Medved said of this phenomenon, "I've looked into this thing and there is no such thing" as a Christian serial killer in real life.[31] But, unfortunately, there is in movie after movie![32])

Consider unbelief organized on a national level: Nazism and fascism were perfect examples, and the untold consequences and costs of World War II speak for themselves. In the late twentieth century, Communism has been secular society's complete expression. Hundreds of millions of people have either died or have been enslaved under the ultimate view of secularism and unbelief.

Today we have more than twenty-four million illiterates and millions more young people who are moral illiterates—they have never been taught any moral standard whatsoever. Remember that George Washington said, "Let us with caution indulge the supposition that morality can be maintained without religion."[33] His warning makes sense because it's never happened—morality has never been maintained without religion. He goes on to say, "Whatever may be conceded to the influence of refined education on the minds of peculiar structure, reason and experience both forbid us to expect that national morality can prevail in exclusion of religious principle."[34] Public schools have attempted to do just that, and the results have been catastrophic.

What do the schools say? They say the problem is very simple. They need more money! Isn't that what they always say? America spends far more money per student than any other nation in the world, and in recent comparative tests of American students with the seventeen industrialized nations of the West, we scored *last* in two categories and first in none. We have passed the level of Albania and have reached the educational level of Zambia and the Ivory Coast.

As literacy rates go down, the murder rate goes up! I remember a few years ago when three murders occurred within a short time span in Fort Lauderdale, where I serve as a minister. Nowadays, murder is all too common. But what made these three murders stand out is that all of them were committed by three different *thirteen* year olds. The first one occurred because a man took a second piece of pizza instead of just the one that had been offered him. The teenager went home, got a gun, came back, and shot the man several times in the chest. Somebody had beat up a friend of the second youngster, so he got a knife and stabbed his friend's attacker to death. Finally, a thirteen-year-old boy was involved in the shooting and killing of a European tourist, for no reason except possibly to rob him. This is the kind of degeneration taking place in our society. People are now afraid to even drive on the streets for fear of being shot at because there are no moral standards anymore in our land. I'm reminded of a brilliant statement by Saadi, the great Persian poet: "I fear God, and next to God I chiefly fear him who fears Him not."[35]

THE HIGH COST OF UNBELIEF

Unbelief has caused our morals to plummet. As moral educator William J. Bennett puts it, "Over the past three decades we have experienced substantial social regression. Today the forces of social decomposition are challenging and, in some instances, overtaking the forces of social composition."[36] Consider the effects of our moral decline listed in Bennett's book, *The Index of Leading Cultural Indicators:*

- 99 percent of Americans will be "victims of theft at least once in their lives."
- 80 percent of Americans "can expect to be the victim of violent crime at least once in their lives."

- Our children account for the "fastest growing segment of the criminal population" of this country.
- Less than 10 percent of "serious crimes results in imprisonment"![37]

Consider how dangerous the public schools of America have become. In his book, *Why Johnny Can't Tell Right from Wrong*, William Kilpatrick says:

> An estimated 525,000 attacks, shakedowns, and robberies occur in public high schools each month. Each year nearly three million crimes are committed on or near school property — 16,000 per school day. About 135,000 students carry guns to school daily; one fifth of all students report carrying a weapon of some type. Twenty-one percent of all secondary school students avoid using the rest rooms out of fear of being harmed or intimidated. Surveys of schoolchildren reveal that their chief school-related concern is the disruptive behavior of their classmates. Teachers have similar concerns. Almost one third of public school teachers indicate that they have seriously considered leaving teaching because of student misbehavior.[38]

What difference does faith make? It makes a very big difference. Hundreds of millions of lives and hundreds of billions of dollars wasted! Indeed, can we afford the cost of unbelief and secularism?

The founders of this country knew that America would not work unless its citizenry was moral. That is why the Congress decreed, "Religion, morality and knowledge being essential to good government, schools shall be established in the Northwest Territories."[39]

JESUS CHRIST IS INCARNATE TRUTH

To halt the moral relativism of our time we must reassert what Jesus Christ said. "You shall know the truth, and the truth shall make you free" (John 8:32).

There are two things in that verse that I think are very important for us to notice. First of all, Jesus is declaring that there is truth. By that, I don't mean a relativistic truth. He didn't say, "You will know *a* truth." He didn't say, "You will know *your* truth." We hear this concept today from those who say, "Well, that's true for you, but it's not true for me." But rather He said, "You shall know *the* truth." God's truth is true for everyone, and the subjective rejection of "somebody else's truth" does not apply to God. Jesus Christ said, "I am the way, the truth, and the life.

No one comes to the Father except through Me" (John 14:6). He is not *a* truth, *part* of the truth, *somebody's* truth but not *somebody else's* truth— He is *the* Truth. How ironic it is that Pontius Pilate could say with a sneer, "What is truth?"—when standing before him was Incarnate Truth.

Furthermore, we see in John 8:32 that we can *know* the truth. Today we are told that we can't know the truth—that we can't know anything for certain. Granted, science only gives probabilities, but through revelation and religion, we can know truth. The Scriptures say, "These things I have written to you . . . that you may *know* that you have eternal life" (1 John 5:13, emphasis mine).

Unfortunately, millions of young people in America believe there are no moral absolutes, that what is sinful to you might not be sinful to me. Turn on just about any talk show on TV and you see this underlying assumption. Tolerance of anything, no matter how perverse or aberrant, is a sacred cow to many modern Americans. And intolerance has become the unforgivable sin.

THE IMMORAL BASIS FOR UNBELIEF

We need also to remember that there is a quality in the hearts of men that causes them to reject God. For example, I recall a number of years ago watching an interview on public television conducted with Sir Julian Huxley. At the time, he was president of UNESCO (United Nations Educational, Scientific, and Cultural Organization). Huxley was the most prestigious evolutionary scientist in the world at the time. The interviewer asked him, "Why do you think that evolution caught on so quickly?" Huxley began, "We all jumped at *The Origin* [*The Origin of the Species* by Charles Darwin] because . . ." Now if you ask a high school science class to finish that sentence, what do you think the students would say? They would say, "The reason we jumped at *The Origin of Species* was that the evidence amassed by Darwin was so intellectually compelling that scientific integrity required that we accept it as fact."

That is not what Huxley said. Rather, I heard him say, "[I suppose the reason] we all jumped at *The Origin* [was] because the idea of God interfered with our sexual mores." I almost fell out of my chair! What does that have to do with science?

Consider also Bertrand Russell, a strongly anti-Christian but brilliant philosopher of our century. He wrote a book titled *Why I Am Not a Christian*.[40] He said that science could not tyrannize over philosophy and tell philosophy that there was no meaning to life because if you accept the evolutionary scientific view, then life has no meaning. Why did he not believe in God? Because science and philosophy disproved His existence? No, because the idea of God interfered with his sin.

Russell was a radical socialist and a philanderer as well. He was involved in multiple marriages and divorces. The judge of one of the divorce courts granting a divorce to his wife said that he was a rogue who had committed adulteries of the type that no decent adulterer would even commit. He seduced virtually everybody who came across his path. Once he was invited to stay at the home of a physician friend for two nights. His second night there he spent seducing the man's teenage daughter.[41] No wonder he didn't want to be a Christian—it would have interfered with his sexual mores.

Man has a fallen nature—a nature that causes people not to want to believe that there is a Creator because they do not want to believe that this Creator is a lawgiver and that this lawgiver is going to be their Judge and hold them accountable for the things they have done.

Friedrich Nietzsche rejected the Scriptures. He rejected Christianity. He hated religion. He hated Christianity, in particular. And he is, of course, the one who said that God is dead.

The amazing thing is that millions of people believed him. He never proved it, he just proclaimed it. It's one thing to declare something; it is another thing to prove it. Somebody wrote graffiti on a building that said, "God is dead—Nietzsche." Someone else came along and wrote, "Nietzsche is dead—God." It is better to debate an issue before settling it, said one philosopher, than to settle an issue before debating it. But Nietzsche did the latter.

No one has ever proved that God is dead or that God doesn't exist. In fact, in case you didn't know, atheism is irrational. To say there is no God is to assert what in logic is called a "universal negative." It is well known that no human being can prove any universal negative. You cannot prove that nowhere in the universe are there little green men. You cannot prove that nowhere in the universe is there a being such as God. In order to prove that, you would have to know what is in every part of the entire universe. In other words, in order to prove there is no God, you would have to be God. And then you would have proved yourself wrong. So nobody has proved that God does not exist.

I debated an atheist on a radio station once. I said to him, "You believe there is no God; you're sure of that?"

He said, "Yes, I am."

I pointed out to him that that's a logical fallacy. It is an irrational state-ment. He didn't know that. And in a few minutes, he had progressed from atheism to agnosticism. (There may be hope for him yet!)

DIVINE ACCOUNTABILITY, A KEY FACTOR IN MORALITY

Knowing that we will stand before God and give an accounting to Him of our lives is a key factor for moral living. The great nineteenth-century statesman Daniel Webster was once asked, "What is the most important thought you ever entertained?" He replied, "The thought of my individual responsibility to God."[42] As one judge put it, "The exis-tence of a Supreme Being—a Spirit, infinite, eternal, omniscient, omnipo-tent—is a first truth of moral science."[43]

SOMETHING GREATER THAN OURSELVES

The Bible is our sure guide for right and wrong. Western civilization is in moral chaos because many members of the cultural elite have put their wisdom in place of biblical truths. As long as we buy into their ideas, we will continue the slide down the slippery slope of situational ethics. Margaret Thatcher, one of England's greatest prime ministers, rightly pointed out:

> The Christian religion—which, of course, embodies many of the great spiritual and moral truths of Judaism—is a fundamental part of our national heritage. For centuries it has been our very lifeblood. Indeed, we are a nation whose ideals are founded on the Bible. Also, it is quite impossible to understand our history or literature without grasping this fact. . . .
>
> But I go further than this. The truths of the Judeo-Christian tradi-tion are infinitely precious, not only, as I believe, because they are true, but also because they provide the moral impulse which alone can lead to that peace, in the true meaning of the word, for which we all long. . . .
>
> But there is little hope for democracy if the hearts of men and women in democratic societies cannot be touched by a call to some-thing greater than themselves.[44]

CHAPTER 3

THE BIBLE AND SOCIETY

"Then He who sat on the throne said, 'Behold, I make all things new.'"
—Revelation 21:5

One day a pickpocket lifted what he thought was a wallet from a man's pocket. But when he arrived home, to his dismay, he discovered it was just a book: a New Testament to be exact. In disgust and anger, he hurled it into the corner. A few days later, curiosity led him to peruse the book. He encountered Jesus Christ in its pages, and he became a Christian. He told this story later at a church meeting, and afterward, a volunteer with a Bible-distribution group sought out the repentant thief. He asked to look at the book itself. When he saw it, he exclaimed that it was the copy of the New Testament that he had given up as lost. This true story, told by W. H. McCutheon, is one of countless examples of the Bible's ability to transform the human heart.[1]

THE IMPACT OF THE BIBLE

The Bible transforms lives, even in the midst of tragic circumstances. I think of Bill Wilson, pastor of Metro-Ministries in Brooklyn, New York. He lives in a dangerous, drug-infested neighborhood. It's his chosen mission field. His primary focus is reaching children before the age of fourteen—before the streets reach them and harden them to the gospel. Each week he buses in fifteen thousand children for an action-filled three-hour Sunday school class—on Saturdays. Many of them become Christians, as do their parents. Bill Wilson comes from a single-parent home. One day in St. Petersburg, Florida, when he was fourteen years old, he and his mother were sitting by a drainage ditch. She got up, saying, "I can't do this anymore. You wait here." She left, and she never came back! Bill had nowhere to go and nothing to do, so he just sat there . . .

for three days! A Christian neighbor saw him and took him home. He bought him food and paid his way to a Christian youth camp. At that camp, Bill Wilson accepted Christ as his personal Savior, a decision that changed the whole direction of his life. Today, some thirty years later, when he picks up children in New York City on his bus route, he says, "You know who I'm picking up? . . . I'm picking up me!"[2] Metro-Ministries is one of the great ministries of our time, and it's based squarely on the Bible.

No book has had a greater and more positive impact on the lives of individuals, of families, of groups of people, of cultures, of nations than the book that tells us about Jesus: the Bible, the Book of books. History is replete with examples of changed lives and changed societies because of the message of the Bible. Here we will examine a few of those.

What if the Bible had never been written? We can see the disaster of a culture in which there is no Bible or in which it's never read.

A TALE OF TWO REVOLUTIONS

In 1789 our Constitution was completed and ratified, and a new nation was born. It was also the year of the godless French Revolution, which saw rivers of blood flowing in the streets of Paris. As H. J. Brine once pointed out:

> The French infidels ruled out the Christian era, did away with the Christian sabbath, and tried to bring in a new era of their own. But they soon quarreled among themselves and destroyed each other; and the influence of Christ triumphed and the Christian era was reestablished.[3]

The French Revolution was a horrible way for people to learn that man is corrupt in his very nature. The false belief in man's goodness led to a shocking reign of terror.

In that same year, on the other side of the world, was another revolution, less famous than those in France and America. A new nation (of sorts) emerged then as well.

This revolution was circumscribed: indeed it was founded by the remnant of the crew of a single ship. The revolution was a mutiny, and the ship was the famed HMS *Bounty* (made famous in the book and movie *Mutiny on the Bounty*). Goaded by the cruelty of Captain Bligh, Fletcher Christian led a group of mutineers to take over the ship and set adrift the captain and loyal officers. The mutineers sailed for an island far out in the South Pacific, four thousand miles east of New Zealand — an island only two square miles in size named Pitcairn Island. There they began a new life, having first scuttled the *Bounty* to avoid detection. They settled down with Tahitian wives. They also took with them some Tahitian men to help settle the island.

Although they were settling a tropical paradise, these men and women turned heaven into hell. Unregenerate human nature being what it is, this group devolved into a drunken, violent, adulterous colony. For ten years there was drunkenness and mayhem and arguments and fights and murder and rape. Then the Tahitian men caught wind of a plot by some of the European men to make them slaves. But the Tahitians incorrectly surmised that the *leadership,* e.g., Fletcher Christian, agreed with that plan. One bloody day, a showdown between these various factions left but *one mutineer* in the midst of the natives, half-breed women, and children. (And even he had been shot and left for dead!)[4] He was the founder of the new nation of Pitcairn Island, and his name was Alexander Smith. However, he later changed it to John Adams, like his counterpart on the other side of the world.

Among the items that the mutineers salvaged from the HMS *Bounty* was a Bible—a Bible now found in the New York City Museum. Smith, who was taught to read late in life by one of his fellow sailors on the island, began to read that Bible. "When I came to the Life of Jesus," Smith later said, "my heart began to open like doors swingin' apart. Once I was sure God was a loving and merciful Father to them that repent, it seemed to me I could feel His very presence, sir, and I grew more sure every day of His guiding hand."[5]

Not only was Smith transformed, he relied on the power of the gospel to transform virtually every person on that island and establish perhaps the most peaceful, tranquil, law-abiding, loving society the world has ever seen. In 1808, when the British navy discovered Pitcairn Island, they were so astonished at the faith of Smith and all the inhabitants of the island, they forbore to prosecute him for mutiny. The name Pitcairn then became a byword for piety in the nineteenth century.[6]

CAN HUMAN NATURE BE CHANGED?

Through the centuries men have debated whether human nature can be changed. The Bible gives a very clear answer to this question, given certain conditions, such as repentance and turning to Jesus Christ.

The twentieth century has seen many people who have been convinced that human nature can be changed, apart from the influence of the Bible. For example, the Communists believed they were going to fashion the "new Communist man" without God or religion, except for the religion of Karl Marx—atheism.

Marx, the intellectual founder of Communism, saw his doctrines as the key that unlocked man's predicament in the world. He proclaimed that Communism was "the true solution" to life's mysteries. What is it that keeps man from getting along with his fellow man? Private property. When that is abandoned, then "self-alienation" is also discarded. Thus, man discovers his true self when he abandons private property, thereby solving the age-old problem of man's natural antagonism toward his fellow man. Marx said, "Communism . . . is the genuine solution of the antagonism between man and nature and between man and man. . . . It is the solution to the riddle of history."[7] So man finally discovers who he is and why he's here—he unlocks the riddle of history—thanks to Communism. No wonder the Soviet Union wouldn't let ministers preach about the Millennium; the Communists had already ushered in paradise through the workers' state![8]

Karl Marx assumed that man was basically good, but corrupted by capitalism and capitalism's class structures. He argued in *The Communist Manifesto* that once the proletariat (the workers) seized power and controlled the state, they would establish a social order that had no classes, and eventually no need for political power. So the state would wither away. He writes:

> When, in the course of development, class distinctions have disappeared, and all production has been concentrated in the hands of a vast association of the whole nation, the public power will lose its political character. . . .
>
> In place of the old bourgeois society, with its classes and class antagonisms, we shall have an association, in which the free development of each is the condition for the free development of all.[9]

Tens of millions of people have been murdered in this century because of this view of man's nature. Marxism did produce a new Communist man—a man so cruel that he could commit the most barbaric crimes against his fellow human beings without the slightest qualms of conscience. When we become aware of what took place in the ghastly labor camps, or gulags, we can understand the nature of the new Communist man, perhaps the cruelest man the world has ever seen.[10]

I have read detailed accounts of what went on in the gulags, and it boggles the mind. What they did to men was bad enough, but what happened to women who were sent there is absolutely shocking. An example of Communist torture occurred just within the last few years. Two

Christian women were being punished by the Chinese authorities for the "crime" of being a part of the unregistered house church movement. They were stripped naked, hung up by their thumbs with wires, and beaten unconscious with cattle prods. The system Marx helped create — based on a false paradigm, which was itself based on a false picture of man's true nature—has probably caused more evil than any system known to man. Recently a former Communist who became a convert to Catholicism summarized that all Communism really has had to show for its time in power is *dead bodies*! Eugene Genovese, who—along with his wife Elizabeth Fox-Genovese—used to publish *Marxist Perspectives* magazine, said this about the former Soviet Union:

> When it all collapsed, the question was, After seventy years, what do we have to show for it? Especially when it became clear that, even on a basic level, the system didn't deliver the goods, the one thing it was supposed to do. So what we had to show for it was *tens of millions of corpses.*[11]

Paul Johnson, the great historian and author of *Modern Times,* writes that the twentieth-century state has "proved itself the great killer of all time."[12] The Communists bear the largest share of that responsibility.

The "new Communist man" was a total failure. A few years ago, after the Communist empire began to break up, five judges came to Fort Lauderdale to see me: the head judge of all the judges in the Soviet Union and four others. Why did they want to see me? Because they had heard that I knew a way to make people good, and they desperately needed to discover what that was. No, Communism provides no new or noble man.

In America, we have decided that the answer to changing human nature is "education." Our democratic society will create the "new democratic man" through education. Of course, the cultural elites decided long ago that the Bible would play no part in that education (even though the Bible played a critical role in the rise of education for the masses in the first place[13]). John Dunphy, writing in *The Humanist* magazine in 1983, shows just how virulent some are in their objection to the Bible being included in education:

> I am convinced that the battle for humankind's future must be waged and won in the public school classroom by teachers who correctly perceive their role as the proselytizers of a new faith: a religion of humanity that recognizes and respects the spark of what theologians call divinity in every human being. These teachers must embody the same selfless dedication as the most rabid fundamentalist preachers, for they will be ministers of another sort, utilizing a classroom instead of a pulpit to convey humanist values in whatever subject they teach,

regardless of the educational level—preschool day care or large state university. The classroom must and will become an arena of conflict between the old and the new—the rotting corpse of Christianity, together with all its adjacent evils and misery, and the new faith of humanism, resplendent in its promise of a world in which the never-realized Christian ideal of "love thy neighbor" will be finally achieved.[14]

Contrary to Dunphy's rosy view of human nature, when we kicked God out of America's schools, we had to install metal detectors instead.

Since 1983, godless humanists like Dunphy have, unfortunately, made even greater gains in our public schools. Have students improved academically? No. Most objective measures of student learning, such as SAT scores, have fallen lower and lower over the years. Have students begun to "love thy neighbor"? Not quite. Most large public school systems have police and security guards due to the threat of student-on-student or student-on-teacher violence. Even then, too many students are walking into schools nowadays with guns and killing their peers. Again, a faulty view of human nature leads to faulty and inadequate solutions. (As to Dunphy's charges that Christianity has brought nothing but "evil and misery," our previous book *What If Jesus Had Never Been Born?* effectively refutes that canard.)

No, education does not produce a new nature in man. Remember, in 1933 the most literate and most highly educated nation in the world was Nazi Germany!

Next, we are told, the new man will be fashioned by psychology and psychiatry. Before you become too excited about that possibility, remember that of all of the professions in America, the highest level of suicide is found in psychiatrists. So if you are contemplating such an act, I don't recommend that you go see one. He might decide to hold your hand and jump first, or put in a call to Dr. Kevorkian. I do not intend to belittle the serious role of helpful therapists and counselors who are legitimately able to help people change. Some of them find the greatest change with the aid of Christianity. Ultimately, the human heart is changed through rebirth, through the gospel of Jesus Christ.

All of the modern secular concepts for changing human nature have failed, and many people now join the centuries-old chorus proclaiming that human nature cannot be changed by man's own doing. They could have avoided the delusion in the first place by reading the Bible. The Old Testament says, "Can the Ethiopian change his skin or the leopard its spots? Then may you also do good who are accustomed to do evil" (Jer. 13:23). When is that? That, my friends, is never. The Bible resoundingly leads the chorus that no man can change his own nature. As Paul says, quoting from the Old Testament, "There is none righteous, no, not one" (Rom. 3:10).

THEN CAME CHRIST

The New Testament tells us the only way to change is from the inside out—through the One who boldly proclaims, "Behold, I make all things new" (Rev. 21:5). He is Jesus Christ. How marvelous, how wonderful He is at changing the human heart.

I think of a young, ambitionless man who worked in a bakery making donuts. He lived to smoke pot or use harder drugs. He even dealt cocaine to help support his drug use. But one day someone invited him to a Bible study. He was converted through hearing the message of the Bible. It totally changed him from the inside out. Not only did he quit the drugs, but he decided to make something of his life. He even went off to college. Today he is a writer, a productive citizen, a committed family man, and an active Christian. While the background and details of the stories may be different, there are millions of people like this young man who found new life in Christ.

Yes, Christ is still making all things new, just as He did with the lives on Pitcairn Island. It is very interesting that, in searching several encyclopedias, I could not find any mention of the religious conversion of Alexander Smith of the *Bounty*, or anyone else. But of course, there is no bias in the media or the educational institutions, is there? Obviously, there is. You have to look to other biographies and histories to discover the significance of what happened after the events on the *Bounty*.[15]

Or go a hundred and fifty years or so forward from Pitcairn Island to the South Asian land of Burma. You may recall a few decades ago the Academy Award–winning motion picture *The Bridge Over the River Kwai,* starring William Holden and Alec Guiness. You remember what happened. The whole battalion of British soldiers were captured by the Japanese in Burma. In the concentration camp, the Japanese systematically overworked the captives, many of whom died.

According to Hollywood, the Japanese commander was initially unsuccessful in his attempt to get these prisoners of war to build a bridge over the River Kwai. Meanwhile, he tried to break the will and spirit of the chief British officer, but was unsuccessful at this too. Although it greatly hurt his pride, the desperate Japanese commander finally put the British officer in charge of building the bridge, and because of that, the bridge was finally built. The men even went out whistling as they went to build the bridge . . . so said Hollywood. But is that what really happened?

Long after the movie had come out, I spoke to the man who had commanded those British forces in Burma. At that time, he was the chaplain of Princeton University, and he had written a book about his experiences, called *Through the Valley of the Kwai*.[16] He told me, heartbrokenly, what Hollywood had done to the truth.

Here is the real story of the bridge over the River Kwai. The captives had been reduced to savagery. They were starving. They were snapping for every crust of bread like animals. And then the British commander discovered in one of their backpacks a New Testament. He began to read it. As he read it, the wonder of the love of Christ began to fill his soul, and he surrendered his life to the Savior and called on Him for His grace and help. He was transformed.

He began to read that New Testament to his men each day. One after another became transformed until virtually the entire camp was transformed by the gospel of Christ. These animal-like men began to save their crusts of bread to give to those who were weaker and sicker than they were. That camp was transformed by Christ, who makes all things new. There was not even a hint of these events in the Hollywood version—but that's the real story.

Christ, indeed, can make all things new. He did it throughout the years that He walked upon this earth. He transformed Nicodemus and told him that he must be born anew. He transformed Peter, the sifting, shifting sand of Simon Peter, into a rock. He transformed the snarling Saul into the apostle Paul. He transformed the "sons of thunder" into the apostles of love. And He has been changing the hearts of one man and woman after another through the centuries.

These people found true meaning in life because God made us and until we come to know Him, we aren't experiencing life as He intended it for us. One of the great converts in Christian history, a former playboy whom we only know as "Saint" Augustine—and rightfully do we call him a saint!—said that since we are created beings we don't really find our purpose in life until we come to terms with the Creator. In his *Confessions,* he wrote (addressing God), "You have made us for yourself, and our heart is restless until it rests in you."[17]

A FORMER COMMUNIST FINDS MEANING IN LIFE

Through the Bible

A well-educated former Communist, Nicholay Ivanovich Revtov, discovered this glorious purpose recently. He was born in the Soviet Union.

After an early life in gangs involved in all manner of criminal activity, he committed his soul to Karl Marx and became a dedicated member of the Party. He then set out to learn as much as he possibly could and earned five academic degrees, two of them doctorates. But this atheist Communist said later, "I missed the best degree in the world, a B.A. (Born Again)."

We may not have an alphabet soup of degrees poured after our name, but each one of us can have *this* B.A. degree even if we never got past the third grade. Nicholay Ivanovich Revtov was visited one day by Buddy Gaines, a member of the staff of Evangelism Explosion, who was in the former Soviet Union. (Evangelism Explosion, sometimes labeled E.E., is a lay-witnessing program I started more than three decades ago at Coral Ridge Presbyterian Church.[18]) There, through an interpreter, Buddy shared the glorious gospel of Jesus Christ. Revtov's empty heart was suddenly filled with the wonder of the love of Jesus Christ. He invited Buddy back again. His wife and his son also accepted Christ. And today Nicholay Ivanovich Revtov is the director for Eurasia for the Evangelism Explosion International ministry. He has recently finished planting E.E. in all of the former nations of the Soviet empire. He found that new life in Christ.

Many people have made a mess of their lives and they know it. They wish there were some way they could start again. And there is, thanks to the Word of God. One lady found it, and she couldn't help but express her wonder in these words:

> I have found in the Book, that wonderful place,
> Called the Land of Beginning Again.
> Where the sins of the past are remembered no more
> And the years, locust-eaten, the Lord doth
>   restore.
> All our filthy rags changed for a garment of
>   grace,
> And the soul is begotten again!
> With a love shed abroad in our heart by the
>   Spirit,
> It is easy to love one another;
> That love thinketh no evil, it envieth not,
> Is so humble-unselfish, with kindness so fraught.
> That transformed by that love, as in Heaven above,
> We shall love one another forever.
> Oh, I wish, yes, I've found, that wonderful place
> Called the Land of Beginning Again.[19]

Have you made that discovery? One skeptic, reared among other vaunting skeptics and unbelievers, made that discovery to his great astonishment. Having been a complete unbeliever who lived in the midst of intellectual atheists in England, he said this:

> But I observed the futile amazement with which every skeptic from Celsus to Wells stood around the cradle of the Christ. I wondered why this helpless Babe was thrust into the world at a time when Roman greed, Jewish hate, and Greek subtlety would combine to crush Him. And yet this most powerful, devastating combination ever known in history served only to advance the cause of the Infant who was born in a stable. . . .
>
> No unbeliever could tell me why His words are as charged with power today as they were nineteen hundred years ago. Nor could scoffers explain how those pierced hands pulled human monsters with gnarled souls out of a hell of iniquity and overnight transformed them into steadfast, glorious heroes [of the cross]. . . . No agnostic could make clear why seemingly immortal empires pass into oblivion, while the glory and power of the murdered Galilean are gathering beauty and momentum with every attack and every age.
>
> Nor could any scoffer explain, as Jesus Himself so daringly foretold, why by telephone, airplane, and radio, by rail, horse, and foot, His words are piercing the densest forest, scaling the highest mountains, crossing the deepest seas and the widest deserts, making converts in every nation, kindred tongue, and people on earth.
>
> No doubter could tell me how this isolated Jew could utter words at once so simple that a child can understand them and so deep that the greatest thinkers cannot plumb their shining depths. The life, the words, the character of this strange Man are the enigma of history. Any naturalistic explanation makes Him a more puzzling paradox, a fathomless mystery.
>
> But I learned that the paradox was plain and the mystery solved when I accepted Him for what He claimed to be—the Son of God, come from heaven a Saviour of men, but above all, my own Saviour. I learned to thrill at the angel's word: "Behold, . . . unto *you* is born this day . . . a Saviour, which is Christ the Lord." Now I have learned the great truth that "though Christ a thousand times in Bethlehem be born, if He's not born in thee, thy soul is still forlorn."[20]

From the change in the human heart ripples forth great changes in society, even tumultuous changes.

TURNING THE WORLD UPSIDE DOWN

In the early days of Christianity, Paul and the apostles were accused of turning the world upside down (Acts 17:6). But the reality is, the world was already upside down. They were merely turning portions of the world rightside up!

Furthermore, Paul and company were engaged in transforming the *world;* they were not satisfied to change just one country. And that is what Christians should be doing, turning the world rightside up. Of course, change begins with the individual. It begins with a heart that is transformed by the gospel of Jesus Christ. Then like a rock tossed into a quiet pond, it causes concentric circles to move ever farther outward, influencing every sphere of life.

C. E. M. Joad was one of the great philosophers of England in this century. He was a brilliant intellect and a militant unbeliever. He joined with George Bernard Shaw and Bertrand Russell and numerous other skeptics to continue an unremitting assault upon the Christian religion. But after all the damage his earlier books had done, in his later life he wrote that humanity's ultimate problem is sin. Earlier he had thought that man was basically good and that, given the right conditions, we could create heaven on earth. But two devastating world wars and the threat of another one brought home to him the reality that man is sinful. The only solution to man's sin, concluded this former skeptic, is the cross of Jesus Christ.[21] His heart was changed as millions of others have been through the years.

BY-PRODUCTS OF CHURCH ATTENDANCE

Interestingly, the more committed people are to Christ as evidenced in regular church attendance, the more they tend to reflect this change of heart. And this change of heart gradually brings a host of benefits. Nationally syndicated radio host Jane Chastain reported recently:

- Churchgoers are more likely to have stable, happy marriages that endure the test of time;
- Church attendance is instrumental in helping young people escape poverty;
- Religious belief and practice contribute substantially to the formation of personal moral criteria and sound moral judgment;
- Those who regularly practice their religion experience less depression, more self-esteem, fewer out-of-wedlock births, less drug abuse, fewer suicides, less crime, and fewer instances of divorce;
- The regular practice of religion has positive health benefits: it increases longevity, lessens the incidence of many killer diseases and improves one's chances of recovery from illness;

- Religious belief and practice is also a major source of strength and recovery and can help repair the damage caused by alcoholism, drug addiction, and marital breakdown.[22]

While we know that there is much anecdotal evidence for these statements, is there scientific evidence to back them up as well? Yes, there is. First we look at the health aspect.

Recently some researchers examined the results of two hundred studies dealing with how religion impacts health. The net effect of their findings is that religion is not only good for your soul, but also for the body! *Christian News* reports:

> Regular church attendance is good for your health, according to scientific studies compiled by *TIME* magazine.
>
> "People who regularly attend religious services have been found to have lower blood pressure, less heart disease, lower rates of depression and generally better health than those who don't attend," the magazine reported in a cover article about changing attitudes toward health.
>
> Supporting the link between religion and health were a series of scientific studies reviewed by Jeffrey Leven, a gerontologist and epidemiologist at East Virginia Medical School, and David Larson, a research psychiatrist at the National Institute for Healthcare Research.[23]

Interestingly, the whole aerobics movement was founded by an evangelical Christian, Dr. Kenneth Cooper, author of *Faith-Based Fitness*.[24] Aerobics has been instrumental in widely promoting good health to many in our culture, believers or otherwise.

Other studies have found similar results concerning the link between faith and health. For example, in a report compiled by the Gallup-affiliated organization Religion in American Life, based in Princeton, New Jersey, the researchers found that regular church or synagogue attendance is generally correlated to a better work ethic, stability in family life, and more volunteer work with charities. They also found that:

- Regular worshipers are 50 percent more likely to reject illicit drugs than nonworshipers.
- Churches and synagogues contribute to America's social services more than any other nongovernmental institution, including corporations.

- Regular churchgoers "demonstrate better-than-average productivity in the workplace."[25]

Again other studies have found similar results.

One study was conducted among five thousand people from Alameda, California, over a span of twenty-eight years to determine the long-term benefits of attending church. The Fort Lauderdale *Sun-Sentinel* summarized the findings with this phrase, "Go to church, live longer."[26] The researchers found that those who reject churchgoing have a 36 percent higher death rate than those who attend regularly! Factors that could contribute to the longer life of regular churchgoers include "improved health practices, increased social contacts and more stable marriages."[27] Again, this finding is not isolated. In the summer of 1996, seventy health care and religion researchers gathered for a conference in Leesburg, Virginia, under the auspices of the National Institute for Healthcare Research to discuss the correlation between faith and health. *The Washington Times* reported that the researchers' presentations showed that "religious commitment is associated with decreased mortality, increased social support, lower rates of depression and higher self-esteem."[28] Thus, we see that the Bible is linked to good health.

U.S. News & World Report had a cover story recently with a picture of a church and this headline: "THE FAITH FACTOR: Can churches cure America's social ills?" In that article, they ask and answer this intriguing question: "What's the surest guarantee that an African-American urban youth will not fall to drugs or crime? Regular church attendance turns out to be a better predictor than family structure or income, according to a study by Harvard University economist Richard Freeman. Call it the 'faith factor.'"[29] The magazine also reports, "Frequent churchgoers are about 50 percent less likely to report psychological problems and 71 percent are less likely to be alcoholics."[30] In short, spread the message of the Bible and you improve the quality of life in society.

In England, the Bible is responsible for "a wave of spiritual awakening" in many prisons, according to the United Bible Society. In one prison alone, Lewes Remand Prison, "more than 600 people have been converted through reading the Bible in the past two years. 'They stand up and say things like "Wow, this is better than crack!" And the changes that take place in their lives as a result of their conversion are amazing to witness,' said David Powe, the full-time Anglican chaplain there."[31]

Even skeptics through the ages have recognized the power of Christianity to improve life for many human beings. I think of William E. H. Lecky of the nineteenth century, who once wrote:

It was reserved for Christianity to present to the world an Ideal Character, which, through all the changes of eighteen centuries, has filled the hearts of man with an impassioned love, and has shown itself capable of acting on all ages, nations, temperaments, conditions; and which has not only been the highest pattern of virtue, but the highest incentive to its practice.[32]

In short, the Bible—by spreading the message of Christ—has had enormous impact on the world for good.

"THE TRANSFORMER OF THE WORLD'S LIFE"

Jesus Christ transforms the world, and we learn about Him through His Word. W. E. Biedersolf wrote about that transformation the Bible brings about through the gospel of Jesus Christ:

What did Darwin mean when he said, "A man about to be shipwrecked on some unknown coast will devoutly pray that the lesson of the missionary will have reached that far"? He meant that where the Gospel has not gone civilization has not gone, and such a shipwrecked man would likely find himself in the soup tureen of a tribe of husky cannibals.

Take Christianity out of civilization; take it out of art, music, literature, and most of all out of the human heart and life, and you'd have mighty little left worthy of the name.

Confucianism, Buddhism and Mohammedanism have proven by their results that their founders were not Divine, but to account for Christianity on any other basis than Divinity is a historical impossibility. You might as well try to paint a Sistine Madonna with a charcoal pencil.

What Jesus Christ always has been He is today, the transformer of the world's life, the reconstructor of human society, the animator of human progress, the one Master moulder of the world's civilization. And by this I know that He is Divine.[33]

CHAPTER 4

THE BIBLE
AND LAW

"The statutes of the LORD are right, rejoicing the heart;
The commandment of the LORD is pure, enlightening the eyes."
—Psalm 19:8

Of the making of laws there is no end. *The Saturday Evening Post* once ran a cartoon showing Moses on the mount, holding the tablet of the Ten Commandments in his hands. He looks up to heaven and says, "Maybe there's only ten of them now, but just wait till the bureaucrats get to work."[1] This joke is more true than you may realize! For centuries our legal system has been based on the foundation of the revelation of God to Moses. Unfortunately, man in his infinite wisdom has added many layers of regulations, often smothering the truly important laws.

In their intriguing book *Positioning: The Battle for Your Mind*, Al Ries and Jack Trout point out the number of new layers that lawmakers are adding on to laws today—showing just how true this cartoon rings:

> The U.S. Congress passes some 500 laws a year (that's bad enough), but regulatory agencies promulgate some 10,000 new rules and regulations in the same amount of time. And the regulatory agencies are not stingy with their words either. Consider this: The Lord's Prayer contains 56 words, the Gettysburg Address, 266; the Ten Commandments, 297; the Declaration of Independence, 300; and a recent U.S. government order setting the price of cabbage, 26,911. At the state level, over 250,000 bills are introduced each year. And 25,000 pass the legislatures to disappear into the labyrinths of law.[2]

In this chapter, we will examine the tremendous impact the Bible has had on law in the Western world. We will be looking at the contributions of godly men to the development of laws throughout history, from Moses to Justinian, from Alfred the Great to William Blackstone. We will see how the Bible was the basis for virtually all law in many of the cultures that preceded ours. As our present-day culture moves away from God, we are witnessing the disintegration of our legal system. The litigation explosion that rocks this nation, draining billions of dollars each year and causing great emotional stress for so many, is a symptom of the continual push to remove biblical influence from the law.

GOD'S REVELATION TO MOSES

The most cursory survey of the history of civilization reveals man's need for a unified code of conduct. A community of people cannot exist unless bound together by standards of behavior. No one knew this better than God, who revealed to Moses the Ten Commandments, which He wrote in stone. No other collection of rules, whether written by man or inspired by the "gods," has had so profound an impact in the realm of law as those words have. In the book *The Story of Law and the Men Who Made It—From the Earliest Times to the Present,* author René A. Wormser states:

> The law of Moses has . . . played a direct and vital part in the creation of our own legal system. Some of our early colonial communities were ruled under the exact and precise law of the Old Testament; moreover, the law of the Jews became one of the chief root sources of both the law of the Continent of Europe and the English law upon which ours is directly based.[3]

Throughout the first civilizations, customs, traditions, and folklore provided the guidelines for proper behavior. Wormser writes that in prior ages, "man's conduct was governed by nothing more than the accumulated experience of his forefathers."[4]

None of them stood the test of time the way the Ten Commandments have. None of them remotely match the legal wisdom God gave to Moses.

Archaeologists have identified fragments of a particular tablet from the ancient city of Nippur, known as *The Code of Lipit-Ishtar,* that dates back to between 1868 and 1857 B.C. The date establishes Lipit-Ishtar, the lawgiver of this particular tablet, as one of the first rulers to actually record laws. This code consisted of laws such as, "If a man rented an ox and damaged its tail, he shall pay one fourth of (its) price."[5] Of the nine rules available, only two deal with people directly.

Another such written code originates from Babylonia. *The Code of Hammurabi* is believed to date back to circa 1750 B.C.[6] Some of its laws were "If a man accuse a man, and charge him with murder, but cannot convict him, the accuser shall be put to death," and "If a man aid a male or a female slave of the palace, or a male or female slave of a common man, to escape from the city, he shall be put to death," and "If a priestess or a nun who is not resident in a convent open a wineshop or enter a wineshop for a drink, they shall burn that woman."[7] Another such law prescribes that the person accused of sorcery throw himself into a river. If the river "overcomes him," well then, he's guilty! Meanwhile, if the accuser is found to be wrong, he is to be put to death. Durant says of Hammurabi's code, "There was nothing in the Code about the rights of the individual against the state; that was to be a European innovation."[8] In reality, such a consideration was first introduced into law by God through His servant Moses in the Ten Commandments.

Max Dimont, author of an essay entitled "Jews, God and History," wrote: "The Mosaic Code . . . was the first truly judicial, written code, and eclipsed previously known laws with its all-encompassing humanism, its passion for justice, its love of democracy."[9] Wormser adds:

> The most important contribution of the Jews to our legal system was the very existence of the Torah, the Pentateuch, adopted by Christianity as part of its basic law. Even Mohammed, creator of a new faith, built it frankly upon the Old Testament and upon the Jewish prophets, calling Jesus one of them. Though it differs from the Old Testament in much detail, yet the Koran has most of its roots in Old Testament moral reasoning; and large parts of the Moslem law, ruling many millions today, are difficult to distinguish from the parent Jewish law.[10]

Dimont elaborates further to show how the code of laws revealed to Moses was for all time:

> The law of Moses anticipates the statehood God promised the Israelites. Though at this juncture of their history the Jews are still nomads, the Code of Moses is not for a nomadic people. These laws of Moses are designed to safeguard a national entity, not merely the family unit, though individual rights are never subordinated to the needs of the state. The lofty framework of these laws permitted the emergence of a democratic form of government virile enough to last eight hundred years until the Prophets in turn renovated them. The American Constitution thus far weathered less than two hundred years.[11]

The Mosaic Law is unlike any of its predecessors. While some noteworthy historians, including Durant, maintain that Moses' law was influenced by that of Hammurabi, I again reiterate that the decalogue (the Ten Commandments) have withstood the test of time, which is not true at all of Hammurabi's law. The principles laid down in the Mosaic Law were far more advanced than their Babylonian counterparts though they were written only a few centuries later, circa 1450 B.C.

THE TEN COMMANDMENTS AND OUR LAWS

Many observers have noted that many of today's laws are derived from the Ten Commandments. One such observer, Will Durant, points to many parallels. He saw the fourth commandment as codifying the Sabbath. He saw the fifth commandment as sanctifying the family so strongly that "the ideals then stamped upon the institution marked it throughout the medieval and modern European history until our own disintegrative Industrial Revolution."[12] Durant saw the seventh commandment as recognizing "marriage as the basis of the family."[13] René Wormser adds that the seventh commandment was meant to reinforce and "protect the family" by prohibiting adultery. Of the eighth commandment Durant writes that it "sanctified private property, and bound it up with religion and the family."[14] As to the ninth commandment, Wormser states that it "enjoins perjury and establishes a religious basis for legal procedure."[15] The tenth commandment "proscribed covetousness," states Wormser, "and from this also a great deal of law has been derived."[16] Hence, the Ten Commandments helped lay many of our societal foundations! It certainly laid the foundation for Western law.

It is to the Holy Bible that we owe our legacy of law. It is the Bible that ushered in an era of compassion, humaneness, liberty, and justice. Professor Israel Drapkin, in his book *Crime and Punishment in the Ancient World,* sums it all up: "The Ten Commandments, [are] the moral and legal foundations of Western civilization."[17]

How is it that the Ten Commandments came to influence so much of the history of law? René Wormser believes that the Jews are among the most widely dispersed people in history. He puts forth the theory that it is a result of them having "been carried off into slavery; and each time some have gone home to Palestine and others have remained to establish a closely knit colony in a foreign land."[18] Like any community, the Jews carried with them their beliefs, customs, and their law wherever they went. Other cultures were profoundly affected by the traditions and laws the Jews brought with them.[19]

Of course, the global spread of the Ten Commandments among so many people, cultures, and nations is due to the spread of Christianity. So as Christianity rose and spread, it took the Ten Commandments along into all the earth. Yet for the first three centuries of the Christian era, the faith was an underground movement. Ten waves of bloody persecution swept over the faithful, but the Romans couldn't stop them. When a Christian Caesar at last ascended to the throne (Constantine in the early fourth century), the laws of the Roman state began to conform to biblical principles. Constantine and Theodosius are among those Caesars who were professing Christians who brought Judeo-Christian principles into law. But of all the emperors of that time, Justinian I stands out for his use of the Bible to undergird the law.

EMPEROR JUSTINIAN I

Emperor Justinian I was the ruler of Constantinople (the eastern half of the Roman Empire) from A.D. 482 to 565. Now I must state from the outset that as a ruler, Justinian I had some serious flaws. Historian and warden of Oxford, J. M. Roberts, in his book *History of the World,* writes of Justinian:

> After it had survived for eight hundred years, he abolished the academy of Athens; he wanted to be a Christian emperor, not a ruler of unbelievers, and decreed the destruction of all pagan statues in the capital. Worse still, he accelerated the demotion of the Jews in civic status and the reduction of their freedom to exercise their religion.[20]

Of course, I don't find these sorts of actions acceptable, especially Justinian's treatment of the Jews. But Justinian's rule serves as an example of how the Bible has influenced the development of law. In the words of Durant, "History rightly forgets Justinian's wars, and remembers him for his laws."[21]

Even Justinian's critics point to the good he did. Charles Diehl says he was "the eminent representative of two great ideas—the imperial idea and the Christian idea; and because he represented those ideas, his name will endure forever."[22] P. N. Ure, in the book *Justinian and His Age,* wrote: "Justinian's codifying of the laws is admitted on all sides to be the main achievement which establishes his claim to a notable place in world history."[23] It is this legacy of streamlining a legal system plagued by hundreds of years of contradiction and layers of legislation that we want to briefly explore.

By the time Justinian came to power, Roman law had accumulated for more than a thousand years. The Romans loved to legislate, and virtually no facet of their life was beyond the taxing tentacles of their ambition. Thus, Justinian inherited a legal mess! There were many layers of various laws, often contradicting other laws, throughout different parts of the Empire. Durant points out that Roman law by this time had become "an empirical accumulation rather than a logical code."[24] To streamline and prune this vast body of existing legislation, Justinian established a commission of great legal minds to develop a new code.

The work was done in three phases. First, this commission wrote up a summary of what they saw as the best laws available. This summary, the *Codex Constitutionum* written in 529, became the law of the land, voiding anything that contradicted it. Historians refer to this as the Code of Justinian in which biblical principles and teachings were enshrined.

The commission then reviewed legal decisions of the best legal minds in Roman history and wrote these up in the *Digesta* or *Pandectae* in 533. George Ostrogorsky, in his book *History of the Byzantine State,* comments, "The appearance of the *Digest* (the *Pandects*) in 533 marked an even greater achievement. This was a collection of the writings of the classical Roman jurists and, together with the imperial edicts, it formed the main body of current law."[25] In the *Digest,* we read:

> Ruling as we do over our Empire, which God has entrusted to us, by His divine authority, we know both the triumphs of war and the adornments of peace; we bear up the framework of the State; and we so lift up our hearts in contemplation of the support given to us by the Lord Omnipotent that we put not our trust in our own arms, nor in those of our soldiers, nor in our leaders in war, nor in our own skill; rather do we rest our hopes in the providence of the Supreme Trinity, from whence proceeded the elements of the world universe and their disposition throughout the world.[26]

The third phase of Justinian's legal reforms was the *Institutiones* published in 533, which was essentially a condensed version of the *Codex* with additional commentary. The *Institutiones* was to be an official handbook for students of the law. Like many important documents in Western history, it begins in the name of the Savior.

> In the name of Our Lord Jesus Christ . . . to the youth desirous of studying the law. . . . Having removed every inconsistency from the sacred constitutions [i.e., imperial laws] hitherto inharmonious and confused, we extended our care to the immense volumes of the older jurisprudence, and, like sailors crossing the mid-ocean, by the favour of Heaven, have now completed a work.[27]

These different publications are known collectively as the Code of Justinian. In addition to eradicating many laws that were contradictory to one another, Justinian made some adjustments and additions to the laws. For example:

- "Freedmen were no longer treated as a separate class group." They came to enjoy "all the privileges of freemen."
- The crime of rape was punished severely: by death, as well as the impoundment of property.
- Attorneys were made to swear on the Bible that they would do their utmost to defend their clients with honor. Furthermore, lawyers were to cease from proceeding with their cases if they found out that they were untruthful![28]

Durant writes that Justinian's Code "enacted orthodox Christianity into law. It began by declaring for the Trinity."[29] George Ostrogorsky says: "Under the influence of Christianity, it was often modified in the direction of greater humaneness, particularly with regard to laws concerning the family."[30] Later Ostrogorsky adds:

Justinian was the last Roman Emperor to occupy the Byzantine throne. He was at the same time a Christian ruler filled with the consciousness of the Divine source of his imperial authority. His strivings towards the achievement of a universal Empire were based on Christian, as well as on Roman, conceptions.[31]

Justinian's enactments affected the world for centuries. Professor of history Norman Cantor writes that the "Justinian Code was the most highly developed system of law in the early medieval world; it is the basis of many of the legal systems of modern Europe."[32] Charles Diehl said of Justinian's accomplishment that despite some flaws and defects "this was a very great work, one of the most fruitful for the progress of mankind."[33] Diehl adds:

If the Justinian law provided the imperial power with the foundation of its moral authority, it also, in the civilization of the Middle Ages, conserved, and, later, taught again to the West, the idea of the State, and the principles of social organization. Also, by permeating the rigor of the old Roman law with the new spirit of Christianity, it introduced into law a regard, hitherto unknown, for social justice, public morality, and humanity.[34]

Durant said, "It continued to the end the code of the Byzantine Empire; and five centuries after it disappeared in the West it was revived by the jurists of Bologna, accepted by emperors and popes, and entered like a scaffolding of order into the structure of many modern states."[35]

Justinian's Code eventually went on to influence English legal history. Percy H. Winfield, in his book *The Chief Sources of English Legal History,* explains:

> In the twelfth century, the great school of Bologna was founded and the teaching of Roman Law revived. . . . The new movement had its missionaries, and one of these, Vacarius, came to England to teach Roman Law at Canterbury and, apparently, at Oxford. He compiled for his students a textbook probably about 1149. . . . It is called *Liber pauperum*, its sources are Justinian's *Codex* and *Digest.* . . . At the close of the twelfth century the teaching of Vacarius was in full flower at Oxford.[36]

René Wormser writes:

> When a renaissance of interest in the Roman law began to draw Europe out of the Dark Ages and to afford a base for the development of modern jurisprudence, it was Justinian's lawbooks which where studied; and his codes formed the foundation stones for the eventual structure of European and a great deal of English and American law.[37]

Israel Drapkin notes: "This Codex is indeed the cornerstone of jurisprudence: the Napoleonic Code was modeled directly on it; in Germany, the Roman law was applied . . . until 1900; and even the English 'common law' has many roots in Roman judicial principles."[38] The significance of all this is simple: the Bible undergirded Justinian's Code of laws. Justinian's Code became the foundation of Western law thereafter. Thus the Bible is at the root of our legal system.

ALFRED THE GREAT

Another example of the Bible's impact on Western law is that of Alfred, King of Wessex (849–899), known to the world as Alfred the Great. Taking his cue from St. Patrick, who helped make the Ten Commandments the law of the land in Ireland, Alfred did likewise for England some four centuries later.

Alfred the Great lived in a tumultuous time. Before and after his reign, England was besieged by conquests and regional conflagrations. The country's biggest threat came from the conquering Norsemen, scourge of the European coast, including the British Isles. These were dark times. Yet King Alfred brought hope to his people. Allen J. Frantzen notes, "By publishing a set of laws, the first issued in England in a century, Alfred renewed a tradition that had lapsed in the legal, political, and social chaos that followed the Viking invasions."[39] But it was more than renewal. Historian J. M. Roberts asserts that Alfred's "innovations were a creative effort of government unique in Europe, and marked the beginning of a great age for England."[40]

Unlike Justinian, Alfred the Great ruled by the highest ethical standard. In his *A History of the English-Speaking Peoples,* Winston Churchill expresses:

> In the grim time of Norman overlord ships the figure of the great Alfred was a beacon-light, the bright symbol of Saxon achievement, the hero of the race. The ruler who had taught them courage and self-reliance in the eternal Danish wars, who had sustained them with his national and religious faith, who had given them laws and good governance and chronicled their heroic deeds, was celebrated in legend and song as Alfred the Great.[41]

Even the highly cynical, anti-Christian Voltaire observed, "I do not think that there ever was in the world such a man more worthy of the regard of posterity than Alfred the Great."[42]

Alfred's character was governed by the Bible, and so were his laws. Lecturer Pauline Stafford explains, "In the lengthy preface to his laws, Alfred quoted extensively from the Old Testament. Its picture of the king as judge ordering human society so that it might please an interventionist God was an ideal model for a late ninth-century king."[43]

Of course, other influences moved King Alfred. Frantzen states, "Alfred's laws synthesize many traditions, including the Mosaic law of Scripture, the synodical records of the early church, and, most important, the written law of his own nation."[44] Churchill adds, "King Alfred's Book of Laws, or Dooms, as set out in the existing laws of Kent, Wessex, and Mercia, attempted to blend the Mosaic code with Christian principles and old Germanic customs."[45]

Philip Schaff, in his book *History of the Christian Church,* points out further ways that Alfred's reforms were infused with biblical principles:

> His code is introduced with the Ten Commandments and other laws taken from the Bible. It protects the stranger in memory of Israel's sojourn in Egypt; it gives the Christian slave freedom in the seventh year, as the Mosaic law gave to the Jewish bondman; it protects the laboring man in his Sunday rest; it restrains bloodthirsty passions of revenge by establishing bots or fines for offences; it enjoins the golden

rule (in the negative form), not to do to any man what we would not have done to us.[46]

It is an interesting point as well that even the structure of Alfred's laws had a specific intention and inspiration. Frantzen notes:

> The complex structure of his code reflects its synthetic purposes. . . . The collection is divided into 120 books, an organizational design which reflects a literary tradition rather than a logical necessity. The division into 120 chapters has been seen as a commemoration of the age of Moses, the archetypal lawgiver, said to have died at age 120.[47]

Pauline Stafford explains, "When Alfred issued his law code he aimed to produce and sustain an earthly order mirroring that of heaven; in the code itself he moves readily from sin to crime. Disturbance of the relationship between humans and God is akin to disturbance of the relationships among humans through murder or theft."[48]

The significance of what he did and why can't be underscored enough. Alfred the Great was the first British king to base law in that country solidly on the Bible. The British legal system would later play a critical role in the legal system of nations around the world, including our own.

THE MAGNA CHARTA

Centuries later, the English reached another milestone in their legal history—the Magna Charta (the Great Charter). In 1215 several nobles were dissatisfied with King John's tyrannical rule. The archbishop of Canterbury, Steven Langton, suggested a *written* agreement between king and subjects that would prevent royal despotism. John Richard Green writes in his *History of the English People* that the Magna Charta "marks the transition from the age of traditional rights, preserved in the nation's memory . . . to the age of written legislation."[49]

As we find with virtually all important documents in Christendom, the Magna Charta begins by acknowledging God:

> John, by the grace of God, King of England, Lord of Ireland, Duke of Normandy, Aquitaine, and Count of Anjou, to his Archbishops, Bishops, Abbots, Earls, Barons, Justiciaries, Foresters . . . and his faithful subjects, greeting. Know ye, that we, in the presence of God, and for the salvation of our soul, and the souls of all our ancestors and heirs, and unto the honor of God and the advancement of Holy Church, and amendment of our Realm . . . have, in the first place, granted to God,

and by this our present Charter confirmed, for us and our heirs for ever:

That the Church of England shall be free, and have her whole rights, and her liberties. . . . We also have granted to all the freemen of our kingdom for us and for our heirs for ever, all the underwritten liberties to be had and holden by them and their heirs, of us and our heirs for ever."[50]

The Bible laid the foundations and principles upon which the Magna Charta was framed.

An important by-product of the Magna Charta is the trial-by-jury system. The reason for the demand of trial by jury was because King John would often capriciously accuse a man and then order a magistrate to find the man guilty! Judge Joseph Wapner, perhaps best remembered for TV's *The People's Court* in the 1980s, served for more than twenty years on the bench of the superior and municipal courts of California. He states:

Taken for granted in America and Great Britain, trial by jury, one of the strongest safeguards against government's arbitrary authority, remains a rare privilege in much of the rest of the world. But where, long before the Magna Charta, did it gain its first, rough expression? That's right, in Leviticus. To be precise, in chapter 19, verse 15: "In righteousness shalt thou judge thy neighbor."[51]

Had the Bible never been written, there would be no Magna Charta, including the system of trial-by-jury.

Another very important development in law that goes back to the Bible also occurred during the Middle Ages, and that was the idea of equality of all before the law. Joseph Reither, former history professor at New York University and author of *World History at a Glance,* writes:

The ideal of human equality is a very new concept among men. It is derived from the Christian teaching reiterated throughout the Middle Ages that the souls of all men are of equal value in the sight of God.[52]

HUGO GROTIUS

Another key leader in the development of Western law was a man who also worked from a biblical base. Hugo Grotius (1583–1645) of the Netherlands is known as "the father of modern international law."[53]

Professor of political science Charles Edwards declares that "by age fifteen Grotius had already revealed an intellect and a scholarly capability which were to make him one of the most distinguished men of his time."[54] And by the age of twenty-six, Grotius was lauded for "his *Mare liberum* (1604), which outlined maritime law, and argued for freedom of the seas for all nations."[55]

Grotius spelled out a form of natural law that applied to the nations. Law professor W. E. Butler, in commenting on Grotius's notion of the Law of Nations, explains that Grotius believed that the "axiom was laid down by God himself through nature, for since not every place is supplied with the necessaries of life, some excel in some things and others in something else. By 'divine justice' it was brought about that one people should supply certain needs of others."[56] Thus, Grotius argued for the freedom of all nations at sea.

His greatest work was the *De Jure Belli et Pacis*. Legal scholar René Wormser observes that it was "a comprehensive work which is quoted to this day."[57] Grotius himself explains that he wrote this work to rectify a grievous wrong that existed in Christendom. He thought that the Christian world was engaging itself in too many wars without just cause. Once engaged in war, it acted in ways in which "all reverence for divine and human laws was thrown away."[58]

Grotius riddles his work with the reality and truth of God. Hedley Bull, the late Oxford professor of international relations, explains why many modern students have difficulty reading Grotius: "The student of international relations today finds the works of Grotius difficult to read, even in English translation, encumbered as they are with the biblical and classical learning with which in Grotius's generation it was thought helpful to buttress theoretical arguments."[59] Here's a sample from Book 1 of Grotius's *The Law of War and Peace:*

> Among all good men one principle at any rate is established beyond controversy, that if the authorities issue any order that is contrary to the law of nature or to the commandments of God, the order should not be carried out. For when the Apostles said that obedience should be rendered to God rather than to men, they appealed to an infallible rule of action.[60]

Charles Edwards, in expounding on the beliefs of Grotius, writes:

> Throughout his treatise Grotius made numerous statements extolling God as the "Author" of nature. In book 2 he cited four ideas of God that he believed had been most generally accepted through the ages: first, that God is, and God is One; second, that God is more exalted than all things seen; third, that God has a concern for human affairs

and judges with righteousness; and fourth, that God is the Creator of all things besides Himself.[61]

In the final words to Book 3, Grotius prays that Christendom will awaken to the injustices that he has brought to light and will repent of them. He prays that God will "inscribe these teachings on the hearts of those who hold sway over the Christian world."[62] He prays that God will give the leaders in Christian lands a mind that knows His law so that they will live in obedience. In his Prolegomena 12, Grotius shows that God is the basis of international law:

> The law of nature which we have spoken, comprising alike that which relates to the social life of man and that which is so called in a larger sense, proceeding as it does from the essential traits implanted in man, can nevertheless be rightly attributed to God, because of His having willed that such traits exist in us.[63]

Grotius has had a profound effect on the course of history. No episode in the history of international relations may have impacted the world more than The Peace of Westphalia (1648), which followed The Thirty Years' War and established, for the first time, the nation–state. The Peace of Westphalia was prefaced with the thoughts and ideas of Hugo Grotius. Hedley Bull explains, "The idea of international society which Grotius propounded was given concrete expression in the Peace of Westphalia, and Grotius may be considered the intellectual father of this first general peace settlement of modern times."[64]

Yet Grotius's impact was much larger than just one seminal event in history. René Wormser said, "Grotius's . . . renown overshadows that of all the modern writers on international law. His service to the subject and to humanity was enormous."[65]

WILLIAM BLACKSTONE

Another towering giant in the field of law was William Blackstone (1723–1780), who wrote a multivolume series of *Commentaries* on British law. Blackstone played a very important role in the shaping of law for about a century and a half. He is still among the most respected of jurists. Blackstone was, in the words of W. N. Welsby, "a sincere believer in Christianity, from a profound investigation of its evidences."[66]

Blackstone's influence stretches even to current legal affairs. Perhaps you've heard about the Alabama judge being sued by the ACLU for the "crime" of having a hand-carved plaque of the Ten Commandments hanging on his courtroom wall? Judge Roy Moore is a hero in my book, and he was the 1997 recipient of the second annual "Christian Statesman of the Year" award from Coral Ridge Ministries.[67] Judge Moore has written an eighty-seven-page affidavit on his defense, using Blackstone as his chief legal source. This unpublished treatise[68]—a very helpful resource—documents very well how the laws of America are based on the laws of England, which in turn were based on the laws of God—in particular, the Ten Commandments.

To this day, Blackstone is still highly thought of as a legal source. Moore writes:

> Since 1793 our United States Supreme Court has referred to Sir William Blackstone over 272 times for direction in the law. Amazingly, in the last six years [1990–1996] our Supreme Court Justices have turned to Blackstone and his *Commentaries* on the Laws of England for nearly 21 percent of these references.[69]

Moore shows how the phrases of "life, liberty, property," which are found (with variation) in our Declaration of Independence, can be found in Blackstone, who was widely read at the time our nation's birth certificate was penned. Moore writes, "All three concepts were based upon a belief in God." According to Blackstone, life was "the immediate gift of God, a right inherent by nature and every individual, and it begins in contemplation of law as soon as an infant is able to stir in the mother's womb. . . . Liberty consists properly in a power of acting as one thinks fit without any restraint or control, unless by the Law of Nature; being a right inherent in us by birth, and one of the gifts of God to man at His creation, when He endued him with the faculty of free will."[70] Moore says that "property was an absolute right in every Englishman and the right of ownership was given of God."[71] Blackstone makes the point that property rights were first given to man through God: "In the beginning of the world, we are informed by holy writ, the all-bountiful Creator gave to man dominion over all the earth: and over the fish of the sea, and over the fowl of the air, and over every living thing that moveth upon the earth. . . . This is the only true and solid foundation of man's dominion over external thing[s]."[72]

Judge Moore points out that the "laws of England as well as the Common Law upon which it was based presuppose a belief in God and that His will is the basis of all law."[73] Blackstone writes, "Thus when the Supreme Being formed the universe, and created matter out of nothing, He impressed certain principles upon that matter, from which it can never depart, and without which it would cease to be."[74]

These principles to which Blackstone refers are "the Law of Nature," which was "coequal with mankind and dictated by God himself."[75] Blackstone sees natural law as the will of God that can be discerned from nature in general:

> This will of his Maker is called the law of nature. For as God, when He created matter, and endued it with a principle of mobility, established certain rules for the perpetual direction of that motion; so, when He created man, and endued him with free will to conduct himself in all parts of life, He laid down certain immutable laws of human nature, whereby that free will is in some degree regulated and restrained, and gave him also the faculty of reason to discover the purport of those laws. . . . Such, among others, are these principles: that we should live honestly, should hurt nobody, and should render to everyone his due; to which three general precepts Justinian has reduced the whole doctrine of law.[76]

Because of the sinfulness of man, because man's understanding was "full of ignorance and error," there was a need for revelation. The Bible was that revelation. "The doctrines thus delivered we call the revealed or divine law," Blackstone writes, "and they are to be found only in the holy scriptures."[77] Thus, there is the law of nature (or natural law) and then there is the law known only by revelation as found in the Bible. Blackstone writes, "Upon these two foundations, the law of nature and the law of revelation, depend all human laws; that is to say, no human laws should be suffered to contradict these."[78] That point needs to be repeated. *Upon these two foundations, the law of nature and the law of revelation, depend all human laws; that is to say, no human laws should be suffered to contradict these.* The revealed laws of God are not to be contradicted by man's law! Would that today's legislators, lawyers, and judges take this injunction to heart.

Blackstone made other significant points pertaining to the Scriptures and law. He showed how the Bible was the original source of:

- Oaths, which were taken on the Bible to ensure veracity of the witnesses. A few decades after Blackstone's *Commentaries*, George Washington asked in his Farewell Address, "Where is the security for property, for reputation, for life, if the sense of religious obligation desert the oaths, which are the instruments of investigation in courts of justice?"[79]
- The whole court system itself, which reflects the one that was "established in the Jewish republic by Moses."[80]

- The importance of future rewards and punishments in terms of people obeying the law. Blackstone said that belief in future rewards and punishments makes all the difference in people obeying the law. This is all the more illuminating when you consider what has happened in our culture in light of the secularization and our consequent slide into lawlessness:

> The belief of a future state of rewards and punishments, the entertaining just ideas of the moral attributes of the Supreme Being, and a firm persuasion that he superintends and will finally compensate every action in human life all which are clearly revealed in the doctrines, and forcibly inculcated by the precepts, of our savior Christ. These are the grand foundation of all judicial oaths; which call God to witness the truth of those facts, which perhaps may be only known to him and the party attesting: all moral evidence therefore, all confidence in human veracity, must be weakened by apostasy, and overthrown by total infidelity.[81]

These statements are all the more incredible when you consider the key role Blackstone has played in British and in American law. When Lincoln taught himself the law, one of the key books he had that helped him was Blackstone's *Commentaries*. Not far from the U.S. Capitol Building along Constitutional Avenue is a statue of Sir William Blackstone. Had the Bible never been written, Western law would never have known Blackstone's monumental *Commentaries*.

TIME TO BREAK THE GLASS?

We have just scratched the surface here on the subject of the Bible and law. It is clear that our legal system comes from the legal system of Europe, England especially, which ultimately comes from the Bible. Key figures through the centuries—from Justinian to Alfred, from Grotius to Blackstone—laid the foundation for Western law squarely on God's Law as found in the Bible.

Tragically, we have been moving away from our biblical moorings in the law, and as a result, our legal system is breaking down somewhat. A political cartoon by Wayne Stayskal brought home the point. The cartoon showed the inside of a legislative hall with the tablet of the Ten Commandments hanging on the wall behind a glass case, similar to that which houses a fire hose. The inscription by the glass encasement read "In case of emergency, break glass." I think it's time to break the glass.

CHAPTER 5

THE BIBLE AND POLITICS

"You are the salt of the earth; but if the salt loses its flavor, how shall it be seasoned? It is then good for nothing but to be thrown out and trampled underfoot by men."

—Matthew 5:13

You are the salt of the earth," said Jesus to His disciples. That is an astonishing statement when you think about it. The setting: a handful of people standing beside a lake in a nondescript corner of the Roman Empire. "You are the salt of the earth." Amazing! Does something of the weight of that rest upon you?

Things are corrupting badly in Mongolia. You had better get going. Africa is a mess. Take off!

It is rotten in Turkmenistan. We need some salt to stop the rot there.

Yet, amazing as it may seem, this astonishing prophecy has turned out to be true. Salt acts as a preservative. It keeps what is good from going bad. The followers of Jesus Christ have in fact proved to be, more than anyone else, the preservatives of decency and morality in the world. It was an incredible statement made by Jesus to just a few people back then. If the Bible had never been written, the positive influence that it has been able to play—for example, in the abolition of the slave trade and of slavery itself—would not have been felt. One aspect of being the salt of the earth includes political involvement (Matt. 5:15–16). I believe that politics is an area of life that Christians are no longer to abandon to unbelievers, which we've done for too long.

Vance Havner once likened humanity to a decaying carcass awaiting the vultures of judgment. So, my friends, it comes down to this: we are either the carcass or the salt. It's good from time to time to ask ourselves which one we are.

THE BIBLE ADDRESSES ALL OF LIFE

Do Christianity and the Church have something to say about politics, or is politics completely outside the purview of the Church? Some people think that the Bible and Christianity address only *spiritual* issues. Simon Kistemaker once pointed out that while the institutional Church can address only so many issues, the range of topics the Bible addresses is limitless. Politics is one of those topics.

Abraham Kuyper, the greatest theologian Holland ever produced, was both an influential Christian and a politician. Not only was he a tremendous scholar, founder of the Free University of Amsterdam, an exegete of the Scriptures, and a minister of the gospel of Jesus Christ, but his talents were so outstanding that he became the prime minister of Holland. He was so effective as prime minister that the government declared a national holiday to celebrate his seventieth birthday.

Kuyper was a Calvinist. John Calvin held very clear views regarding the relationship between the Church and the state. Calvin affirmed that the triune God is sovereign over the whole of the cosmos in all of its spheres and kingdoms—not merely the Church, but every sphere of life. Kuyper wrote:

> The Son is not to be excluded from anything. You cannot point to any natural realm or star or comet or even descend into the depth of the earth, but it is related to Christ, not in some unimportant tangential way, but directly. There is no force in nature, no laws that control those forces that do not have their origin in that eternal Word. For this reason, it is totally false to restrict Christ to spiritual affairs and to assert that there is no point of contact between him and the natural sciences.[1]

Thus, politics is not a domain separate from Christian influence.

GOD IS THE SOURCE OF ALL POLITICAL POWER

The ultimate source of all authority is not the state, nor the people: it is God. As we read in the Scriptures, all authority and power come from God. The power man exercises is delegated by God. Understanding this fact is vitally important, because history makes it clear that every humanistic or nontheistic state that has placed the authority to govern (and you need to remember that the right to govern is the right to coerce) in an all-powerful state or even in the people has sown within itself the seeds of totalitarianism.

The authority of the state comes from God, and the state is answerable to God; when a people lose sight of that truth, totalitarianism will follow. The state, then, is an agency of God's common grace, whereby He restrains wickedness; its purpose is to enact and to execute the laws that God has given in His Word, the moral laws that He has written upon the hearts of men. Our responsibility is to honor the state, for Scripture says government is put in place by God. We are to obey our laws, pay our taxes, and pray for those in authority over us.

THE STATE HAS LIMITED POWERS

The fact that God is the source of political power leads us to another principle: God has limited the state's authority and power. The state does not encompass *all* of society; there are other spheres of authority. There are the family and the Church; there are schools, businesses, and other creative endeavors that the state does not naturally have the authority to control, as we see happening in totalitarian regimes—and increasingly in the United States.

This limitation means, of course, that when people in leadership overstep their authority, the Christian is bound to disobey. If the state commands the Christian to do that which is contrary to the clear teaching of God's Word, then he must obey God and not man (Acts 5:29). Today and throughout history some governments have forbidden Christians to pray, to worship God, or to proclaim the gospel to others. In these and all other circumstances where the state countermands the commandments of God, the Christian must obey God and defy the state because the state is limited in its authority.

CHURCH AND STATE

What, then, is the relationship between the state and the Church?

Again, John Calvin's views are clear and, in my opinion, accurate. The Lutheran scholar, author, and law professor Dr. John Eidsmoe summarized Calvin's teaching about the state in *God and Caesar:*

Unlike many Anabaptists, Calvin recognized that the authority of the state comes from God. Unlike many Catholic theologians, Calvin believed that the authority came directly from God to the state rather than through the church. The believer was a citizen of both kingdoms and under the authority of both the state and the church. However, the state's authority over the believer is limited to that which God has given to the state; if the state steps beyond that authority, it acts without legitimacy, and believers are to resist it.[2]

This view helps explain why so many of the sons and daughters of Calvin's teaching would go on to become the settlers and founders of America. (We'll discuss them further in Chapter 6.)

I believe there should be a separation of the Church and the state, as Calvin taught. But separation of the Church and the state does not mean a separation of *God* from the state, which is what we find in our country today. The Bible very clearly states that the nation that forgets God "shall be turned into hell" (Ps. 9:17). The Founding Fathers of this country never meant to establish a nation separated from God. The Declaration of Independence acknowledges God as the giver of inalienable rights to men. Benjamin Franklin arose during the writing of the Constitution of the United States and declared in a well-known speech:

> I have lived, sir, a long time, and the longer I live, the more convincing proofs I see of this truth—that God governs in the affairs of men. And if a sparrow cannot fall to the ground without His notice, is it probable that an empire can rise without His aid? We have been assured, sir, in the Sacred Writings, that "except the Lord build the House, they labor in vain that build it." I firmly believe this; and I also believe that without His concurring aid we shall succeed in this political building no better than the builders of Babel.[3]

Franklin requested that the Constitutional Convention, which wrote America's governing document, should be opened with prayer, imploring the aid of Almighty God. Franklin's actions demonstrate the fallacy of those who would say that we should do away with prayer before the opening of the sessions of the House of Representatives and the Senate, on the premise that it is contrary to our Constitution. Nothing could be more ridiculous nor ultimately more damaging to any nation.

THE FOUNDING FATHERS AND THE SINFULNESS OF MAN

The founders of America, because of their clear understanding of the teachings of the Bible, knew that man basically was evil, so they designed a form of government that could keep that evil in check.

They granted the federal government specifically enumerated powers only, while all other powers were reserved to the states or to the people. They also created the three branches of government, with their built-in checks and balances. Why did they do that? Because they recognized the dangers of concentrating power in the hands of a few, who could manipulate government to further their own ungodly ambitions.

We see this view of human nature expressed in the Federalist Papers, written by James Madison, Alexander Hamilton, and John Jay in order to convince the states to ratify the Constitution. Madison, the chief architect of the Constitution, learned his political philosophy from the great Presbyterian parson John Witherspoon. In Federalist Paper #51, Madison makes the point that men aren't angels and, therefore, even government itself (since it's run by men) must be held in check. Madison states that government is "but the greatest of all reflections on human nature."[4] Madison goes on to argue that "if men were angels,"[5] then government wouldn't even be necessary! He continues:

> If angels were to govern men, neither external or internal controls on government would be necessary. In framing a government which is to be administered by men over men, the great difficulty lies in this: you must first enable the government to control the governed; and in the next place oblige it to control itself.[6]

The biblical doctrine that man is sinful led the founders of this country to build safeguards that protect the governed from the government. But today the division between the powers of the states and the federal government is being obliterated, the distinctions between the three branches of the federal government are being blurred, and more and more power is being collected into fewer and fewer hands.

What is the purpose of government, then? It has been instituted by God because of sin—to restrain the wicked and to protect justice. The purpose of government is to glorify God and to allow lawful citizens to go about their tasks and live for Him. One of the reasons for our lack of impact on our country is that many Christians are not sufficiently committed to Jesus Christ to do everything that they can to change our land.

A LESSON FROM FRANKENSTEIN

The Church seems to be somewhat ineffective in the political realm today. Christianity is today under attack in the very nation that gave the world the model of religious liberty. What happened along the way from Plymouth Rock to the 1990s? Who is responsible? We could blame atheism, humanism, secularism, Communism, or cultism. We could point a finger at the ACLU or the NOW or the People for the American Way. Are they the culprits?

Perhaps a little story may shed some light on this. I am sure you know the story of Dr. Frankenstein and his famous monster. Just imagine, if you will, the final scene in which the monster has gone berserk and has wreaked havoc upon the townspeople. He has left several people dead, has attacked his maker, and has destroyed the home. The whole house is now ablaze and is setting the sky alight with its flames. About this time a friend of Dr. Frankenstein arrives from a distant city. He sees the carnage and chaos and asks, "Dr. Frankenstein, what has happened here?"

"A monster, a monster! A monster did this. It was terrible! He just went berserk, killed people, and destroyed the home."

The friend exclaims, "A monster? Where did this monster come from?" Silence. "Where did it come from, Dr. Frankenstein?"

"Well . . . I made it myself," he replies.

In case you don't see the application, we have to acknowledge that a great deal of the blame must rest upon us—must be laid at the doorstep of the Church. We have failed to obey the Great Commission in this country as a whole. We have failed to obey the Bible's cultural mandate to be involved in every sphere of activity. We have retreated from politics, government, the media, and higher education, and we have left them to unbelievers. We have failed to fulfill our responsibilities as citizens; we have failed to obey the command of Christ to render unto Caesar the things that are Caesar's.

Now, we didn't create this monster with our own hands, but we allowed it to grow up and to take power, and with the power of the government, the colleges, the media, the courts, and the legislatures in its hands it has wreaked this carnage in America today. Therefore, I think we must realize that much of the fault is ours.

The reason Christianity has lost ground in our nation is clear. We have allowed secular humanists to take the offensive while the Christian Church cowers. The Christians have been running as fast as they can away from the conflict. No wonder the other team is winning!

CHRISTIAN RETREAT FROM THE PUBLIC SPHERE

For decades, religion has left all of the public spheres and has retreated within the stained-glass walls of the church or the prayer closet. Up until about fifteen years ago, we virtually abandoned government, media, and public education, and we left these fields to the unbelievers to take over and then to destroy. There have been many efforts in the last decade or two to try to play "catch up," and there have been many successes along the way. But the humanist agenda has made incredible inroads, particularly in our public schools.

Of course, there are many preachers who have failed to preach. I have had laymen lament to me that their preachers will not speak about the important issues of the day because the subjects are too controversial, and the preachers don't want to step on anyone's toes. And they don't want to jeopardize their tax-exempt status by appearing to endorse a particular candidate or political party.

But we can't lay all the blame at the feet of the preachers because there are many laymen who simply don't want to be bothered with these important issues. They don't want to hear about what's happening in our government and how it is affecting our society. They are only interested in their own personal problems.

As a result of our culture's continued assault on Christianity, the Christian faith has been isolated more and more into a tiny, private sector of life and removed from the whole public spectrum of our existence. Christians have got to wake up to the fact that they have been deluded, deceived, and outmaneuvered. We have got to assert the truth of what our Constitution means. I am not in favor of the government selecting a church and making the national Church of America and financing it. Nor am I in favor of the Church controlling the state. I am astounded to see apparently intelligent people fearful that Christians are aiming for just that because we would then have an American ayatollah running the government. I assure you that I do not want the bishop of Washington running the United States. But I am in favor of the influence of Jesus Christ being felt throughout this land in every sphere of its activity. I am in favor of the law of God being proclaimed. I am in favor of Christians becoming informed, of Christians becoming active, of Christians voting, of Christians serving their country, of Christians bringing their convictions to bear upon every part of the American life.

I believe that unless we act as salt, this nation is going to continue to decay until it reaches the point of no return. Voices on all sides are doing their dead level best to force the salt back into the salt shaker! I for one am determined that I will not let that happen to me. I want you to know that there are those who want to silence me. But I have determined that I will not be silent, and I will continue to speak out. I believe that we have very little time left before all of us will be silenced completely, if we do not act now.

THREE MODEL CHRISTIAN STATESMEN

Someone once said that "history is biography"—meaning that throughout history, key men and women shape the course of history. Three of the greatest statesmen in the last two hundred years were shaped by the Bible. I want to focus the rest of this chapter on each of these three key leaders—George Washington, Abraham Lincoln, and William Wilberforce. In particular we want to look at how the Bible impacted their character and their politics.

THE FAITH OF GEORGE WASHINGTON

One of the great Christian statesmen of all time was George Washington (1732–1799), the father of our country and a man of noble character and virtue. Revolutionary War hero Henry Lee once described Washington as "First in War, First in Peace, and First in the Hearts of his Countrymen."[7]

While some in our society today, even a few Christian authors, call George Washington a Deist, the facts of history easily refute that. Deists believed that although "a god" made the world, this god was not personal and never interfered in the affairs of man. Deism, which exalted human reason over divine revelation, was totally contradictory to Christianity with its belief in the Incarnation.

Washington was a committed vestryman in the Episcopal church. He was a Trinitarian in good standing with his church. Some of George Washington's own prayers, recorded in a book entitled *The Daily Sacrifice* in his own handwriting, show without a doubt that his relationship with the Lord was important to him.[8] The following sample of those prayers shows that Washington was definitely not a Deist:

SUNDAY MORNING . . . Almighty God, and most merciful Father, who didst command the children of Israel to offer a daily sacrifice to Thee, that thereby they might glorify and praise Thee for Thy protection both night and day, receive O Lord, my morning sacrifice which I now offer up to Thee. . . .

Since Thou art a God of pure eyes, and will be sanctified in all who draw nearer to Thee, who dost not regard the sacrifice of fools, nor hear sinners who tread in Thy courts, pardon, I beseech Thee, my sins, remove them from Thy presence, as far as the east is from the west, and accept of me for the merits of Thy son Jesus Christ. . . .

Bless my family, kindred, friends and country, be our God and guide this day and forever for His sake, who lay down in the grave and rose again for us, Jesus Christ our Lord. Amen.

SUNDAY EVENING . . . O most Glorious God, in Jesus Christ my merciful and loving Father, I acknowledge and confess my guilt, in the weak and imperfect performance of the duties of this day. I have called on Thee for pardon and forgiveness of sins. . . . Let me live according to those holy rules which Thou hast this day prescribed in Thy holy word. . . .

Continue Thy goodness to me this night. These weak petitions, I humbly implore Thee to hear, accept and answer for the sake of Thy Dear Son, Jesus Christ our Lord, Amen.

MONDAY MORNING . . . Daily frame [shape] me more and more into the likeness of Thy Son, Jesus Christ, that living in Thy fear, and dying in Thy favor, I may in Thy appointed time attain the resurrection of the just unto eternal life.[9]

Washington's devotional life would put the average Christian today to shame. He normally arose early in the morning to pray. He spent a great deal of time on his knees. A few portraits of him kneeling in prayer at Valley Forge are well known and reflect his commitment to prayer.

George Washington once said to a group of Indians, "You do well to wish to learn our arts and ways of life, and above all, the religion of Jesus Christ. . . . Congress will do everything they can to assist you in this wise intention."[10] Imagine if the politically correct crowd got ahold of this statement—Washington is saying here that Jesus is superior to the Indian gods. This would not exactly endear him to the cultural elites of today who elevate Native American religion over Christianity, even as they elevate virtually anything above Christianity!

In a letter sent to the governors of all the states, Washington wrote:

I now make it my earnest prayer that God would have you and the State over which you preside in his holy protection; and that he would most graciously be pleased to dispose us all to do justice, to love mercy, and to demean ourselves with charity, humility, and pacific temper of mind, which were the characteristics of the Divine Author of our blessed religion; without a humble recognition of whose example, in these things, we can never hope to be a happy nation.[11]

Referring to this very quote, the statesman Henry Cabot Lodge stated: "Washington either believed in the divinity of Christ or when he wrote those words he deliberately stated something which he did not believe."[12]

Our first president did not separate his politics from his religion; rather, his religious views motivated his politics. Just as virtually all our presidents have done, he called for national days of fasting and prayer and national days of thanksgiving (to God) and prayer. He saw the proper role that religion played in promoting morality.

George Washington was generally quiet about his religion, and I personally think that the quiet dignity of his faith may have in some way helped create the misunderstandings about what he believed. Nelly Custis, the granddaughter of Martha Washington, was upset to learn that some people questioned his faith. She wrote to historian Jared Sparks to rebut the notion that he was not a Christian: "His life, his writings, prove that he was a Christian. He was not one of those who act or pray, 'that they may be seen of men.' He communed with his God in secret."[13] Had the Bible not been written, Washington would not have been the same man. He spoke reverently of the "blessed Religion revealed in the word of God";[14] it was the religion that helped make him the great leader he was.

WAS LINCOLN A CHRISTIAN?

Abraham Lincoln (1809–1865) is everlasting in the memory of his countrymen. He was greatly influenced by the Scriptures. Read any of his speeches and they virtually drip with the Word of God. Many Americans actually think the quote "A house divided against itself cannot stand" was Lincoln's, but he was simply quoting a Bible verse (Matt. 12:25), which his audience probably recognized. (In the nineteenth century, Americans were far more biblically literate than we are today — unfortunately.) John G. Nicolay, Lincoln's private secretary, said, "He praised the simplicity of the Gospels. He often declared that the Sermon on the Mount contained the essence of all law and justice, and that the Lord's Prayer was the sublimest composition in human language."[15]

Earlier in his life, Lincoln was not a Christian. When he came to Springfield, Illinois, he fell in with some agnostic and skeptical friends who gave him *Volney's Ruins* — a book of great unbelief that viciously and articulately attacked the Scriptures. That book had a tremendously chilling effect upon Lincoln's faith. Nonetheless, Lincoln found in the Scriptures the power to mold and change his life, and later, during the midst of the calamitous war, he became a Christian.

Joshua Fry Speed, who was Lincoln's "most intimate and unselfish friend,"[16] remarked that Lincoln had been a skeptic as a young man, but in the summer of 1864, Speed noticed a change:

> As I entered the room, near night, he was sitting near a window, intently reading the Bible. Approaching him I said: "I am glad to see you so profitably engaged." "Yes," said he, "I am profitably engaged." "Well," said I, "if you have recovered from your skepticism, I am sorry to say that I have not." Looking me earnestly in the face, and

placing his hand upon my shoulder, he said: "You are wrong, Speed; take all of this book upon reason that you can and the balance on faith, and you will live and die a happier and better man."[17]

The Speeches and Other Works of Abraham Lincoln

Most of the speeches and writings of Lincoln clearly reflect the influence of the Bible. It's interesting to read the Second Inaugural Address etched in stone at the Lincoln Memorial and see Scripture quoted there, in light of today's schizophrenic view of absolute separation of Church and state (which so often translates to "officially sanctioned atheism").[18]

Like Washington, he declared national days of fasting and prayer or thanksgiving and prayer. Note the Bible's impact, as we read excerpts from two calls for prayer and fasting and from an order Lincoln gave to Union soldiers to observe the Lord's Day:

> Proclamation of a National Fast Day, August 12, 1861
> Whereas it is fit and becoming in all people, at all times, to acknowledge and revere the supreme government of God; to bow in humble submission to his chastisements; to confess and deplore their sins and transgressions, in the full conviction that the fear of the Lord is the beginning of wisdom; and to pray with all fervency and contrition for the pardon of their present and prospective action . . .[19]

> Proclamation of a National Fast Day, March 30, 1863
> We know that by his divine law nations, like individuals, are subjected to punishments and chastisements in this world, may we not justly fear that the awful calamity of civil war which now desolates the land may be but a punishment inflicted upon us for our presumptuous sins, to the needful end of our national reformation as a whole people? We have been the recipients of the choicest bounties of Heaven. We have been preserved, these many years, in peace and prosperity. We have grown in numbers, wealth, and power as no other nation has ever grown; but we have forgotten God. We have forgotten the gracious hand which preserved us in peace, and multiplied and enriched and strengthened us; and we have vainly imagined, in the deceitfulness of our hearts, that all these blessings were produced by some superior wisdom and virtue of our own. Intoxicated with unbroken success, we have become too self-sufficient to feel the necessity of redeeming and preserving grace, too proud to pray to the God that made us:
> It behooves us, then, to humble ourselves before the offended Power, to confess our national sins, and to pray for clemency and forgiveness.[20]

Order for Sabbath Observance, November 15, 1862
The President, commander-in-chief of the army and navy, desires and
enjoins the orderly observance of the Sabbath by the officers and men
in the military and naval service. The importance for man and beast of
the prescribed weekly rest, the sacred rights of Christian soldiers and
sailors, a becoming deference to the best sentiment of a Christian people, and a due regard for the Divine will, demand that Sunday labor in
the army and navy be reduced to the measure of strict necessity. . . .
The first general order issued by the Father of his Country [Washing-
ton] after the Declaration of Independence indicates the spirit in which
our institutions were founded and should ever be defended. "The general hopes and trusts that every officer and man will endeavor to live
and act as becomes a Christian soldier, defending the dearest rights
and liberties of his country."[21]

His Second Inaugural Address

The last months of Lincoln's life—for he lived only a year and a half
after that day when he consecrated his heart to Christ—saw a tremendous change in him. In fact, during this time he was reelected president
and after the reelection, of course, he delivered his second Inaugural
Address, which, in my opinion, is Lincoln's finest speech. One Lincoln
biographer, Henry Whitney, author of *Lincoln the Citizen*, once described
this speech as "an almost unbroken invocation to God for His assistance
and succor in behalf of our bleeding nation."[22] The words are inscribed
on the walls of the Lincoln Memorial. It includes these words:

The Almighty has His own purposes. "Woe unto the world because of
offenses! for it must needs be that offenses come; but woe to that man
by whom the offense cometh." If we shall suppose that American slavery is one of those offenses which, in the providence of God, must
needs come, but which, having continued through His appointed time,
He now wills to remove, and that He gives to both North and South
this terrible war, as the woe due to those by whom the offense came,
shall we discern therein any departure from those divine attributes
which the believers in a living God always ascribe to Him? Fondly do
we hope—fervently do we pray—that this mighty scourge of war may
speedily pass away. Yet, if God wills that it continue until all the
wealth piled by the bondman's two hundred and fifty years of unre-
quited toil shall be sunk, and until every drop of blood drawn with the
lash, shall be paid by another drawn with the sword, as was said three
thousand years ago, so still it must be said, "The judgments of the
Lord are true and righteous altogether."

. . . With malice toward none; with charity for all; with firmness in the right, as God gives us to see the right, let us strive on to finish the work we are in; to bind up the nation's wounds, to care for him who shall have borne the battle and for his widow, and his orphan—to do all which may achieve and cherish a just and lasting peace among ourselves, and with all nations.[23]

The last bill that he signed into law was the bill that mandated that the words "In God We Trust" should henceforth appear on all of our coins. His last meeting with his cabinet on the day that he was shot was one in which he said that there would be no recriminations, no vengeance taken on the South—"malice toward none; charity for all." If he had lived, the restoration of the South probably would have gone differently.

His last speech ended with the words that a proclamation for a national day of thanksgiving was in preparation and would soon be sent to Congress. In that same cabinet meeting, he had said that now that the abomination of slavery was removed, the next point on the agenda would be the curse of alcohol that so plagued the land.

The Cruelest Shot Ever Fired

But that night he and his wife went to Ford's Theater. Lincoln was not interested in the play. That very day news had come that the war was over. Now he looked forward to times of peace. But he had said on several occasions that he would not outlive this conflict—that when this great issue was settled, he would die. Sitting there in that theater, he leaned forward and said to Mary his last words: "Do you know what I would like to do now? I would like to go with you to the Near East."

The same day Lincoln said the scourge of alcohol should be removed, a young man had gone to a tavern and had several drinks. His name was John Wilkes Booth. Another young man had left his post outside the president's theater box and had gone across the street to a tavern to have a drink. Now the first of these two men—in the absence of the second—quietly opened the door of the president's box. Lincoln continued speaking to his wife: "We could go to Bethlehem where He was born." Booth stepped quietly into the presidential box. "We could visit Bethany. We could follow in those hallowed footsteps." Booth lifted the gun and aimed it at the back of Lincoln's head. "And we could go up to Jeru—"[24]

The maddest pistol in history rang out and a bullet pierced the head of Abraham Lincoln. He was carried across the street. He had written to the New York Avenue Presbyterian Church explaining that he had now come to a faith in the Savior and requested to make a public profession that Easter Sunday—but on Good Friday, he died.

Secretary of War Edwin Stanton, looking down at the body lying at an angle across the bed in a room across the street from Ford's Theater, said, "There lies the most perfect ruler of men that the world has ever seen."[25] Now Lincoln belonged to the ages.

WILLIAM WILBERFORCE: CHRISTIAN STATESMAN

William Wilberforce (1759–1833) was probably the greatest Christian statesman of all time, yet I have discovered that there are many Americans who are not familiar with him at all. This ignorance is indeed very sad because he was a great man among great men and is worthy to be known. He is, of course, well known in England, where he lived. For those Americans not familiar with him, I hope to paint a vivid and memorable picture. He is a great model to emulate.

William Wilberforce inherited considerable wealth from his grandfather and from an uncle. He was, therefore, among the landed nobility of England. He was indeed a polished gentleman; a man of exemplary conduct and morals.

He grew up in the Church of England, as did almost everyone in England at that time. His mother was not too religious. In fact, she was actually fearful of her son becoming "too religious." Therefore, at one time she kept him away from some friends that were considered a little over zealous in their religion. He continued with the nominal sort of religion "in-name-only" that was so typical of the age in which he lived.

Parliament at Twenty-One

When he grew up he went to Cambridge. Upon leaving there he ran for Parliament at the age of twenty-one. Although he ran against men who were much older and much more experienced in political matters than he, Wilberforce had a God-given talent of speaking that he had perfected with many years of study and practice and used to win the election. At the age of twenty-one, he entered the House of Commons, where he was to serve for the next forty-five years!

When he was about twenty-five years old, his mother decided to take a trip to the Continent to visit Switzerland and Italy. He decided to go along during the summer, and he invited an old schoolmaster named Isaac Milner to join him. Milner suggested to Wilberforce that to pass the time as they made their way slowly across France they read the famous devotional classic by Philip Doddridge, *The Rise and Progress of Religion*. Wilberforce was struck by the beauty of what Doddridge taught, and of the meaning of the atonement of Jesus Christ.[26]

Though it impressed his mind and opened his intellect to an understanding of the gospel that he had never had before, he resisted the book's message because he lived in a high and giddy circle. He hobnobbed with the finest of the aristocracy. He was in demand at all of the parties and balls. And he did not want this Christ to get too close.

He left his family in Italy and returned to England. The following summer he returned to the Continent and again invited Isaac Milner to accompany him. This time they decided to read together the Greek New Testament. As they read it, the Holy Spirit of God took the Word of God and drove it deeper into the heart of William Wilberforce, and that Word finally changed his life. He returned from the Continent, this time a transformed man; Christ had come to live in his heart. And thereafter, it was the goal of William Wilberforce to live for Christ.

Should He Stay in Politics?

At first his family and friends thought that he was mad, because real Christianity was so rare in those days, especially among the upper class. Though the Wesleyan revival had touched the lower classes, the upper classes in England were almost unaffected. The rumor flew around Parliament that Wilberforce was bereft of his senses. But his colleagues soon found that he was not melancholy, as had been reported, but rather, he was filled with joy. He was loving and sober and gracious and kind beyond any person that they knew. In fact, he was seen to be the most loving and compassionate man in all of England.

Wilberforce was seeking some sort of guidance. He had been elected to Parliament at age twenty-one, and then at twenty-five he had been elected to represent the largest county in all of England: Yorkshire. But now that he was a Christian he felt he should resign his position in Parliament because it was too worldly.

He went to see John Newton, author of the familiar hymn "Amazing Grace." Newton had grown up in a very rough-and-ready way. He had been a slave trader, transporting slaves from the west coast of Africa to the markets of the Western world, until God reached out and transformed this rough and godless man into a minister of the gospel.

Wilberforce wrote him a letter and then went to see him. To his amazement Newton advised him that he should not leave his post as that would be tantamount desertion of the position to which God had called him; rather, he should serve Christ there with all of his talents and all of his energies. Newton told Wilberforce, "The Lord has raised you up to the good of his church and for the good of the nation."[27] So Wilberforce decided not to resign his position in Parliament.

Wilberforce was a lifelong friend and classmate of William Pitt (the younger), another remarkable young man in a remarkable age. In his mid-twenties, Pitt was elected prime minister of England. Wilberforce and Pitt were like brothers, except Pitt never accepted Christ.

Slavery — His Great Concern

One day Pitt visited Wilberforce at his country home. Pitt declared, "Wilberforce, England needs a crusader to wake her up. This slave trade is horrible business. I agree, it will be a long, hard fight, but someone must take the lead. *William, you are that man*."[28] Now Newton had impressed upon Wilberforce's mind this problem of slavery, having been so intimately involved with it himself in earlier days.

Wilberforce felt, after much prayer, that indeed God was calling him to a lifetime crusade. Wilberforce said that slavery in England was like a wisdom tooth. It would be exceedingly difficult to get it out because there were a great many financial and economic matters that tied almost all of England into the slave trade. In fact, many of the members of Parliament were involved with it in one way or another. But he began to earnestly give himself to the task.

Wilberforce was also concerned about how he could be used by God to stop moral decline. In 1787, he wrote, "Almighty God has set before me two great objectives, the abolition of the slave trade and the reformation of morals."[29] And so he formed two societies: The Committee for the Abolition of the Slave Trade and The Society for the Reformation of Manners, which was designed to raise the moral standards of Englishmen. (I guess this was the first Moral Majority that ever existed.)

But Wilberforce gave himself wholeheartedly to the freeing of slaves. He began an intensive study of the problem of slavery, working night and day. He made a chart of each hour of every day broken down in quarter-hour segments. He indicated on it the time spent in prayer, the time spent in the Word of God, the time spent studying the slave trade, the time spent working for the great causes of God.

His Great Goals

Wilberforce gave himself over to truth and righteousness and humanity. These were the great goals of his life. He set aside political ambitions. He could have easily become prime minister after Pitt, but he turned his back on that possibility in order that he might pursue more noble goals. He refused, along with forty other members of Parliament, to ever accept any of the emoluments and benefits that the government could bestow upon them. Of the forty men that took that vow, Wilberforce was the only one of the group to remain true to his pledge.

In 1797, he married Barbara Spooner. He moved to Clapham, and his group began to grow as a few other Christians who had been moved by his example were brought into Parliament. At first he was virtually the only evangelical Christian in all of Parliament, but by the time he left, there were over one hundred Christians in each of the houses.

Wilberforce wrote a book at this time that had enormous impact on the upper classes of England, rather laboriously titled *A Practical View of the Prevailing Religious System of Professed Christians in the Higher and Middle Classes of This Country Contrasted with Real Christianity.* With a title that long (twenty-four words!), a book is never going to go, right? Well, it went through twenty editions! In fact, it is still in print today under the abbreviated title *Real Christianity.* It had a tremendous impact on people, one of whom was the great Edmund Burke, who joined with Wilberforce and others in opposing, among other things, the war in America. (Wilberforce came into Parliament right during the Revolutionary War. He opposed the war and called for peace.)

Abolition of Slave Trade

After several years of studying and thoroughly preparing himself, finally Wilberforce got up on the floor of Parliament and introduced a bill for the abolition of the slave trade. His speech, lasting four and one-half hours, was one of the most moving speeches that had ever been given on the floor of Parliament. But the vote went overwhelmingly against his motion. The bill was defeated because of the tremendous financial interests in slavery among the members of Parliament.

As John Wesley lay dying, he wrote to Wilberforce to encourage him:

MY DEAR SIR,—Unless the Divine Power has raised you up to be as *Athanasius contra mundum,* I see not how you can go through your glorious enterprise in opposing that execrable villainy which is the scandal of religion, of England, and of human nature. Unless God has raised you up for this very thing, you will be worn out by the opposition of men and devils; but if God be for you, who can be against you? Are all of them stronger than God? Oh, be not weary of well-doing. Go on in the name of God, and in the power of His might, till even American slavery, the vilest that ever saw the sun, shall vanish away

before it. That He who has guided you from your youth up may continue to strengthen you in this and all things, is the prayer of, dear sir,
Your affectionate servant,
JOHN WESLEY[30]

The next year Wilberforce got up in Parliament, spoke again, made the motion again, and again was defeated. The next year he spoke again, and again he was defeated. The next year he spoke again, and again met with defeat. He skipped a year, then spoke again and was defeated; and again and again and again for two decades! He continued to battle for the abolition of slavery. Slowly, the vote began to change.

Finally, in 1807, twenty years after he began his great crusade, the vote was taken and there was an overwhelming majority in favor of the abolition of the slave trade. Parliament leaped to its feet when the vote was announced and gave Wilberforce perhaps the greatest ovation that had ever been given to anybody in its history. He was so moved and overwhelmed with gratitude to God that this long crusade of twenty years had finally met with the blessings of heaven, that he sat at his table with his head in his hands, tears streaming down his face.

Of course, this was only the first step in his long-range goal, which was to bring about not only the abolition of the slave trade but also the emancipation of the slaves, who, even after the vote to abolish the slave *trade*, were still in chains throughout the British Empire.

The Battle for Emancipation of Slaves

Wilberforce continued the battle, which was to last for another twenty-five years. He became the object of all sorts of persecution and obloquy. Every kind of cartoon imaginable was drawn about him. He was attacked in the newspapers; he was attacked physically; his family was threatened; he was the target of attempted murder. He had to hire bodyguards. In spite of all of that he continued with his crusade.

Finally, some fifty-nine years after he had written his first article in the newspaper opposing slavery, he reached the end of his life. Having resigned from Parliament in 1825, he went on a visit to London where he was struck with what would be his final illness. While he was struggling for life, about a mile away at the House of Commons, the bill for the emancipation of all of the slaves in Great Britain was once again before the House. Finally the vote was cast; the measure had been victorious. Immediately a runner was sent to Wilberforce's house, and there in his bed he received word that after a lifetime of effort on his part, seven hundred thousand British slaves had been set free!

A few days after he received the word of the emancipation of the slaves, he died. His body was interred at Westminster Abbey, and the memorial there reads in part:

> To warm benevolence, and to universal candour,
> He added the abiding eloquence of a Christian life.
> Eminent as he was in every department of public labour,
> And a leader in every work of charity,
> Whether to relieve the temporal or the spiritual wants
>   of his fellow men
> His name will ever be specially identified
> With those exertions
> Which, by the blessing of God, removed from England
> The guilt of the African slave trade,
> And prepared the way for the abolition of slavery
>   in every colony of the Empire.
> —*Epitaph to Wilberforce in Westminster Abbey*[31]

A VIEW TO THE FUTURE

We as Christians must be involved in the political process. In fact, as we'll see in the next chapter, Christians helped to shape the political process and the freedoms we enjoy in the first place. The Bible, especially in times past, has had a great deal of impact for good on politics. It is time for Christians to reassert that impact and to regain our role as salt in the culture. The very future of society depends upon it.

CHAPTER 6

THE BIBLE AND THE FOUNDING OF AMERICA

"Blessed is the nation whose God is the LORD."

—Psalm 33:12

On the eve of the International Year of the Bible in 1983, *Newsweek* did a cover story on the role of the Bible and the founding of America. At that time it made this insightful statement:

> For centuries [the Bible] has exerted an unrivaled influence on American culture, politics and social life. Now historians are discovering that the Bible, perhaps even more than the Constitution, is our founding document: the source of the powerful myth of the United States as a special, sacred nation, a people called by God to establish a model society, a beacon to the world.[1]

I agree. An honest look at history, especially at primary sources, reveals that to be the case. *Newsweek* isn't the only news magazine to make this point. A few years after that article was published, *TIME* magazine, which is not usually a friend to Christianity, in an article entitled "Looking to Its Roots," said this: "Ours is the only country deliberately founded on a good idea. That good idea combines a commitment to man's inalienable rights with the Calvinist belief in an ultimate moral right and sinful man's obligation to do good. These articles of faith, embodied in the Declaration of Independence and in the Constitution, literally govern our lives today."[2] So we see that even some secularists acknowledge that the Bible gave us the Constitution.

The purpose of this chapter is to look at our founding documents, in particular the Declaration of Independence and the Constitution, and trace clear biblical influence. No historical movement operates in a vacuum, and American constitutionalism certainly did not. There were several forces working together to shape this nation, but I maintain that chief among them were the Judeo-Christian Scriptures. America began with a long line of actions by "people of the book," the Bible. As historian Clarence Carson writes in *A Basic History of the United States:*

> Since Christianity is a religion of the book, the written word assumes a special importance for Christians. Learning assumes a special importance. Careful construction of the meaning of words assumes a special importance. The original meaning, the original documents, the earliest applications, all assume a special importance. This is so especially for the scriptures, but the attitude and belief tend to be extended to more worldly books, documents, and words as well. While this attitude is true for all Christians, it is even stronger for Protestants than for others, and they set the religious tone for the United States.[3]

To understand how the Bible shaped our founding documents, let's start with that pivotal group, the Pilgrims, who played such a critical role in the founding of this nation. To understand them, we have to back up and look at the spiritual climate in which their movement was born.

THE PILGRIMS

In an address to honor the memory of the Mayflower Pilgrims, President Teddy Roosevelt said on August 20, 1907, "The coming hither of the Pilgrims 300 years ago, followed in far larger numbers by their sterner kinsmen, the Puritans, shaped the destinies of this Continent, and therefore profoundly affected the destiny of the whole world."[4]

Henry Cabot Lodge, the senator and author, wrote in 1881, reflecting on the Pilgrims who settled Plymouth:

> They were poor and friendless, separatists from the Church and exiles from England; but they bore with them the seeds of a great nation and of a great system of government . . . the vanguard of a great column, bearing a civilization and a system of government which was to confront that other system founded far away to the south of the rivers of Virginia, and which, after a conflict of two centuries and a half, was destined to prevail throughout the length and breadth of a continent.[5]

Unfortunately, young people today know virtually nothing about the true story of the Pilgrims because of the incredibly secularized version of history presented in the schools. The "separation of Church and state" (a phrase that does not appear in our Constitution) has come to mean the "separation of God and state." If separating God from our government means that the true history of America is turned on its head, then so be it, say the secularists today. New York University professor Paul Vitz made a comprehensive study of sixty leading social studies textbooks used in our schools. Dr. Vitz headed up a blue-ribbon panel that discovered the deep bias in textbooks against religion in general, the Christian religion in particular, and the Protestant religion most specifically, about which the authors seem to have a virtual paranoia. Dr. Vitz wrote, "One social studies book has thirty pages on the Pilgrims, including the first Thanksgiving. But there is not one word [or image] that referred to religion as even a part of the Pilgrims' lives." Thanksgiving has been revamped so that it is no longer a celebration of the Pilgrims giving thanks to Almighty God, it's a celebration of the Pilgrims giving thanks to the Indians. Listen to what the National Education Association, the teachers union, says about Thanksgiving:

"Celebration of Diversity in Thanksgiving"

> The National Education Association believes that Thanksgiving is the recognition of unity and the rich American diversity that was embodied in the settlement of America.[6]

Diversity is a modern buzzword for the tolerance of different types of people, including people whose lifestyles flout the Word of God. God—who was the very center of the original *holiday*—is removed from the picture. When the educational establishment takes this kind of approach to teaching history, the average young person growing up today learns virtually nothing about the real founding of this country, unless they happen to pick it up from other sources—church, Sunday school, or books like this one.

The Pilgrims set sail from Holland (via England) to come to these shores after fleeing their native England twelve years earlier. William Bradford was their governor for thirty or more years, and he wrote the most important history of that period, titled *Of Plymouth Plantation*. Before they set sail from Holland, Bradford described their motives in coming. He said they cherished "a great hope and inward zeal of laying some good foundations, or at least making some ways toward it, for the propagation and advance of the gospel of the kingdom of Christ in the remote parts of the world, even though they should be but stepping stones to others in the performance of so great a work."[7]

How prophetic! A small, harassed congregation has nothing to cling to but the Lord and His Word. They create a settlement in the New World to serve as "stepping stones" in spreading the gospel.

But just *who* were these Pilgrims? I dare say that few people today understand that the Pilgrims were a *church*. They were one local church, who, with their pastor, determined to move their congregation. It was a "church-relocating project"—not only did they move their church from England to America, they also translated their covenant for church government into the first written charter for local self-government: the Mayflower Compact.

To understand that church and why they moved, we go back to shortly before the year 1600 during great foment in the Church of England. The issues between Henry VIII and Rome came to a head in the 1530s, so the Church of England cut its ties with Rome. Nonetheless, there was little change in Church teaching during the reigns of Henry VIII and later, Elizabeth I.

But there was a tremendous movement taking place, the Puritan movement, that theologically and ideologically began with Luther, and more specially with the Reformer of Geneva, John Calvin, and had begun to influence the people in their thinking. Many who had fled to Geneva as refugees and had returned to England wanted to purify the church, its doctrine, and its worship.

The Puritans were foremost a people driven by a love for the Scriptures. The Bible was the standard by which these godly men and women measured everything. Reflecting on the Puritans in 1874, Leonard Bacon wrote this in his "Genesis of the New England Churches": "The more they studied the New Testament, the less they could find bearing a resemblance to that or any other National Church."[8]

The Puritan movement met with a great deal of opposition from the established church in England; a small group of them despaired of ever being able to really purify the Church at all. They decided that the only thing to do was to separate from the Church of England. They were called Separatists. We know them today as Pilgrims, of course, for they were wanderers across the earth. The very name "Pilgrims" comes from the Bible (1 Peter 2:11).[9]

The Separatist movement had its beginning in the English counties of Lincolnshire, Yorkshire, and Nottinghamshire. There, particularly in the little town of Scrooby in Nottinghamshire in 1606, a group of people withdrew from the Church of England and formed themselves into a covenanted people with God, regardless of what persecution or suffering they would endure as a result. A young man by the name of John

Robinson joined the church as assistant to Reverend Richard Clyfton, who shortly thereafter left for Amsterdam.

William Bradford, who had become a godly young man by the age of twelve, also joined the church at that time. He was so deep in his studies of the Word of God that every Sunday he walked twelve miles from Austerfield to Babworth in order to hear what he described as the "illuminating ministry" of Richard Clyfton. This was the first step in his "holy, prayerful, watchful walk with God."

The Separatists were all devoted followers of the teachings of Calvin. The Geneva Bible was smuggled into England and was widely read by the people in the three counties that I mentioned previously. Scrooby had a precious treasure: the Bible in English. But owning this Bible was against the law—an Englishman was not allowed to have the Bible in his own language in his own hands.

As the people of Scrooby read the Scriptures, they saw things that were not right in the Church and things that were not right in England. The movement that eventually brought these people to our shores to found the most important early settlement in America began when Christians studied the holy Scriptures.

But no sooner had they organized themselves into a secret Separatist Church in 1606, than they were persecuted by the Church and civil authorities. They had to hide and move from place to place; their homes were watched; they were thrown into jail. Robinson and his followers finally decided there was nothing else for them to do but leave England if they were to worship according to the Word of God.

They planned to cross the sea to Holland and religious liberty, where others had gone before. They arranged for an English captain to take them there, but when they got into the longboats to go out to the ship, he betrayed them. They were robbed of their money and possessions, brought back to the magistrates, and thrown into prison. They were finally released, and after facing many other difficulties, they finally arranged with a Dutch captain to sail to Amsterdam. Group by group they made their way at last to Holland in 1608 and remained in Amsterdam one year. Later they settled in Leyden, where they stayed until 1620. Unlike other Englishmen in Holland at the time, they were lights, a shining example of how to live the gospel.

After eleven years of peace and relative prosperity, the Pilgrims realized they had to move on again. The Dutch were very worldly, and there was a great deal of impiety and ungodliness among them. The Sabbath was grossly profaned. Their children were growing up and intermarrying with these worldly people. The Pilgrims were afraid they were going to lose their congregation. They decided they would move to the New World, where they could worship and live according to Scripture.

A CIVIL BODY POLITIC

In the New World the Pilgrims sought to establish a peaceful, Bible-based colony. That is what Plymouth was all about. One group went first, while John Robinson stayed to minister to the bulk of the congregation, which would join the others later. On July 21, 1620, on board the *Mayflower,* John Robinson preached his farewell sermon (based on Ezra 8:21–22) for those about to sail to America. In that sermon, Robinson reminded the flock of the spiritual covenant that they had made when they became a congregation. That spiritual covenant was soon echoed in their political covenant, known as the Mayflower Compact. Edward Winslow, one of the Pilgrims about to sail for America, said of Robinson's good-bye message: "Here also he put us in mind of our church covenant, at least that part of it whereby we promise and covenant with God and one another to receive whatsoever light or truth shall be made known to us from his written Word."[10]

After a fearful journey of sixty-six days, never coming up on the deck of the *Mayflower* because of the great gales and storms, the Pilgrims at last sighted the inhospitable shores of the New England coast in winter. They harbored there in the bay, but before going ashore, they met in the captain's cabin and drew up in the first contract of government (or a *covenant*, as they would call it), America's "birth certificate": the *Mayflower Compact*. They declared that the purpose of their voyage was to glorify God and to advance the Christian faith.[11]

Daniel Webster, one of our greatest senators, said:

> Finally, let us not forget the religious character of our origin. Our fathers were brought hither by their high veneration for the Christian religion. They journeyed by its light, and labored in its hope. They sought to incorporate its principles with the elements of their society, and to diffuse its influence through all their institutions, civil, political, or literary. Let us cherish these sentiments, and extend this influence still more widely; in the full conviction, that that is the happiest society which partakes in the highest degree of the mild and peaceful spirit of Christianity.[12]

The Pilgrims did indeed become "stepping stones" — in Bradford's own words — for others to come, for the furtherance of the gospel. Not only did the rest of Robinson's congregation come to Plymouth in later voyages (although Robinson himself died in 1625, before he was able to come), but many waves of more God-fearing men and women also settled in the New World.

THE PURITANS

The Puritans, who were spiritual cousins of the Pilgrims, migrated to America in the 1630s, and soon outnumbered them. They have been maligned and misrepresented by later generations. C. S. Lewis said, "Nearly every association which now clings to the word *puritan* has to be eliminated when we are thinking of the early Protestants. Whatever they were, they were not sour, gloomy, or severe; nor did their enemies bring any such charge against them."[13] The Puritans sought to apply biblical principles to civil government and laid an important foundation for this country. Their knowledge of the Bible made them wary of human nature. Constitutional attorney and historian John Eidsmoe explains in his book *Christianity and the Constitution:* "Puritans refused to give anyone too much power because of their belief in human depravity. Power had a corrupting influence and could be used to oppress others. For that reason, the authority of their rulers was carefully monitored."[14]

The Puritans intended to create a theocracy, which historian Clarence Carson simply defines as a "rule by God through the elect, those chosen by Him."[15] As the Puritans saw it, they were creating a covenant in their colonies with God and with each other in order to live in obedience to God's Word. This covenanting, articulated in compacts and constitutions, helped pave the way to our written national covenant, the Constitution. John Winthrop—the earliest major leader of the Puritans, who spoke about how "we must consider that we shall be as a City upon a Hill, [for] the eyes of all people are upon us"[16]— writes this about the covenant they sought to establish:

> Thus stands the cause between God and us. We are entered into a covenant with Him for this work. We have taken out a commission. The Lord hath given us leave to draw our own articles. . . . We have hereupon besought Him of favor and blessing. Now if the Lord shall please to hear us, and bring us in peace to the place we desire, then hath He ratified this covenant and sealed our commission, and will effect a strict performance of the articles contained in it: but if we shall neglect the observation of these articles . . . the Lord will surely break out in wrath against us; be revenged of such a sinful people, and make us know the price of the breach of such a covenant.[17]

Carson elaborates on the key link between the idea of a spiritual covenant and our Constitution:

> Understanding the doctrine of the covenant is necessary both to a grasp of the Puritan mission and to meaning of a constitution in America. The doctrine of the covenant is that people may make an agreement with God and with one another. It is similar to a contract among men, but much more profound. For by a covenant men bind themselves to God to do His will, and God binds Himself to them. These are overtones of this doctrine in such great documents as the Mayflower Compact and the Fundamental Orders of Connecticut, the charters issued by kings, and the United States Constitution.[18]

Self-government was part of the foundation of Puritan New England. The meeting house, where the people attended church services, was always centrally located. It was often the seat of political power also. John Fiske writes, "All had for many generations been more or less accustomed to self-government and to public meetings for discussing local affairs. That self-government, especially as far as church matters were concerned, they were stoutly bent upon maintaining and exceeding. Indeed, that was what they had crossed the ocean for."[19] The New England colonies consisted of a network of townships. Fiske points out that in these townships, "the people directly govern[ed] themselves"[20]—so much so that Jefferson observed: "Those wards, called townships in New England, are the vital principle of their governments, and have proved themselves the wisest invention ever devised by the wit of man for the perfect exercise of self-government, and for its preservation."[21]

WILLIAM PENN AND "THE HOLY EXPERIMENT"

But it wasn't just the Pilgrims and Puritans in New England who brought Christianity to the colonies. The early American settlements were dominated by Christians of various denominations seeking refuge and religious freedom, fleeing the religious persecution of state churches in Europe. This was true up and down the Atlantic coast, from Massachusetts to Georgia (although only in New England did Christians try to create a theocracy).

Consider the example of William Penn, the founder of Penn's "woods," or as we know it today, "Pennsylvania." Penn was a convert to Quakerism, a Christian sect that was sadly persecuted by other Christian sects (even the Puritans were guilty of persecuting them). When his father died in 1670, he left William Penn a fortune. The Crown owed his father £16,000. Seeing how he and his Quaker friends suffered persecution in England, Penn conceived the idea of requesting from the British government a wilderness in the New World in exchange for the forgiveness of the debt. His request was granted.

A godly man, Penn, like the Pilgrims before him, made a peaceable and fair deal with the Indians when he settled in the New World. He wrote a letter to the Indians in the area: "My Friends: There is one great God and Power that hath made the world and all things therein, to whom you and I and all people owe their being and well-being, and to whom you and I must one day give an account, for all that we do in the world; this great God hath written His law in our hearts by which we are taught and commanded to love and help and doe [sic] good to one another and not to do harm and mischief one unto another."[22] William Penn paid the Indians a reasonable price for the land and signed a lasting treaty with them. Soon that wilderness proved to be a place of refuge for Quakers and other persecuted Christians.

Penn wrote the Pennsylvania colony's first constitution. Here is the opening of that document, known as the *Fundamental Constitutions of Pennsylvania:*

> Considering that it is impossible that any People or Government should ever prosper, where men render not unto God, that which is Gods [sic], as well as to Caesar, that which is Caesars; and also perceiving that disorders and Mischiefs that attend those places where force in matters of faith and worship, and seriously reflecting upon the tenure of the new and Spiritual Government, and that both Christ did not use force and that he did expressly forbid it in his holy Religion, as also that the Testimony of his blessed Messengers was, that the weapons of the Christian warfare were not Carnal but Spiritual.[23]

B. F. Morris, who wrote *The Christian Life and Character of the Civil Institutions of the United States*, observes, "The frame of government which Penn completed in 1682 for the government of Pennsylvania was derived from the Bible. He deduced from various passages 'the origination and descent of all human power from God.'"[24]

THE ROLE OF CALVINISM

Most of the early settlers of the American colonies were Christians of various sects. Calvinism in particular played a unique role among the churches that shaped the colonies. Calvinism (the teachings of John

Calvin) was espoused not only in the Presbyterian church but also by the Congregationalists, the Episcopalians, and the Baptists. We should also remember that all of the Pilgrims on the *Mayflower* were Calvinists. John Robinson, their pastor,[25] was a Calvinist of the first order.

Calvinism was predominant in America's earliest days and was still predominant 150 years later, at the time of the Revolution. One scholar has said that there were three million people in America in 1776 and of those approximately nine hundred thousand were Scottish Presbyterians; about six hundred thousand of them were Puritan English; some four hundred thousand were German and Dutch Reformed—all Calvinists.[26] There were also many French Huguenots, who were also Calvinists. Whether Presbyterian or Episcopalian or others, two-thirds of Americans in 1776 embraced Calvin's theology. No wonder that historian George Bancroft called John Calvin "the father of America."[27]

William Bradford, the governor of Plymouth; John Winthrop, the second governor of Massachusetts Bay Colony; Thomas Hooker, the founder of Connecticut; John Davenport, the founder of New Haven; Roger Williams, the founder of Rhode Island—all were Calvinists.

Presbyterianism, another branch of Calvinism, gave the pattern for our government. Everywhere that Presbyterianism has gained dominion, it has produced a republic, a fact to which many historians will attest.[28] The American government is a republic. In the Church, the laymen are given the right to govern the church. The Presbyterian elders, voted in by the congregation, rule the church, just as the representatives voted in by the electorate rule the country. Because of the key role Presbyterianism, and thus Calvinism, played in the founding of this nation, the German historian Leopold von Ranke said, "John Calvin was the virtual founder of America."[29] In a larger sense, though, it isn't just Presbyterianism; it's Christianity that is republican. De Witt Clinton, who served as the governor of New York and in the U.S. Senate, once said, "Christianity, in its essence, its doctrines, and its forms, is republican."[30]

KEY WAYS CHRISTIANITY SHAPED AMERICA'S FOUNDING DOCUMENTS

With the living religion of the Puritans in the seventeenth century in mind, how did the Christian faith shape America at the founding of the United States in the latter half of the eighteenth century? Put the question this way: Was the Christianity that shone like a light in 1620 snuffed out by 1776? The answer is absolutely not. In fact, the first major communications between the colonies up and down the coast was a by-product of the Christian revival known as the Great Awakening. Jonathan Edwards and George Whitefield were the key ministers in this movement that spiritually and culturally united the otherwise separate colonies. Let's examine now exactly how Christianity shaped this nation.

The Founding Fathers' Education — Thoroughly Christian

Virtually all of the men who wrote the Declaration of Independence, the Articles of Confederation, the Constitution, and the Bill of Rights — all the major founding documents of this nation — had received a strong, well-integrated Christian education. In the lower grades, the Bible was the chief textbook, and the church or home the classroom. Many educational elites of our day would no doubt mock such a scenario, but the result was a highly literate society.

Christianity made the United States the leader in universal "public" education around the world. Schools and universities blanketed the land, since our forefathers believed that all men needed to read the Bible to understand the doctrines of the Christian faith. Education was necessary for all so that all could study the precious Word of God and be faithful servants of Christ.

As far as higher education is concerned, America was committed to Christian education. The Christian origins of Harvard, Yale, Dartmouth, Columbia, Princeton, and many other of our great universities is well documented.[31] Of America's first 126 colleges, 123 were Christian. Faith wasn't separate from learning. Taking their cue from the Bible, educators applied faith to all aspects of life, including politics. The Scriptures were the bedrock of all higher learning at that time. For example, included in Harvard's "Rules and Precepts" is this item:

Every one shall so exercise himself in reading the Scriptures twice a day, that he shall be ready to give such an account of his proficiency therein, both in *Theoretical* observations of the language, and *Logic,* and in *Practical* and spiritual truths, as his Tutor shall require, according to his ability; seeing *the entrance of the word giveth light, it giveth understanding to the simple,* Psalm 119:130.[32]

Even the Founding Fathers who didn't go to church did have a biblical worldview. Today we have many people *attending* church who lack a biblical worldview.

One great Christian who taught many of the Founding Fathers was Reverend John Witherspoon, the Presbyterian minister who served as the president of the College of New Jersey (later known as Princeton). Witherspoon was the only minister to sign the Declaration of Independence. Witherspoon said, "Cursed be all learning that is contrary to the cross of Christ."[33] Witherspoon's best-known pupil was the chief architect of the Constitution, James Madison. A Virginian, Madison was expected to attend college at William and Mary. Instead, he chose the more Presbyterian-oriented education at the College of New Jersey under the leadership of Witherspoon. After he graduated, Madison spent one more year at the College of New Jersey, where he translated the Bible from Hebrew and Greek to English. Madison's views on government were thoroughly shaped by Witherspoon and other Presbyterians. Thus, Madison's political worldview was one shaped by the Bible more than any other source. Gary DeMar, author of *America's Christian History: The Untold Story*, writes about the leaders Reverend Witherspoon trained: "Witherspoon taught a vice president, 21 senators, 29 representatives, 56 state legislators, and 33 judges, three of whom became members of the United States Supreme Court."[34]

"God-Given"—Not State-Given—Rights

The Founding Fathers proclaimed the individual to have certain "God-given" rights that could not under any circumstances be taken away by the state. The power of the state was acknowledged to be finite and under the constraint of God. The state was seen as God's servant to execute justice, but it remained within a limited sphere of influence lest it usurp the place of God in the hearts of the people. Romans 13:1–4 lays the foundation for the government's authority, and Acts 5:29 lays the foundation for civil disobedience, when appropriate.

The Puritan Work Ethic

The United States was filled with men and women who believed in the Puritan work ethic. This Christian ethic maintained that every profession and job was to be done with excellence, diligence, and faith. Every task was to be done to the glory of God. Money was to be wisely used and debt avoided. From this ethic, America grew into the most prosperous nation ever to appear in the entire history of the world. God blessed America and rewarded her work.

The Christianity of the Founding Fathers

The late Dr. M. E. Bradford of the University of Dallas, author of *A Worthy Company*, has documented that fifty to fifty-two of the fifty-six men who signed the Declaration of Independence were Trinitarian Christians, men of good standing in a local, orthodox church. Of the fifty-five men who signed the Constitution, again he found in his research that fifty to fifty-two were professing *orthodox* Christians. Remember Dr. Bradford's findings the next time your hear that most of them were Deists.[35] William J. Federer, editor of *America's God and Country,* summarizes the Christian affiliation of the writers of the Constitution: "29 were Anglicans, 16 to 18 were Calvinists,[36] 2 were Methodists, 2 were Lutherans, 2 were Roman Catholic, 1 lapsed Quaker and sometimes Anglican, and 1 open Deist—Dr. Franklin who attended every kind of Christian worship, called for public prayer, and contributed to all denominations."[37] Many of these men were trained in the leading colleges of the day—virtually all of which were evangelical Christian colleges!

For anyone wishing to read more on the faith of our Founding Fathers, there are many good resources available today.[38]

THE BIBLE AND THE DECLARATION OF INDEPENDENCE

The Declaration of Independence, written primarily by Thomas Jefferson, was the bloom of a tree that had grown for centuries. In one sense, you can trace its roots as far back as 1215, when the archbishop of Canterbury first penned the Magna Charta, the historic document demanding liberties from the king for the citizens. In another sense the Declaration was a uniquely American document, produced after decades of growing independence in the colonies, particularly in New England.

John Fiske, in *The Beginnings of New England,* said that as early as 1639, Bostonians were complaining about the magistrate having too much power. So Reverend Nathaniel Ward of Ipswich wrote up "The Body of Liberties," which were adopted in 1641.[39] The very opening of the Body of Liberties describes itself as "The free fruition of such liberties, immunities and privileges as humanity, civility, and Christianity call for. . . ."[40] John Palfrey, in his *History of New England,* states, "Ward was capable of the great business to which he was set. . . . When . . . he announced the principle that life, liberty, or property was not to be invaded except by virtue of express law . . . it was almost a Declaration of

Independence."[41] The Massachusetts Body of Liberties contained "ninety-eight separate protections of individual rights, including: 'no taxation without representation,' 'due process of law,' 'trial by a jury of peers,' and prohibitions against 'cruel and unusual punishment.'"[42]

John Winthrop, the great Puritan leader, gave a speech on liberty in 1645, in which he discussed spiritual liberty and civil liberty:

> The other kind of liberty I call civil or federal; it may also be termed moral, in reference to the covenant between God and man, in the moral law, and the political covenants and constitutions, amongst men themselves. This liberty is the proper end and object of authority, and cannot subsist without it; and it is a liberty to that only which is good, just, and honest. This liberty you are to stand for, with the hazard (not only of your goods, but) of your lives, if need be. Whatsoever crosseth this is not authority but a distemper thereof. This liberty is maintained and exercised in a way of subjection to authority; it is of the same kind of liberty wherewith Christ hath made us free.[43]

The liberty the founders of America knew was not the same as licentiousness; it was liberty under law.

In the first legislative act in the colony of Pennsylvania, William Penn also made clear the link between Christianity and civil liberties:

> Whereas the glory of Almighty God and the good of mankind is the reason and end of government, and therefore government itself is a venerable ordinance of God, and foreasmuch as it is principally devised and intended by the Proprietary and Governor and freemen of Pennsylvania and territories thereunto belonging, to make and establish such laws as shall best preserve true Christian and civil liberty, in opposition to all unchristian, licentious, and unjust practices, whereby God may have his due, Caesar his due, and the people their due.[44]

American liberty, as articulated in the Declaration of Independence, owes its very existence in large part to Christianity. Alexis de Tocqueville, the Frenchman who visited America in 1830 and later wrote *Democracy in America*, made a very important observation about freedom: "Despotism may govern without faith, but liberty cannot."[45] Dissolve the bonds that faith creates and the state will create the control.

The Founding Fathers didn't turn to revolutionary writers like Rousseau or Voltaire, but to Christian writers like John Locke who said that "the Christian Religion, as delivered in the Scriptures, and free from all corrupt mixtures, is the most reasonable institution in the world,"[46] and to

Blackstone, or Algernon Sidney who said, "The Liberty of a people is the Gift of God and nature."[47]

When the thirteen colonies united and announced their separation from England, they articulated a carefully thought-out Christian philosophy of government: a coherent set of convictions rooted in the biblical understanding of God as Creator, of man's God-given rights and responsibilities, and of the true purposes of a righteous civil government. John Locke said, "As men, we have God for our King, and are under the Law of Reason; as Christians, we have Jesus the Messiah for our King, and are under the law revealed by him in the Gospel."[48]

If the Bible had never been written, it is highly unlikely that so sublime and liberating a document as the Declaration of Independence would have been written. Gary DeMar, president of American Vision, points out, "The Declaration is a religious document, basing its argument for rights on theological grounds. Rights, the Declaration maintains, are a gift from the Creator: 'We are endowed by our Creator with certain inalienable rights.' The logic is simple. No Creator, no rights."[49]

THE BIBLE AND
THE CONSTITUTION

In one sense, the first constitution written in America was the Mayflower Compact: it was the cornerstone of our republic. Before they even set foot in the New World, the Pilgrims penned this now-classic agreement for self-government:

> In the name of God, Amen. We, whose names are underwritten, the loyal Subjects of our dread Sovereign Lord, King James . . . Having undertaken for the Glory of God, and Advancement of the Christian Faith, and the Honour of our King and Country, a voyage to plant the first colony in the northern Parts of Virginia; do by these Presents, solemnly and mutually in the Presence of God and one of another, covenant and combine ourselves together into a civil Body Politick, for our better Ordering and Preservation, and Furtherance of the Ends aforesaid.[50]

From the time of this revolutionary political covenant until the time the United States Constitution was composed in the summer of 1787, Christians in New England wrote up about one hundred different compacts, covenants, and constitutions. In the words of historian Charles Hull Wolfe, all of these charters for self-government "laid the groundwork for a uniquely free and Christian America."[51]

One of these agreements, the New England Confederation of 1643, states, "We all came into these parts of America, with one and the same end and aim, namely, to advance the Kingdom of our Lord Jesus Christ."[52]

Another agreement, the Fundamental Orders of Connecticut, which was initiated in 1638 and adopted in 1639, was inspired by a sermon delivered by Reverend Thomas Hooker, the founder of Connecticut.

> Forasmuch as it has pleased Almighty God by the wise disposition of His divine providence so to order and dispose of things that we the inhabitants and residents of Windsor, Hartford and Wethersfield and now cohabiting and dwelling in and upon the River Connecticut and the lands thereunto adjoining; and well knowing where a people are gathered together the Word of God requires that to maintain the peace and union of such a people there should be an orderly and decent government established according to God, to order and dispose of the affairs of all the people at all seasons as occasions shall require; do therefore associate and conjoin ourselves to be as one public State or Commonwealth, and do, for ourselves and our successors and such as shall be adjoined to us at any time hereafter, enter into combination and confederation together to maintain and preserve the liberty and purity of the Gospel of our Lord Jesus which we now profess, as also the discipline of the churches, which according to the truth of the said Gospel is now practiced among us.[53]

This constitution was signed on January 14, 1639, almost 150 years before the U.S. Constitution was drafted. It has been called "the first written constitution in the history of nations."[54] Perhaps the greatest significance of the Fundamental Orders of Connecticut is that it vests the government's authority in the consent of the people. "We the People" in the U.S. Constitution of 1787 articulates the same concept.

The link between the Puritans' constitutionalism and the American Constitution is no minor point. Their governing documents were political versions of their spiritual covenants. And all of these political compacts and constitutions paved the way for *the* Constitution. Modern secularists like to point out that the Constitution doesn't mention God. But regardless of that fact, constitutionalism as enjoyed by Americans is a major contribution of the Puritans, who were unquestionably committed Christians. The framework for America's liberty under law was created by Christianity. Let's examine some of the biblical principles contained in the Constitution.

BIBLICAL PRINCIPLES ENSHRINED IN OUR CONSTITUTION

Government by Law

Which governing principles did the Founding Fathers (and their Puritan and Presbyterian forerunners) discover in the Bible, as they searched its pages? The first one we note is the creation of a government by law and not by man. That is the whole purpose of the Constitution—it institutes government by law, which is the meaning of a republic. If you ask the average person today what kind of government we have, he or she will tell you that we have a democracy. Do you realize that the Founding Fathers believed that democracy was among the worst forms of government? That point is so alien to modern secularists that they have no idea what it means. The Founding Fathers believed that because of the sinfulness of man, when a society was ruled by men, it was on its way to tyranny. They feared mob rule.

The Ten Commandments were important to them, as the decalogue has been important to many rulers ever since they were first introduced into civil government outside of Israel by St. Patrick in A.D. 432 in Ireland. Shortly after A.D. 565 they became part of the civil law in Scotland by Columba. In A.D. 600, because of the work of the monk Augustine (not the man we know as St. Augustine), they became part of the civil law of England. They also became part of the law of America.

As one of the signers of the Constitution, James McHenry, summed up, "The Holy Scriptures . . . can alone secure to society, order and peace, and to our courts of justice and constitutions of government, purity, stability, and usefulness. In vain, without the Bible, we increase penal laws and draw entrechments [protections] around our institutions."[55]

All Men Created Equal

The second principle they observed is that all men are created equal. The founders of this country believed in equality before the law. Neither the state nor the law was to be a respecter of persons. This was a radical departure from what they had known. In England the citizens certainly didn't have equality. While someone from virtually any background could be elected to the House of Commons, the same was (and is) not true for the House of Lords. There was the nobility and the hoi polloi . . . the unwashed masses . . . the many.

That social system was completely eschewed by the Founding Fathers who believed that *all* men were created equal. The Bible says that "God shows no partiality" (Acts 10:34). Therefore, they saw that men were created equal before God, and they enshrined that equality in our founding documents. It took another one hundred years before that principle was fully lived out and all men were considered by the law to be equal, but the principle was established at America's founding.

Our Inalienable Rights

The third principle the founders observed is the existence of inalienable rights. "We hold these truths to be self-evident, that all men are created equal"; that they are "endowed by their Creator with certain inalienable Rights," wrote Jefferson in his Declaration. I should say that his statement really is not quite accurate. Those truths are not self-evident. If they were self-evident to mankind, they would have been self-evident to everyone. But these were radical departures from anything that had been seen before. Jefferson and his colleagues believed natural law *was* self-evident. It's the same idea that Paul has in mind when he says that God's law is written on every heart (Rom. 2:15). But beyond what man can discern as "natural law" is the revelation of divine law that is in the Scriptures.

The Founding Fathers believed that people had rights that came from God. For example, God guarantees our rights in the Ten Commandments. The right of private property is guaranteed in the commandment "Thou shalt not steal." The sanctity of life and our right to life is guaranteed in the commandment "Thou shalt not kill." And so the various rights that we have come from the guarantees God has given us in the Ten Commandments. Do away with the Commandments and you do away with our inalienable rights.

So you see that when the Supreme Court says that we cannot put the Ten Commandments on the walls of our schools, they are, indeed, chipping away at the inalienable rights that we have from God . . . though most people do not recognize what is happening.

Liberty

Liberty is what America is all about. But most people don't realize that its source is in the Judeo-Christian Scriptures. Paul said, "Where the Spirit of the Lord is, there is liberty" (2 Cor. 3:17). "Stand fast therefore in the liberty by which Christ has made us free," the Bible says in Galatians 5:1. Everywhere the shackles of sin had been broken, shortly thereafter, those who had been set free by Christ and had been given spiritual freedom began to seek political and civil freedom as well. So it was the tremendous impetus of Christian redemption that moved people to seek liberty in every part of their lives, and it was guaranteed to us in the Constitution. It was an extent of liberty never before seen anywhere else in the world, and it came from the Word of God! Political liberty assumed the dignity of self-governing individuals.

Separation of Powers

Another biblical principle the founders knew to be true is that men are sinful. Jeremiah said, "The heart is deceitful above all things and desperately wicked; who can know it?" (Jer. 17:9). James Madison said, "There is a degree of depravity in mankind which requires a certain degree of circumspection and distrust." As we saw earlier, this biblical principle led to the division of powers, so that not too much authority rested in the hands of any one man or group of men.

How were those powers to be separated? Madison said that Montesquieu offered the answer. But long before Montesquieu, God said through His servant Isaiah, "For the LORD is our Judge, the LORD is our Lawgiver, the LORD is our King" (Isa. 33:22). So here we see the tripartite division of government—in the roles of judge, lawgiver, and king. The Founding Fathers placed the authority for these roles not in the hands of men but in separate institutions under the rule of law: those are the judiciary, the legislative, and the executive branches of government.

How many powers does the federal government have? Today it almost seems to be an infinite number because of Supreme Court decisions and runaway legislation, but the Founding Fathers, in the Constitution, gave the federal government specifically *twenty* powers. There are only twenty things that the federal government was supposed to be able to do: all of the rest remained with the states or the people. Even the enumerated powers were limited by checks and balances.

Making the Shekel Great

The Bible's view of economics was also important to the Founding Fathers. Man's sinfulness and greed create the tendency to inflate money. The Old Testament had warned them about that. We read, for example, in Amos 8:5: "Saying, When will the new moon be gone, that we may sell corn? and the sabbath, that we may set forth wheat, making the ephah small, and the shekel great, and falsifying the balances by deceit?" (KJV). The Old Testament condemns making the shekel great—inflating the money—and thus using deceit in finances. The founders were thus afraid of inflating money. From the time of the Revolution, which began in 1775, until the Constitution was written in 1787, the government had printed money. This paper money, called the Continental, had become debased—hence, the expression, "not worth a Continental." The Continental by this time was worth less than a penny because of inflation. They knew that there must be inflation-proof currency. Therefore, the United States government was not empowered to print money. It could "coin money" out of gold and silver or print bills that were redeemable in gold or silver, but it could not print worthless paper. Now, because of various acts of modern politicians, the government is able to do that, and consequently we suffer the rigors of inflation off and on. The only way we are going to recover from that cycle is to return to the system that the Founding Fathers gave us.

The founders of this nation gave to us the great heritage founded upon God's Word, the Bible, the founding document of America. But the nation has been hijacked by atheists and skeptics and unbelievers and secularists of every sort, who even now deceive the minds of millions into supposing that this was a secular and godless country that was established at Philadelphia.

"FIGHTING WORDS"

These days, to claim that America is, or ever was, a "Christian nation" is to utter "fighting words."[56] A few years ago, someone wrote to Sandra Day O'Connor to ask if it was true that the Supreme Court had declared that this was "a Christian nation." When O'Connor wrote back in the affirmative, citing the 1892 Trinity decision, it unleashed a firestorm of criticism in the press. It is not politically correct to teach that this ever was a Christian nation.

It's ironic that in this country, which was so profoundly shaped by Christians, we find Christians on the defensive. The secularist engaged in Christian-bashing in America is rather like a petty ingrate standing atop a large pyramid constructed by the sweat and blood of Christians, hurling stones at their descendants.

In the Anti-Defamation League's 1994 report, *The Religious Right: The Assault on Tolerance & Pluralism in America,* they dedicate the entire second section to a closer look at the "religious right's attack on church/state separation." This section tries to argue the point that the religious right has rewritten America's history, and that the "separation of church and state" as now understood in secular America is what the founders of this nation intended. Those of us who proclaim the profound impact Christianity has had on the founding of this nation are now being accused of rewriting history.

AMERICA: A CHRISTIAN NATION

But the question is just *who* is rewriting history—the Christians or the humanists? As we've reviewed earlier, many of the great political thinkers of our country's past—whether Christian or otherwise—saw the important link between God and freedom, between Christianity and liberty. All of these statements culminate with the climactic pronouncement from the Supreme Court in 1892. After spending some ten years pouring through thousands of documents from our history, the Court finally declared in the Trinity decision:

> This is a religious people. This is historically true. From the discovery of this continent to this present hour, there is a single voice making this affirmation. . . . We find everywhere a clear recognition of the same truth. . . . This is a Christian nation.[57]

For years now, I have spoken on and written about some of the massive evidence for the fact that it is unquestionably true that America was founded as a Christian nation. I learned two new things about the Trinity decision after all these years of studying these matters, and I think they are exciting and worth knowing. Today, the Supreme Court dispatches cases with a rapidity that is almost bewildering. Do you realize that before cases of the utmost importance to the American people are brought before the Supreme Court the justices have one hour to argue their case? Thirty minutes for one side and thirty minutes for the other and it is done! But in 1892 there was not that pressure upon the Court. They spent ten years researching the Trinity decision!

The second thing I learned was that all seven of the judges concurred in the Trinity decision that America really was a Christian nation. (Raising the number of justices to nine was a part of Franklin Delano Roosevelt's famous attempt to "pack the court" in the 1930s.)

Although it is politically incorrect, the idea that America was founded as a "Christian nation" was reaffirmed by the courts as recently as a decade ago. In 1986, U.S. District Judge Frank McGarr, a federal judge in Chicago, said this in a ruling: "The truth is that America's origins are Christian and that our founding fathers intended and achieved full religious freedom for all within the context of a Christian nation in the First Amendment as it was adopted rather than as we have rewritten it."[58]

Who is the greatest chief justice of the Supreme Court that we have ever had? I think lawyers would agree, without much doubt, that it was Chief Justice John Marshall, who presided over the Supreme Court from 1801 to 1835. Marshall said, "No person, I believe, questions the importance of religion to the happiness of man even during his existence in this world. . . . The American population is entirely Christian, and with us, Christianity and religion are identified. It would be strange, indeed, if with such a people, our institutions did not presuppose Christianity, and did not often refer to it, and exhibit relations with it."[59]

I believe that Christians need to be strengthened with the knowledge that they are not as they would be led to believe today—some Johnny-come-lately trying to intrude their religious perspective on life into this happy, secular culture—but rather, they represent the foundations of America and the ideas that made this country great in the first place.

To anyone with an open mind, willing to study the primary sources of the founding era (from the settlement at Jamestown through the founding era in the 1770s and 1780s and even beyond), the Bible unquestionably played a critical role in the shaping of the nation. It is beyond controversy that the overall world-and-life view held by the founders of this nation—whether they believed in the deity of Christ or not—was that which had been derived from the Scriptures and was, indeed, enshrined in the religion of the Lord Jesus Christ. It is no wonder that our national motto is "In God We Trust."

A BLESSED NATION

I agreed with the U.S. Congress when they declared 1983 to be the "Year of the Bible." Here's what our nation's top lawmakers said then:

The Bible, the Word of God, has made a unique contribution in shaping the United States as a distinctive and blessed nation. . . . Deeply held religious convictions springing from the Holy Scriptures led to the early settlement of our Nation. . . . Biblical teaching inspired concepts of civil government that are contained in our Declaration of Independence and the Constitution of the United States.[60]

CHAPTER 7

THE BIBLE AND SCIENCE

"Cursed is the ground for your sake."
— Genesis 3:17

"For we know that the whole creation groans and labors with birth pangs together until now."
— Romans 8:22

In the great Christmas carol "Joy to the World" we are reminded by Isaac Watts that Jesus makes His blessings known "as far as the curse is found." The third stanza rings out:

No more let sins and sorrows grow,
Nor thorns infest the ground;
He comes to make His blessings flow
Far as the curse is found,
Far as the curse is found,
Far as, far as the curse is found.[1]

That curse was pronounced by God upon rebellious man. He had placed our original parents in a perfect world—a garden in Paradise with every conceivable blessing. Adam and Eve had the opportunity to return God's love by their obedience to His single command—to not eat from the Tree of Knowledge of Good and Evil. But they ate the fruit and died, and God pronounced a curse. That curse is what Christ came to lift from us.

THE NATURE OF THE CURSE

What is the nature of the curse? It is both physical and spiritual. The spiritual dimension and how Christ resolved it we will address in Chapter 13. As to the physical dimension, the curse plunged nature into destruction and woe—including physical death, which eventually would catch up with Adam and us all. It includes all of the diseases, illnesses, and weaknesses that finally lead to death. We see the evidence of that curse all around us in nature. Such is the world now under the curse of God. Man had disobeyed God, the fountain of every blessing, and was banished from the Garden to wander in the arid and desert wastelands.

The effects of the curse are everywhere, present from childbirth to marriage, through work and old age, until finally death takes us to our graves.

A CRITICALLY IMPORTANT CHRISTIAN INNOVATION: MODERN SCIENCE

Christ has brought a great blessing to mankind that reverses many of the physical effects of the curse. And that blessing is *science*. Surprised? Public schools today teach that science is antithetical to religion, especially Christianity, so the vast majority of Americans are ignorant of the fact that science is a blessing from Christ and His Church.

As we pointed out in *What If Jesus Had Never Been Born?*, not only is modern science a Christian blessing to the world, not only did it develop in the midst of Christianity, it also could have developed nowhere else. It could not have come into existence, for example, among the animists who worship rocks and trees and monkeys and things, supposing that all of these have gods in them.

Science could not have developed among those who worship Allah because of Islam's belief in fatalism, the idea that everything is predetermined, that no matter how hard mankind tries to change things, whatever will be will be. The purpose of science is to inquire, test hypotheses, and find ways to apply knowledge; those activities would be considered futile in a world controlled by fatalism. Science would never have been birthed in India or among the Buddhists or Hindus because of their belief that the world is an illusion. You don't spend your whole life studying and working with an illusion.

Science could have developed only in a Christian civilization—although there were incipient beginnings in ancient Greece, but those activities did not lead to the kind of beneficial science that we know as modern science. Modern science began in Christian civilization in Western Europe in the late Middle Ages.

Modern science could not even have risen in our modern culture because modern man believes that life is irrational and illogical.

Modern man rejects the notion of absolutes; therefore, he rejects the very foundation of science. Think about it: if there are no absolutes in nature, then results in experimentation are relative. *Everything* is relative. How different the worldview was of those who created modern science. Chemistry professor and author Dr. Donald Chittick explains why the Christian faith helped give rise to modern science:

> A proper philosophical base for investigating the universe was needed and the Christian doctrine of creation provided that base. The Creator established laws for people and laws for the natural world. A created universe was expected to have design, order, and purpose. Man, using his created rational mind, could study this ordered universe in a rational way and seek to discover its laws; and modern science is based on the assumption of scientific law. In addition, moral laws given by the Creator established the ethical base for science. Scientists must be honest and truthful.
>
> By contrast, if the universe were not created, it must have come to its present state by the impersonal interaction of the material of the universe itself. No intelligence would have been involved. With such a philosophy, there would be no reason to expect such a universe to operate in a rational way. Man's mind would also be a product of the same chance universe. It would not be capable of rationally studying anything. Hence, a materialist philosophy of this sort would tend to discourage one from becoming a scientist.[2]

J. Robert Oppenheimer—one of the physicists responsible for splitting the atom and developing nuclear power—is one of many non-Christians who have pointed out that Christianity gave birth to modern science. Francis Schaeffer summarizes Oppenheimer's argument: "The early scientists also shared the outlook of Christianity in believing that there is a reasonable God, who has created a reasonable universe, and thus man, by use of his reason, could find out the universe's form."[3]

In October 1962, Oppenheimer wrote an intriguing essay titled "On Science and Culture" for *Encounter* magazine, a publication of Christian Theological Seminary in Indianapolis. He points out, "as all serious historians would agree," that the scientific revolution began in the late Middle Ages and early Renaissance. Why? A large part of it had to do with the Christian view of good works. He says of the origins of the scientific revolution:

> It took something that was not present in Chinese civilization, that was wholly absent in Indian civilization, and absent from Greco-Roman civilization. It needed an idea of progress, not limited to better

understanding for this idea the Greeks had. It took an idea of progress which has more to do with the human condition, which is well expressed by the second half of the famous Christian dichotomy — faith and works; the notion that the betterment of man's condition, his civility, had meaning; that we all had a responsibility to it, a duty to it, and to man. I think that it was when this basic idea of man's condition, which supplements the other worldly aspects of religion, was fortified and fructified between the 13th and 15th centuries by the rediscovery of the ancient world's scientists, philosophers, and mathematicians, that there was the beginning of the scientific age.[4]

FOUNDERS OF SPECIFIC SCIENTIFIC FIELDS

We know there was some science being practiced before the Reformation, but science as a discipline did not burst out in all of its splendor until after the sixteenth century.

I read about a modern astronomer who looked through one of our newest and largest telescopes and saw galaxies that had never been seen before, nebulae that thrilled the heart and mind, stars uncharted, and when he stepped back, he said, "How magnificent, how glorious, how wondrous is the mind of man to build such a telescope!" That, my friends, is the faith known as humanism.

Not so with the early modern scientists (and, if the truth be known, even many scientists alive today). These dedicated observers of nature had a strong belief in God and His Word. They were inspired to seek out in nature those laws the Creator had set forth in nature. As Francis Bacon, the "father of the scientific method," once put it, "There are two books laid before us to study, to prevent our falling into error; first, the volume of the Scriptures which reveal the will of God; then, the volume of the Creatures, which express His power."[5]

In particular, the real growth of modern science was during the seventeenth century, under the influence of the Puritans, who believed that the Bible applied to all of life, not just the spiritual. As historian Robert G. Frank Jr. points out, "The predominant forms of scientific activity during England's Puritan decades can be shown to be a direct outgrowth of a Puritan ideology."[6]

Let's look at a few quick examples of some of the key founders of various branches of modern science. The magical arts of alchemy in the Middle Ages were the forerunners of chemistry, but who gave us the modern chemistry that has produced so many medicines and healed so many diseases? It was Robert Boyle, born in 1627. Boyle was a humble

Christian, a man diligent in his study of the Bible. He wrote and translated works on the gospel, wrote books on apologetics, and was a propagator of the Christian faith. In his will he left a large sum of money to found the "Boyle lectures" for proving the Christian religion.[7]

In the realm of physics, Sir Michael Faraday is acknowledged as one of the greatest scientists of all time. He was especially gifted in scientific experimentation. He discovered electromagnetic induction, without which we would have no motors or engines. He invented the generator. His discoveries gave us the ability to drive cars and use all sorts of devices that have improved the quality of our lives.

Faraday was a devout Christian, as we can see from what he wrote about the Bible and about faith: "The Bible, and it alone, with nothing added to it nor taken away from it by man, is the sole and sufficient guide for each individual, at all times and in all circumstances. . . . Faith in the divinity and work of Christ is the gift of God, and the evidence of this faith is obedience to the commandment of Christ."[8]

Lord Kelvin, one of the great physical scientists of all time, was also a man of deep faith. Kelvin formulated a new temperature scale, named after himself, which begins at "absolute zero" and is used in several different scientific fields. He formulated the science of thermodynamics, giving us the first and second laws of thermodynamics, including entropy. Lord Kelvin was the first scientist to use the concept of energy. He held twenty-one honorary degrees, was knighted, and given a barony. He was the greatest scientist of his time, and yet he could say: "With regard to the origin of life, science . . . positively affirms creative power."[9]

Most people know little about Joseph Lister other than a vague association with the product "Listerine." He was an English surgeon who made a great contribution to the development of antiseptic surgery and the use of chemical disinfectants, innovations that still are responsible for saving many lives. He was simultaneously president of the Royal Society of London and the British Association of Science. Lord Lister said, "I am a believer in the fundamental doctrines of Christianity."[10]

These were devout men of faith. When you get into your car and start the engine, turn on the lights, drive to a hospital, receive anesthesia, have a Caesarian section and have it done in a germ-free environment, remember that you owe it to Christ. "He makes His blessings flow far as the curse is found."

Let's delve further into a handful of other scientists who were Christians. The Bible influenced their lives . . . and their science.

JOHANNES KEPLER

The great astronomer Johannes Kepler (1571–1630) was a man of God and the Bible. As with so many other great minds, the Scriptures played a crucial role in his life and in the development of his ideas. Kepler, the founder of celestial mechanics, once said, "My wish is that I may perceive the God whom I find everywhere in the external world in like manner within me."[11] Writer Charles E. Hummel articulates Kepler's significance:

A brilliant mathematician and astronomer, he contributed to the scientific revolution with his work on the planetary orbits, laws of motion and scientific method. Kepler's accomplishments formed the foundation of modern theoretical astronomy. He was also a devout Christian whose unwavering faith in God sustained his life and motivated his research.[12]

Professor Job Kozhamthadam, S.J., summarized Kepler's work and significance when he wrote:

Kepler's great ambition was to create a true heavenly physics, as opposed to a heavenly metaphysics or even a heavenly mathematics. To be sure, metaphysics and mathematics had a place in his study of astronomy, but he wanted more; he wanted a system that would give a physical explanation of heavenly phenomena. He wanted to know why the planets moved as they did and what laws governing that motion were.[13]

According to Will and Ariel Durant, it was in 1604 that Kepler "reached his basic and epochal discovery—that the orbit of Mars around the sun is an ellipse, not a circle as astronomers from Plato to and including Copernicus had supposed."[14]

Kepler was emphatic that religion, like science, should be rational. Kozhamthadam elaborates that Kepler argued that "it would be a contradiction for it to do otherwise. God is supremely rational, and the human being is also rational, being created in the image and likeness of God. Hence religion, which is the expression of the deep relationship between God and humankind, cannot be but rational."[15]

The Bible was vital to Kepler's intellectual foundation. Kozhamthadam points out two biblical themes that were important to Johannes Kepler:

The idea that God is the source of light and life is an old one that occurs very clearly in both the New and Old Testaments. The Psalmist says: "The Lord is my light and my salvation" (Ps. 27:1). Again, he proclaims: "For with Thee is the fountain of life . . ." (Ps. 36:9). The New Testament, especially the Gospel of St. John, has many direct references to this theme. The Bible not only considers God the source of light and of life, but even identifies God with them. . . . Kepler also accepted this idea and often wrote about it. He spoke of Christ as "the Son of God . . . that true light that enlightens every person coming into the world."[16]

Kepler saw astronomy as a glimpse of God's glory. Richard J. Blackwell writes that Kepler argued "that astronomy provides a second means to see the power and glory of God, and thus it complements the goals of religion. Furthermore, truth in religion is based on the word of God in Scripture, while truth in natural science is based on evidence and reason."[17]

Kepler viewed all of science as man attempting to "think God's thoughts after Him." Kepler was the father of modern satellites, of modern space travel. He revolutionized the world with his ideas; had the Bible never been written, I doubt he would have formulated such ideas.

GALILEO GALILEI

Another great pioneer and innovator in science was Galileo Galilei (1594–1642). Often he's presented to modern man as if he were a nonbeliever, but that is not true, as we'll see momentarily. Charles E. Hummel comments on some of Galileo's achievements:

> While others talked about the need for new methods of science, Galileo endeavored to discover a demonstrative science of motion. He was not a philosopher but a scientist; he did not propose a new theory of science but a new science as he laid the foundations for modern mathematical physics. Yet in doing so he pioneered a path that ultimately led to a new conception of the scientific enterprise.[18]

Galileo's discoveries and propositions have had a profound impact on science and man. Galileo is responsible for hundreds of discoveries. Will and Ariel Durant highlight quite a few of them, which include:

- Affirming the "indestructibility of matter,"
- Formulating the "principles of the lever and the pulley,"
- Discovering that a "moving body will continue indefinitely in the same line and rate of motion unless interfered by some external force." We know this concept as *inertia*.[19]

The Durants conclude their litany of Galileo's discoveries by announcing that "no man since Archimedes had ever done so much for physics."[20]

Aside from his many contributions, Galileo declared that the earth was not the center of the solar system, but that the earth revolved around the sun. The Roman Catholic Church believed Galileo's assertion to be contradictory to the Scriptures, accused him of heresy, and tried him. Ultimately Galileo was "condemned to imprisonment at the pleasure of the Holy Office," and his book titled the *Dialogue* was prohibited. Galileo did not deny the Scriptures nor did he propose a concept that was opposed to them; however, the Roman Catholic Church believed him to have committed heresy. As one keen observer noted, "The maintenance of ecclesiastical authority, not the scientific issues themselves, led to that tragic trial."[21] (Since that trial, of course, the Catholic church has come to agree with Galileo on the matter. Even within the last decade or so, Pope John Paul II reiterated Galileo's innocence.)

It wasn't the Bible that Galileo had trouble with. His problem was actually with the view of the universe that the Catholic church assumed was biblical. In reality, the church's view on that point was more Aristotelian than biblical. Read Galileo's own words, and you will see that his defense of the Bible was *without compromise*. In a letter explaining his views on the mixture of science and religion, Galileo wrote:

> Holy Scripture could never lie or err, but its decrees are of absolute and inviolable truth. I should only have added that although Scripture can indeed not err, nevertheless some of its interpreters and expositors may sometimes err in various ways, one of which may be very serious and quite frequent, [that is,] when they would base themselves always on the literal meaning of words.[22]

Contrary to a modern caricature, Galileo was a man of God and the Bible. The Scriptures impacted his work profoundly. They were the measure of his accuracy as a scientist.

ISAAC NEWTON

When we think of history's greatest scientists, Isaac Newton comes immediately to mind. Sir Isaac Newton (1642–1727), the father of calculus and dynamics and other branches of science, was a scientific genius of the first order. He formulated the theory of gravitation and the laws of motion. He discovered that white light is composed of the colors of the spectrum. He made important contributions to mathematics, astronomy, and physics. Newton also studied the Bible fervently. Professor Derek Gjertsen comments on Newton's affinity for the Scriptures:

> Newton's knowledge of the Bible and its associated literature was impressive by even the highest standards of scholarship. . . . There is also the evidence of the *Variantes,* with its collation of variant readings from the Apocalypse sufficient to impress a professional Bible scholar like John Mill. More direct evidence can be seen in Newton's Library. He owned thirty Bibles. . . . There were also two editions of the *Cambridge Concordance* (1672 and 1698) and Walton's six-volume *Biblia Sacra polyglotta* (1655-7).[23]

Isaac Newton is one of the many great men of God[24] who was also a great man of science; one of many who felt there were two key sources of knowledge—one revealed in the Bible and the other revealed in nature.[25] Gale Christianson elaborates on Newton's views:

> On this scene of increasing cosmic order, with its heightened interest in nature as a tangible manifestation of divinity, the idea also emerged that there is a double revelation of God: the one contained in His words found in Scripture, the other to be found in nature and its general laws.[26]

Professor Christianson says that Newton believed that in order to "truly know the Creator one must study the natural scheme of things—the original ordering of matter and the laws that govern its composition and motion."[27] It was to this endeavor that Newton dedicated his life—to know both God and the nature of things. By his dedication to both science and the Bible, Isaac Newton greatly blessed the world.

CARL VON LINNAEUS

Scripture has often inspired people to new innovations—sometimes even to establish entire fields of study or schools of thought. Such was the case of Carl von Linnaeus (1707–1778), who created a labeling system for natural science—a labeling system he ultimately got from the Bible. Each organism was given a Latin name in two parts; the genus and the species. For example, *canis familiaris* is the name of a household dog. You will recognize *homo erectus* and *homo sapiens* as terms from his "binomial nomenclature." These classifications are so commonplace that we don't even realize the importance of the innovation.

The Durants wrote that Linnaeus "mapped the teeming world of life with the care and devotion of a scientific saint."[28] Writer and researcher Ian Taylor explains:

> Linnaeus essentially laid the foundation of natural history by devising a system of classification whereby any plant or animal could be identified and related to an overall plan. He introduced a method of naming each type of living, or once-living, thing that forms the basis of the system used internationally today. Until the time of Linnaeus, common plants and animals were referred to by names that not only differed from language to language but even differed within the same country.[29]

Linnaeus created a universal language that *all* scientists could understand and use to communicate ideas and findings in their selected fields of study. Harvard Professor Stephen Jay Gould (one of today's leading evolutionary scientists) articulates, "Linnaeus produced his unmasking of nature at two levels—first, by designating species as basic units and establishing principles for their uniform definition and naming; and, second, by arranging species into a wider taxonomic system based on a search for natural order rather than human preference or convenience."[30]

This monumental innovation by Linnaeus was inspired, as I pointed out, by the Bible. In 1729, Linnaeus happened across an opportunity that would be instrumental in his later works. Alice Dickinson, in her book *Carl Linnaeus: Pioneer of Modern Botany,* explains what occurred after Linnaeus's serendipitous interlude with Dr. Olaf Celsius, a professor of theology:

> At this time, Olaf Celsius was preparing a book, *Hierobotanican,* on the plants of the Bible. Linnaeus was able to help him in this enterprise. He plunged into the project vigorously, bringing all his botanical knowledge and youthful energy to the task. Working with Celsius on the writing of this book was one of the best experiences young Linnaeus could have had at this time. In the course of the project he learned much about the preparation of a botanical manuscript—something that was soon to prove useful to him.[31]

He also learned something about the Bible and botany. Ian Taylor, in tracing the source of Linnaeus's system of classification, wrote, "The Book of Genesis, originally written in Hebrew, used the word 'min' which subsequently became translated into English as 'kind.' Linnaeus, familiar with the Latin Vulgate [a translation of the Bible used by Roman

Catholics] translation, used the corresponding word 'species' in his system of Latin classification."[32]

Stephen Jay Gould believes that Linnaeus's "definition fractured the conceit of a human-centered system with basic units defined in terms of our needs and uses."[33] Gould continues by explaining that Linnaeus "proclaimed that species are the natural entities that God placed on earth at the creation. They are His, not ours—and they exist as they are, independent of our whims."[34] And, because he felt that any change of species would deviate from his understanding of the book of Genesis, the Durants point out that "he laid down the principle that all species had been directly created by God and had remained unchanged throughout their history."[35]

Because of Linnaeus's extensive knowledge of plants and the Bible, he was of great assistance to a commission working on a translation of the Scriptures. Alice Dickinson reports that Linnaeus visited Stockholm, "where the Swedish Royal Bible Commission was working to make a more accurate translation of the Bible. He had an encyclopedic knowledge of the plants mentioned in the scriptures and of their uses. His help was invaluable to the commission."[36]

The Bible provided the framework for this pioneer of science to carry out his work. Today Linnaeus's schema has been built upon, yet it remains the foundation for science to name and classify living things. Alice Dickinson observes: "In *Fundamenta Botanica (Botanical Foundations),* published in 1736, and in greater detail in *Critica Botanica (Botanical Opinions),* published in 1737, Linnaeus set forth many of his rules. It is astonishing how many of them are recognized as sound and are followed by botanists today."[37] Dickinson concludes the book on Linnaeus by stating, "So, even today, Carl Linnaeus stands tall. . . . His contribution is a lasting one."[38]

Linnaeus saw the tenth edition of his monumental book *Systema Naturae* in 1758. In this edition, binomial nomenclature was used exclusively. The significance of this is that 1758 marks the beginning of scientific nomenclature. According to the International Rules of Zoological Nomenclature, all names given to animals before 1758 were disqualified. Thus, Linnaeus, a firm believer in the Bible, laid the cornerstone of all scientific names which are used today.

THE COMPUTER: CHARLES BABBAGE AND BLAISE PASCAL

Charles Babbage (1792–1871) is often considered to be the father of modern-day computer science. *Encyclopedia Americana* tells us that in

1822, "he announced the construction of a small, model calculating machine by which intricate arithmetical calculations could be correctly and rapidly performed."[39] He too was a man of God and the Bible.

Babbage wrote a book, entitled *Ninth Bridgewater Treatise,* in which he explained his idea for a machine that was to be the first inkling of the computer. Lecturer David Knight writes that the amazing "thing about his book is that he imagines the world as a great computer whose programme we are trying to guess, so that what seem to us miracles—arbitrary exercises of Divine Power—may be better understood as programmed in."[40] Babbage himself wrote: "We take the highest and best of human faculties, and exalting them in our imagination to an unlimited extent, endeavour to attain an imperfect conception of that Infinite Power which created everything around us."[41]

Anthony Hyman, introducing a selected work of Babbage's, states, "In 1837 Babbage wrote *The Ninth Bridgewater Treatise* in which he presented God as Programmer."[42] In the book, *Memoirs of the Life and Labours of Charles Babbage ESQ. FR.S.,* H.W. Buxton tells how Babbage feared that his views might be thought fatalistic:

> [Babbage] saw the possibility that his views might be misinterpreted and that they might be supposed to lead a belief that a fatal *necessity* governs the arrangement of the material universe. He, however, entertained no such views, and firmly believed that whenever man failed to trace the finger of God in his works, the failure was the result of ignorance. . . . Setting aside the idea of *chance* as unscientific, and having no prototype in Nature, being a mere expression of our ignorance of causality, the stability of the Universe must be regarded either as necessary or contingent; in other words it must be either the result of necessity or of an Almighty design.[43]

"Mr. Babbage regarded the phenomena of the Cosmos," writes Buxton, "as the immediate and direct consequence of an eternal decree of the Divine intelligence."[44] Buxton continues:

> [Babbage] was essentially a mathematician and regarded mathematics as the best preliminary preparation for all other branches of human knowledge, not even excepting theology, for he believed that the study of the works of nature with scientific precision, was a necessary and indispensable preparation to the understanding and interpreting their testimony of the wisdom and goodness of their Divine Author.[45]

In addition, Blaise Pascal (1623–1662) made significant contributions to mathematics and technology that also helped with the development of the computer. Pascal invented the first adding machine, which was an important type of forerunner for the computer. Pascal's Christianity was well documented. He even wrote an important book of great spiritual insight that is still read today, *Pensées*[46] (French for "thoughts"). In his honor, a computer language is named after Blaise Pascal. Thus, we see that the fathers of the computer, a major advancement for humankind, derived many of their ideas from the Christian faith.

SAMUEL F. B. MORSE

The telegraph, including the development of Morse code, was one of the greatest innovations in the world of communications. Had the Word of God not been set to paper for man to read, Morse code would not have been created. Samuel F. B. Morse (1791–1872) was the man responsible for the development of the modern telegraph and Morse code. He was a man of God and the Bible. Morse biographer Paul J. Staiti writes, "Samuel F. B. Morse's extraordinary life and work were shaped by the circumstances of his birth. . . . Samuel deeply absorbed his family's orthodox Calvinism, which he eventually translated and applied to all his adult actions."[47]

Morse began work on his telegraph in 1832. It was not an easy task. "Years of work and study were needed to perfect his device."[48] Finally, "On May 24, 1844, he astonished Congress, gathered in the Supreme Court chamber, by sending words from Numbers 23:23: 'What hath God wrought!'"[49] On that day, "the first intercity line in the world"[50] communicated the very words of Scripture. This was no small accomplishment, all to the glory of God.

While Morse himself did not *choose* the Scripture verse transmitted over his telegraph (an assistant did), he certainly did *approve* of this verse. William Kloss writes of Morse that "the famous words were certainly appropriate for him. Taken from the Bible (Num. 23), they were part of a prophetic utterance of vindication that must have given him consolation."[51] The great inventor saw his work as a service to the Lord, and it was no accident that he transmitted that particular Bible verse. Morse wrote: "That sentence was divinely indited, for it is in my thoughts day and night. 'What hath God wrought!' It is His work, and He alone could have carried me thus far through all my trials and enabled me to triumph over the obstacles, physical and moral, which opposed me."[52] Morse also said, "I know, for I have *felt,* the substantial support of immediate and cheerful submission to God's will under the pressure of severe trials."[53] In a letter, Morse revealed how his faith helped clear his mind from distracting thoughts: "Anguish of mind can only exist while rebellion is in the heart. [But] an unqualified, sincere 'Thy will be done' will calm the severest tempest that can agitate the soul."[54] His Christian faith helped free this great man to concentrate on his scientific work.

The telegraph, perhaps unimportant to us today, was a major step in the development of modern communications. Morse was the first to develop cabled communications. Paul J. Staiti explains that the "telegraph, one of the most remarkable triumphs in nineteenth-century technology, was for Morse the most explicit demonstration of God's benevolent design for the future of mankind."[55] As the *Encyclopedia of American Biography* points out, "By mid-century . . . the telegraph was internationally recognized as a masterpiece of mechanical invention."[56] Thanks to Morse, mankind established the first network of instant communication through the telegraph poles (forerunners of today's telephone poles). Indeed, what hath God wrought!

MATTHEW FONTAINE MAURY

Another man of the Word who influenced our world is Matthew Fontaine Maury (1806–1873). Maury has been called "the father of modern-day physical oceanography."[57] He is also known as the founder of hydrology. As we shall see, he derived many of his ideas from the Bible.

He began his career as an officer in the U.S. Navy. While enlisted in the navy he was provided the opportunity to "circumnavigate the earth."[58] After an injury left him unable to sail, he was given an assignment at the Depot of Charts and Instruments. During Maury's tenure in this department, he "began collecting information systematically from naval vessels and merchant ships on currents, weather, winds, and other useful data recorded in Maury's specially designed ships' logs."[59] From this collection of data Maury became the first person to chart shipping routes throughout the world. According to *Facts on File: Dictionary of Marine Science,* "These charts made possible shorter passages using areas of the ocean that had the favorable winds—the first establishment of 'sea lanes.'"[60] This designation of shipping lanes was an enormous contribution to the safety and reduced time that ships would spend at sea. Maury also contributed to the laying of electrical cable across the Atlantic Ocean. Gardner Soule, in his book *Men Who Dared the Sea: The Ocean Adventures of the Ancient Mariners,* writes, "Maury also was measuring the depths and sampling the bottom of the Atlantic Ocean as part of the preparations for the laying of an electric cable across the ocean—a way of communication that would transmit messages across the ocean in minutes, instead of the two or more weeks of a sailing ship."[61]

All this we owe to the Bible. Frances Leigh Williams, in his book *Matthew Fontaine Maury, Scientist of the Sea,* explains, "In his role as a scientist, he spoke of his personal belief in religion *as the basis* for any comprehensive understanding of the natural world."[62] Maury got his idea that the sea has "lanes" and currents from a verse in the Bible. Psalm 8:8 speaks of "the fish of the sea that pass through *the paths of the seas.*" In an address given "at the laying of the cornerstone of the University of the South," Maury spoke these words:

> I have been blamed by men of science, both in this country and in England, for quoting the Bible in confirmation of the doctrines of physical geography. The Bible, they say, was not written for scientific purposes, and is therefore of no authority in matters of science. I beg your pardon: the Bible *is* authority for everything it touches. What would you think of the historian who should refuse to consult the historical records of the Bible because the Bible was not written for the purposes of history? The Bible is true; and science is true. . . . And when your man of science with vain and hasty conceit announces the discovery of disagreement between them, rely upon it the fault is not with the Witness or His records, but with the "worm" who essays to interpret evidence which he does not understand. . . . As a student of physical geography, I regard earth, sea, air, and water as parts of a machine, pieces of mechanism, not made with hands, but to which, nevertheless, certain offices have been assigned in the terrestrial economy. It is good and profitable to seek to find out these offices . . . and when, after patient research, I am led to the discovery of any one of them, I feel with the astronomer of old [Kepler] as though I had "thought one of God's thoughts," — and tremble. Thus as we progress with our science we are permitted now and then to point out here and there in the physical machinery of the earth a design of the Great Architect when He planned it all.[63]

Would that more students of today could hear such words! Maury's work benefits humanity to this day, and it began with the Word of God.

JAMES SIMPSON

The scientist who discovered chloroform helped lay the foundation for modern anesthesiology. James Simpson (1811–1870), a Scotsman nurtured on the Bible, was also one of the chief founders of gynecology. He was professor of Obstetric Medicine at Edinburgh University.

Up until Sir James Simpson's contribution, ether was the gas that fueled this painful revolution. Roberto Margotta, in his book *The Story of Medicine,* states that it "was not until 1842 that modern surgical anaesthesia began, with the use of ether."[64] Professor Roderick McGrew writes, "Dr. James Young Simpson, who held the chair of surgery in Edinburgh, experimented with ether in childbirth, but he wanted something better."[65] He tried many different experiments until he finally learned of a new anaesthetic, chloroform, which had been independently described by Eugene Soubeiran and Justus von Liegig in 1831, and by the American Samuel Gutherie in 1832.

What is interesting about Simpson's innovation is what he based it upon. According to Roberto Margotta:

> In November 1847, he informed the association of surgeons of Edinburgh about his discovery, thus incurring the wrath of the Scottish clergy. The Calvinists maintained that Genesis stated, "with pangs shall you give birth to children." Simpson replied by reminding his opponents that God made Adam fall into a deep sleep before taking the rib from him; in other words God anaesthetized him.[66]

And so we see the Bible has given birth to another innovation that has helped to remove the effects of the curse.

GEORGE WASHINGTON CARVER

Like so many other discoverers and innovators, George Washington Carver (1864–1943) was a man who accomplished many things in the service of others. Carver, a great American, was a humble and sincere Christian, a man of the Word. His work and life touched many people. The *Encyclopedia of American Biography* summarizes some of the man's achievements:

> Carver sought to enable poor southern farmers, especially Negroes, to make a better living from the soil. He stressed soil improvement and crop diversification and did pioneering work in the production of useful synthetic materials. When the boll weevil attacked southern cotton and thus devastated the South's one-crop economy, he urged the planting of soil-enriching peanuts and sweet potatoes, from which he was able to develop more than 400 synthetic materials, including dyes, soap, cheese, and a milk substitute. . . . He developed the so-called Carver's Hybrid, a variety of cotton that yielded fat bolls on stems long enough to provide protection against rain-splashed soil.[67]

From the sweet potato alone he was able to develop over one hundred products, "including tapioca, starch, vinegar, molasses, library paste, and rubber. Pecan nuts were used to produce 60 useful products."[68] The *Encyclopedia Americana* says of Carver, "He gave his inventions freely to mankind, refusing large sums offered for their commercial exploration."[69] For Carver's unselfish innovation, we are once again indebted to the Holy Bible.

In a letter to a Seattle minister affirming his own belief in the biblical explanation of creation, Carver wrote: "My life time study of nature in its many phases leads me to believe more strongly than ever in the biblical account of man's creation as found in Gen. 1:27: 'And God created man in his own image, in the image of God created He him; male and female created he them.'"[70]

Carver believed that working toward his discoveries was one way he could draw nearer to God. He wrote, "We get closer to God as we get more intimately and understandingly acquainted with the things he has created. I know of nothing more inspiring than that of making discoveries for one self."[71]

Biographer Rackham Holt called Carver a "seeker after truth." He showed how Carver, in the tradition of all the great scientists who were Christians, was merely "thinking God's thoughts after Him." Holt writes:

> The seeker after truth did little but draw aside the veil and think God's thoughts after him. "I discover nothing in my laboratory," Professor Carver said. "If I come here of myself I am lost. But I can do all things through Christ. I am God's servant, His agent, for here God and I are alone. I am just the instrument through which He speaks, and I would be able to do more if I were to stay in closer touch with Him. With my prayers I mix my labors, and sometimes God is pleased to bless the results."[72]

Carver was also a tremendously popular and successful professor. Linda McMurry said she believes it was his perspective on the subject that lent itself to success:

> To Carver the great creative forces of the universe were divine in origin, and the man who attuned himself to these forces could harness their power and become an agent for the creation of the miraculous. To study agriculture was to study one means of harnessing the forces of nature for the benefit of man. Carver's lectures on even the most mundane subject became religious as well as educational experiences.[73]

In illustrating the lessons that he taught to poor black sharecroppers, Carver often quoted Scripture. McMurry reports that he cited such passages as, "'Look unto the hills from whence cometh thy help,' 'There is much food in the tillage of the poor, but there is that which is wasted for want of judgement,' and 'God said, Behold, I have given every herb bearing seed, which is upon the face of all the earth . . . to you it shall be for meat.'"[74]

Carver also conducted Bible studies. Linda McMurry reports that Carver's was "a joyous religion of love that went far beyond the Protestant work ethic or the fear of eternal damnation. As a result, students who had previously found religion repressive sought out Carver for Bible discussions."[75] During his Bible studies the "creation was explained in the 'light of natural and revealed religion and geological truths.'"[76]

Carver's discoveries were timely and desperately needed by families struggling in the South. "By finding nonfood uses for these soil-enriching plants, he enabled Southern farmers to diversify their crops."[77] His revolutionary work with the peanut remains legendary. He showed how a small part of creation could yield large benefits to mankind. All that he did, like so many great scientists, was done to the glory of God.

VIRTUALLY EVERY MAJOR BRANCH OF SCIENCE

And there are others whose work we could explore: suffice it to say that the Bible played an important part in the development of *scientific* truth. The world has been blessed with this knowledge, and had the Scriptures never been written, I very much doubt that modern science would have been born. As we pointed out in our previous work *What If Jesus Had Never Been Born?*, virtually every major branch of science was created by a Bible-believing Christian. (See page 101 of that work for the comprehensive list.)

OBSERVATIONS OF A RENOWNED SURGEON

One of the great scientists of this century was the American surgeon Dr. Howard A. Kelly, professor of gynecology at Johns Hopkins University from 1889 to 1919. In his time Kelly was a very well-respected scientist. Listen to what this great doctor said about the Bible and science in his book, A *Scientific Man and the Bible:*

I accept the Bible as the Word of God because of its own miraculous character, born in parts in the course of the ages and yet completed in one harmonious whole. *Without the Bible, all God's precious parables in nature, His other book, are utterly lost, and nature, exploited merely for lucre or for the pride of science, is degraded and ruined.* I testify that the Bible is the Word of God because it is meat for the spirit just as definitely as bread and meat are food for the body. *The Bible appeals to me strongly as a physician, because it is such excellent medicine; it has never yet failed to cure a single patient if only he took his prescription honestly.* . . . In opposition to false science and false religions it fixes the origin of sin at a particular time and in an individual, Satan, and at the very outset promises sin's cessation forever when that arch traitor shall be rendered forever impotent. . . . Whatever there is in civilization that is worth while rests on the Bible's precepts. Everywhere and in all its teachings the Bible claims to be the authoritative Word of God, and as such I accept it.[78]

CONCLUSION

Has the Bible been helpful in the cause of science? The Bible essentially created science! And the science the Bible birthed has done much to ameliorate the effects of the curse. But no matter how much progress has been made and no matter how much progress will yet be made, of course, we'll never get to the point that all the effects of the curse are removed. We may be able to postpone death nowadays, but we can't postpone it inevitably. We may be able to manage pain, but we can't do away with it forever. Meanwhile, the Christian knows that when we get to heaven, there will be unspeakable joy:

And God will wipe away every tear from their eyes; there shall be no more death, nor sorrow, nor crying. There shall be no more pain, for the former things have passed away. (Rev. 21:4)

On *that* day, the curse will be completely removed! *Joy* to the world!

CHAPTER 8

THE BIBLE AND LITERATURE

"Then [Jesus] spoke many things to them in parables."
—Matthew 13:3

The very end of the classic novel *Jane Eyre* by Charlotte Brontë closes with one of the characters uttering a prayer familiar to the readers of the New Testament:

> "My master," he says, "has forewarned me. Daily he announces more distinctly,—'Surely I come quickly!' and hourly I more eagerly respond,—'Amen; even so come, Lord Jesus!'"[1]

This is just one of *thousands* of examples where a classic work of literature—a novel, play, or poem—has a direct or indirect reference to the Bible. (Not surprisingly, the recent filmed version of this novel chose to leave out this prayer.)

In the Bible we read some of the most important stories ever told—from Cain and Abel to Noah's ark, from David and Goliath to the passion and resurrection of our Lord Jesus Christ. In addition to such nonfiction accounts, Jesus Christ told many parables—stories that made a spiritual point. With them He communicated God's truth to the masses. The Bible contains some of the most important stories ever told.

Through the centuries we have received a rich heritage of Western literature. What book has influenced that body of work more than the Bible? Lecturer and writer Terry Glaspey says in his *Great Books of the Christian Tradition:*

> The great literature of our culture is littered with references and allusions to the Bible. As one great critic put it, you cannot understand most of the great literature of our civilization if you are not familiar with the Bible and with Shakespeare. The Bible's thoughts, ideas,

personalities, and phrases are the coin in which much of our conversation is transacted.[2]

Yet we live in a time of widespread contempt toward Christianity. (This is a subject important enough that we devoted an entire book to it—*The Gates of Hell Shall Not Prevail: The Attack on Christianity and What You Need to Know to Combat It*.[3]) Because of the hostility against the faith today, some view Christians as being "anticultural." But, as Glaspey points out, a "tradition which can boast the likes of Bach, Dostoevsk[y], Rembrandt, Kierkegaard, Rouault, Flannery O'Connor, Donne, Handel, Dante and Pascal cannot fairly be dismissed as narrow, sterile and lacking in creative thrust."[4]

Indeed, you can hardly consider any of the great classics in literature without encountering the Bible. From Dante to Dostoevsky, from John Bunyan to C. S. Lewis, the influence of the Scriptures is unavoidable. Some of the greatest moments in literature can be traced back to the Bible's influence.

The sixty-six books in the Scriptures leave no facet of the human condition unexamined. This rich source of human experience is the well from which so many great writers have drawn. In an essay entitled "Religion and Literature," T. S. Eliot wrote, "The Bible has had a *literary* influence upon English literature *not* because it has been considered as literature, but because it has been considered as the report of the Word of God."[5] Had the Bible never been written, then Western literature would certainly never have developed as fully as it has.

In this chapter we will consider five great writers of Western literature who were heavily influenced by the Bible. They are Dante, Shakespeare, Milton, Bunyan, and Dostoevsky. After that, we will briefly deal with other writers, such as Swift, Dickens, and C. S. Lewis, and how the Bible influenced their work.

THE BIBLE AND DANTE

Dante Alighieri (1265–1321) wrote the classic *The Divine Comedy*. Born in Florence, Italy, Dante was one of the most profound poets ever to set pen to paper. Dante spent most of his life in Florence, until he was exiled for alleged fraudulent use of public funds, "a charge," according to David Higgins, "trumped up by his political enemies."[6] While he was in exile, Dante produced his masterpiece. According to Yale Professor Harold Bloom, "Only Shakespeare, again by common consent, is judged to be Dante's rival as a great Original in representation."[7]

As John Bunyan did in *The Pilgrim's Progress, The Divine Comedy* chronicled Dante's personal spiritual pilgrimage. John Humphreys Whitfield, in his *A Short History of Italian Literature,* writes, "It is a human pilgrimage through an inhuman world."[8] The poem, written between 1307 and 1321, takes its readers along a journey into hell, purgatory, and heaven. Therefore, the poem itself consists of three canticles entitled: *Inferno, Pergatorio,* and *Paradisio.* Dante was the first writer ever to treat a poem as he did. Colin Manlove, author of *Christian Fantasy: From 1200 to the Present,* states, "It is perhaps strange that Dante was the first to explore the Christian universe in this way."[9] To which he adds, "There had been numerous legendary journeys to hell, purgatory and heaven before Dante, but . . . there is little that foreshadows his fullness and subtlety of treatment."[10] What is amazing is that it is not *just* a brilliant poem. Professor and scholar of Italian literature Ernest Wilkins stated, "The *Comedy* is the greatest of all poems, yet it is only secondarily a poem: it is primarily an instrument of salvation."[11]

Dante was influenced by the Roman classics; for example, Virgil is his guide throughout his journey. But, more important, the Bible influenced *The Divine Comedy.* Edward Moore of Oxford wrote that Dante quoted or referred to the Vulgate, or Latin version of the Bible, some five hundred times.[12] Moore adds:

> Dante's language is full of Scriptural phraseology. And it is scarcely necessary to add that his reverence for the authority of the Scripture is unbounded, and any statement therein found, either directly, or as transformed by the strange processes of allegorical interpretation and application then universally recognized as valid, is for him an absolute final and self-sufficient warrant for any point with which it deals.[13]

Moreover, there are many passages in *The Divine Comedy* that reflect a biblical worldview. For example, on the short-lived nature and vanity of earthly fame, Dante writes, "The Noise of worldly fame is but a blast of wind, that blows from diverse points, and shifts its name, shifting the point it blows from."[14] Worldly fame is of no eternal consequence: what matters is the state of our eternal souls. As Jesus once asked, "For what will it profit a man if he gains the whole world, and loses his own soul?" (Mark 8:36).

The Divine Comedy reflects what Dante believed to be true, yet he did not want his literature to upstage the Bible. Manlove tells us, "While it is true that he both maintained and at least partly believed that the *Commedia* was a vision of the truth granted him by God, he did not intend that his images of the worlds beyond death should usurp the place of scriptural certainties."[15] So although he felt he received his work by divine inspiration, such inspiration was not, of course, comparable to the Scriptures, which were God-breathed (2 Tim. 3:16).

The Divine Comedy repeatedly emphasizes the importance of human beings choosing the right path—to choose the will of God, not our own will; to choose heaven, not hell. Here's how Dante opens the poem:

> Half way along the road we have to go,
> I found myself obscured in a great forest,
> Bewildered, and I knew I had lost the way.[16]

He continues a few lines later:

> I cannot tell exactly how I got there,
> I was full of sleep at that point of the journey
> When, somehow, I left the proper way.[17]

We have important choices on this earth. Either we turn to Him and follow in His guided path, or we turn away from the will of God—and follow the path to our own eternal destiny in hell. Francis Newman believes that this choice is much of Dante's point in the *Inferno*. He states: "In [the] *Inferno* Dante presents this fact in realized action: the sinners condemn themselves to live forever in the kind of material world they were meant to transcend."[18]

As Dante in his literary vision approaches hell, he sees the well-known sign that comes from Dante's *Inferno*, "Abandon all hope, ye who enter here."[19] In the very bowels of hell, he finds there two characters being perpetually chewed up by Satan—Judas Iscariot and Brutus, the betrayers of Jesus and Julius Caesar, respectively. One wag pointed out that in the depths of hell, Judas, Brutus, and Satan are not basking in the glow of the midday sun on an island in the Mediterranean; rather, as Dante put it, they are "in that bottom which devours."[20] The choices we make have eternal consequences.

The next place Dante visits in his dream is purgatory, where the soul goes of a person who will ultimately be redeemed; however, he must first be *purged* of his sins through the prayers and good deeds of loved ones on earth. Of course, the Protestant view is that there is no such place as purgatory because Jesus paid for our sins once and for all (Heb. 9:28). He said to the dying thief who repented and believed on Him, "Assuredly, I say to you, today you will be with Me in Paradise" (Luke 23:43).

While the whole of this pilgrim's journey is a moving experience, perhaps no episode moves us more than the third leg of this spiritual expedition. Dante begins *Paradisio* by saying:

> The glory of him who moves everything
> Penetrates the universe and shines
> In one part more and, in another, less.[21]

Later in *Paradisio*, Dante writes:

> There must be such language for your mind
> Because it learns only from what is sensible
> Matter which, afterwards, it makes fit for the intellect.
> For this reason Scripture condescends
> To your capacities, and attributes
> Feet and hands to God.[22]

He is telling us that God communicates in ways that we can understand.

The most revealing part of the poem comes at the end, when he sees a "simple light":

> In that light a man becomes such
> That it is impossible he should turn away
> Ever to look upon any other thing.
> So I was faced with this new vision;
> ... My mind was struck by a flash
> In which what it desired came to it.
> At this point high imagination failed;
> But already my desire and my will
> Were being turned like a wheel, all at one speed,
> By the love which moves the sun and the other stars.[23]

The inability of Dante to articulate what he sees in heaven lay in the greatness of what he has encountered. We can surely see such overtones of this in the Scriptures: "Men have not heard nor perceived by the ear, Nor has the eye seen any God besides You" (Isa. 64:4). Surely there are experiences in all of our lives that are so overwhelming that we are at a loss for words. Compare that with the poetic experience of seeing God in heaven. Susan Gallagher and Roger Lundin, in their book *Literature Through the Eyes of Faith*, elaborate: "The heavenly world appears too stunning and beautiful to be depicted adequately by the poet [Dante]. God and his creation are more majestic than any images the poet can create and more astonishing than anything he can imagine."[24] They conclude by saying, "In Dante's world, if the poet is to be faulted, it is because his vision falls short of the splendor it tries to depict."[25]

Colin Manlove says it well: "Dante's journey reveals more and more of the harmony of the universe that man but for his sin and mortality would know as his true home."[26]

C. S. Lewis once said, "Dante is eminently the poet of beatitude. He has not only no rival, but none second to him."[27] Lewis also said, "I think Dante's poetry, on the whole, the greatest of all the poetry I have read."[28]

THE BIBLE AND THE BARD: SHAKESPEARE

William Shakespeare (1564–1616) has no literary peer in the English-speaking world. Generations of readers have been moved by Shakespeare's ability to portray virtue and vice in their true light. Scholars observe that some eight hundred quotes from the Bible found their way into his writings: Would his work have been as great without them?

There is no exact record of Shakespeare's date of birth, but "it probably preceded his baptism on April 26, 1564, in Stratford-on-Avon, by only a few days."[29] (For centuries the Church had the most accurate records of births through baptismal records.) In the fifty-two years of Shakespeare's life he contributed a body of work that includes 37 plays (comedies, histories, and tragedies), 6 poems, and 154 sonnets.[30] Millions of people have read or watched productions of *Romeo and Juliet, Hamlet, Othello, Macbeth,* and *The Merchant of Venice.*

In an essay entitled "Political Philosophy and Poetry," the late Professor Allan Bloom of the University of Chicago said of William Shakespeare: "There is a whole series of fundamental human problems, and I suggest that Shakespeare intended to depict all of them and that the man who . . . could understand all the plays individually would see the consequences of all the possible important choices of ways of life and understand fully the qualities of the various kinds of good soul."[31] This analysis understates the breadth and width with which Shakespeare approached his writings on the human condition. Shakespeare's universal perspective had an equally universal point of reference: the Holy Bible. Anyone with a cursory knowledge of the Scriptures will read Shakespeare's comedies, histories, tragedies, poems, and sonnets and be keenly aware of the hundreds of biblical references he employed. Professor of English Peter Milward declares, "There is hardly a book of the Old or the New Testament which is not represented at least by some chance word or phrase in one or other of his plays."[32] Peter Alexander, at the conclusion of his book *Shakespeare's Life and Art,* said, "That he was familiar with the Bible in translations popular in the Reformed Churches, there can be no doubt, and his intimate knowledge of the Anglican Prayer Book has been demonstrated by Mr. Richmond Noble."[33]

During the time of Shakespeare there were eleven translations of the English Bible available. Scholars agree that it is difficult to know exactly which translation of the Bible Shakespeare preferred. Professor of English literature Naseeb Shaheen states, "The vast majority of Shakespeare's Biblical references cannot be traced to any one version,"[34] which he attributes to "the many Tudor Bibles [which] are usually too similar to be differentiated."[35] Yet after a careful line-by-line comparison of Shakespeare's works and the many Bible translations available to him, Milward and Shaheen both say that in the tragedies and histories it appears Shakespeare referred most often to the Geneva Bible. I find that fascinating in light of the fact that the Geneva Bible was virtually prohibited by Queen Elizabeth I and King James I. Although King James is best known for the Bible translation of 1611 that bears his name, he most certainly hated biblical Christianity. Historian Dr. Charles Wolfe observes that the King James Version was created in part to counteract the influence of the hated (i.e., hated by the Crown) Geneva Bible.

In addition to the Geneva Bible, Milward believes that the Bishops' and Rheims Bibles also influenced Shakespeare.[36] Of Shakespeare's comedies, Shaheen has determined that he "refers more often to the Psalms than to any other book of the Bible, and whenever his references resemble a particular version of the Psalms, it is almost always to the Psalter rather than the Geneva" that he refers.[37] Thus Shakespeare referred to no less than three or four versions.

Shakespeare did not just refer to the Scriptures casually: his plays were often saturated with biblical themes. Although little is known of Shakespeare's youth or education, some writers feel the Scriptures were influential in his formative years. In exploring the educational background of Shakespeare, Philip Edwards determined the English Bible (in its "Geneva" or "Bishops'" version) that was "probably the most important English element in Shakespeare's *education.*"[38] So the Bible wasn't just important in his plays, it had been important in his education.

One of the Bible stories that had the most influence on him was Cain and Abel. In *Hamlet,* the title character's father had been slain by his own brother Claudius, which Milward compares to "the first murder of Abel by his brother Cain."[39] In two other tragedies, *Macbeth* and *King*

Lear, Milward observes that beginning with Shakespeare's history plays, "there is a direct line of development leading to the tragedies, and culminating in *Macbeth* and *King Lear* . . . [which is] noticeably Biblical in its overtones. There is, in the first place, a significant series of references to the murder of Abel by his brother Cain, from *Genesis* iv."[40] So powerful was "the story of Cain" to Shakespeare, writes S. Schoenbaum, that he "refers to it at least twenty-five times" in his works.[41]

Two very popular parts of *Hamlet* illustrate the similarities between Shakespeare's writing and the Bible. In Act 1, scene 3, Polonius says to his son these very famous words:

This above all: to thine own self be true,
And it must follow, as the night the day,
Thou canst not then be false to any man.[42]

Milward, in his line-by-line comparison, explains that Shakespeare's line "to thine own self be true" very much "corresponds to the advice of Ecclesiasticus xxxvii.13: 'Take counsel of *thine own* heart; for there is no man more faithful unto thee than it.'"[43] Ecclesiasticus is part of the Apocrypha of the Bible, a relatively small portion of the Old Testament that Roman Catholics hold to be part of the Word of God. (Protestants don't share that view of the Apocrypha.) For Shakespeare, writing this line was the same as echoing a passage from Holy Writ.

Another well-known passage from *Hamlet* is Hamlet's speech given in Act 3, scene 1:

To be, or not to be, that is the question.
Whether 'tis nobler in the mind to suffer
The slings and arrows of outrageous fortune,
Or to take arms against a sea of troubles
And by opposing end them. To die: to sleep.[44]

As before, Milward believes, "The whole of this famous soliloquy of Hamlet is deeply rooted in the Book of *Job*, as his [Hamlet's] problem in its deepest aspect is that of Job."[45]

Writing about Shakespeare's play *Richard II,* Alexander states, "It is clear from the Biblical allusions that Shakespeare had in mind the whole problem of charity and pity, which lies at the heart of literature no less than of religion, and its dramatic treatment."[46] In the third part of *Henry the Sixth*, King Henry's son Richard states:

No, God forbid, that I should wish them sever'd
Whom God hath join'd together: ay, and 'twere pity
To sunder them that yoke so well together.[47]

These lines refer to what Jesus said about marriage in Matthew 19:6: "What therefore God hath joined together, let not man put asunder" (KJV).

In Shakespeare's comedy *Measure for Measure*, we find that "the play's title . . . is based on Jesus' words in Matthew 7:2, 'With what measure ye mete, it shall be measured to you.'" Shaheen explains that the expression "measure for measure" was commonplace in Shakespeare's day.[48] Russell Fraser, in his book *Shakespeare: The Later Years,* says of the play *As You Like It:* "The Bible, endlessly his primer, elucidates this plot, however, also giving him his point of departure."[49]

There are literally hundreds of such examples that illustrate how Shakespeare referred to and was influenced by the Bible. Whole books have been written specifically on this subject; I've quoted here from a few of them. Milward states, "It may be said that Shakespeare's view of human life is neither more nor less than the Biblical view, with the imperfections of the Old Testament supplemented by the teaching and life of Christ in the New Testament."[50]

Tragically, Shakespeare is in decline right now in American education. The National Alumni Forum (NAF) reports:

> Shakespeare and other Great Authors have been dropped from English major requirements at two-thirds of the 67 colleges and universities responding to an NAF survey. The survey contacted the *U.S. News [& World Report's]* "top fifty" schools as well as others for added balance.[51]

This is a tragic trend. Jonathan Yardley, writing in *The Washington Post,* commented on the NAF study: "The final piece of evidence that the lunatics are running the academic asylum is now firmly in place."[52] Literally, instead of Shakespeare, some courses are studying such noteworthy subjects as soap operas, Graceland, "White Trash," and gangster films. I believe this is further evidence of the anti-Christian (and anti-Western) bent found among our cultural elites. Modern academics are apparently trying to distance themselves even farther from the culture the Bible was instrumental in shaping.

THE BIBLE AND THE BLIND PROPHET: JOHN MILTON

John Milton (1608–1674) was one of the greatest writers of all time. The Bible was the key source of his writings, especially his masterpiece, *Paradise Lost,* published in 1667. His writings were prophetic, in the sense that he saw things that the ordinary person didn't and was then able to articulate them.

"There are men who stand aside from the period which happens to give them birth," said author F. W. Boreham. "Their genius is disconcerting, terrifying, majestic. The world holds aloof from them. They are the citizens, not of an age, but of the ages. And the ages are quick to identify their own, hail them, applaud them, crown them. Of such pure and deathless spirits, John Milton is the supreme and peerless representative."[53]

"Never before," said Dr. Edward Garnett, "nor since has such a splendid figure crossed the broad stage of English life."[54] Author and lecturer Terry Glaspey describes *Paradise Lost* as one of "the most important poems of all time and influential in creating some of our popular cultural conceptions of God and the devil."[55]

John Milton lived during turbulent times in seventeenth-century Britain. Milton was seven years old when Shakespeare died. He was ten when Sir Walter Raleigh was executed. He was twelve when the *Mayflower* set sail for these inhospitable shores. The young poet lived and worked to see the republic established in England. Milton was a great herald of political liberty, writing for the Puritans under Cromwell during the British civil war. He championed political and religious liberty. He had a strong desire that what he believed to be the biblical form of government (a purity in government, church, and life) be brought to England. He lived to see it accomplished under Cromwell when the monarchy was overthrown and the republic was set up. Later he lived to see Cromwell die, the republic overthrown, and the monarchy reestablished, after which England sank back into abasement and shallowness. After the death of Cromwell, Milton was thrown into prison. His writings were publicly burned. He lost most of his property at this time.

England was up to her knees in the mire of sin, and it seemed that Paradise indeed had been lost. Through all of this hardship, Milton came to see that any earthly paradise is but a *poor shadow* of that Paradise to which, by the grace of God, he hoped to go. Even though his long labors for freedom in England had already cost him the sight of one eye, he soon faced a dilemma. He was commissioned to write a particularly long and arduous work in defense of the freedom of the government, yet he was told by the doctors that if he did, he would lose the sight of his other eye. Choosing blindness rather than dereliction of duty, this young man persevered until he slipped, never to emerge, into total blackness.

He gave himself completely to the fulfillment of his task. Seeing what his calling was, he studied diligently, and part of his study was another reason for the loss of his sight. From the time he was twelve until the time he was forty-four years old—when he lost his vision—he gave himself every day completely to study. His learning was so vast and his erudition so great that it forms for many today an obstacle to the reading of his poetry, because few of us have given ourselves to anything like the tremendous classical learning that filled the mind of Milton. He saw the chief object of studying as godliness:

> The end then of learning is to repair the ruins of our first parents by regaining to know God aright, and out of that knowledge to love him, to imitate him, to be like him, as we may the nearest by possessing our souls of true virtue, which, being united to the heavenly grace of faith, makes up the highest perfection.[56]

Though the Greeks had their ethics and their heroes—their *Odyssey* and their *Iliad*—nothing compares with the tremendous universal poem that Milton was to write. *Paradise Lost* did not deal with just one nation or one people, but with all mankind; and it involved not just humans, but angels and seraphim and demons and God and His Son. Never had anyone given himself, said Boreham, to such a colossal task and followed through it (in spite of all of the handicaps) with such stupendous perseverance throughout his life.

Though his vision was taken from him, Milton had prayed that God would open unto him an inward sight and fill his soul with eyes that he might see things invisible and reveal them to men who, though they had physical sight, were often blind to that vast universe that lay behind the tangible. So, Milton was a poet of the invisible, and he splashed on a vast canvas the history of the world from eternity to eternity. He saw things that had never been seen before. And with that inner sight he has opened the eyes of millions. There is a grandeur to his poetry. The word *Miltonic* has been coined to describe the sublimity of that "cathedral speech" (as it was called), the like of which has never been seen before and probably never will be seen again.

The first thing that grasps the minds of any who read or study the life of Milton is the fact that here was a man who was dominated by one basic source of inspiration—not only for his writing, but also for his life. That source was the Scriptures. There is no doubt that he held the Scriptures from Genesis to Revelation to be the absolute infallible revelation of the living God; and all that man was and had been, and ever hoped to be was written in their pages. He has been called one of the highest examples of Puritanism—a man who had a vision, which he drew from those Scriptures.

The glorious work that was to be Milton's great life enterprise and contribution to the world had grown silently throughout thirty years in the poet's soul. Milton saw the tremendous power and deception of sin that had come into the world and had created such havoc and misery upon the earth. He saw it in all of its subtlety. He saw that it had come forth from the mind of Satan. The book begins in hell, right after Satan and his demons (one-third of the angels) have lost the battle against God and His faithful angels in heaven:

> The dismal situation waste and wild:
> A dungeon horrible, on all sides round
> As one great furnace flamed, yet from those flames
> No light, but rather darkness visible
> Served only to discover sights of woe,
> Regions of sorrow, doleful shades, where peace
> And rest can never dwell, hope never comes
> That comes to all; but torture without end
> Still urges, and a fiery deluge, fed
> With ever-burning sulphur unconsumed:
> Such place Eternal Justice had prepared
> For those rebellious, here their prison ordained
> In utter darkness, and their portion set
> As far removed from God and light of heaven
> As from the center thrice [the very center] to the utmost pole.
> O how unlike the place from whence they fell!!

Then Satan speaks to a fellow demon, equally suffering in torment:

> In equal ruin: into what pit thou seest
> From what height fallen, so much the stronger proved
> He with his thunder, and till then who knew
> The force of those dire arms? . . .
> All is not lost; the unconquerable will,
> And study of revenge, immortal hate,
> And courage never to submit or yield:
> And what is else not to be overcome?
> That glory never shall his wrath or might
> Extort from me. To bow and sue for grace
> With suppliant knee . . .[57]

In other words, although Satan has lost the battle between himself and God, and although he's in the most miserable place imaginable, he still retains his "unconquerable will." He goes on to say that it's "better to reign in hell than to serve in heav'n"![58]

Satan and his minions go on from there to plot their revenge against God. Their plan is to sabotage His new creation, man. Satan causes man to sin, and sin brings forth death.

Milton also saw the reality of Jesus Christ, the second Adam. His great masterpieces, *Paradise Lost* and *Paradise Regained*, are about two principal characters: the first Adam, by whose disobedience all mankind was plunged into sin and death and misery; and the second Adam, Jesus Christ, who was the beginning of a whole new creation. Thus, Jesus came to destroy the works of the devil. His heavenly love undoes the hellish hate for all those who come to accept His grace. Christ's servant, John Milton, helped bring these and other biblical truths to light.

If you have never read *Paradise Lost* or *Paradise Regained*, then I highly recommend you do. Be forewarned, however, that it is difficult reading. The advantage of reading them is gaining a perspective on what life on earth is all about, from eternity to eternity.[59] In light of its archaic language, I would like to make a bold and perhaps controversial suggestion: I think that some bright, Christian professor with a good grasp of Miltonic English (perhaps a professor of English language) would do the world a favor by "translating" Milton's great epics into more modern English. It may help the two great masterpieces get back into the spotlight, where they belong. In any event, if the Bible had never been written, this titan of a writer wouldn't have given us what scholars call "the greatest epic in the English language."[60]

THE BIBLE AND JOHN BUNYAN

One of the most famous, most widely read, most frequently published books in the history of the world begins as follows:

As I walked through the wilderness of this world, I lighted on a certain place where was a den, and laid me down in that place to sleep; and as I slept, I dreamed a dream. I dreamed, and, behold, I saw a man clothed with rags, standing in a certain place, with his face [away] from his own house, a book in his hand, and a great burden upon his back. I looked, and saw him open the book, and read therein; and, as he read, he wept and trembled; and, not being able longer to contain, he brake out with a lamentable cry, saying, "What shall I do?"

In this plight, therefore, he went home, and restrained himself as long as he could, that his wife and children should not perceive his distress; but he could not be silent long, because that his trouble increased. Wherefore, at length, he brake his mind to his wife and children; and thus he began to talk to them: "O, my dear wife," said he, "and you, the children of my bowels, I, your dear friend, am in myself undone by reason of a burden that lieth hard upon me; moreover, I am certainly informed that this our City will be burnt with fire from heaven; in which fearful overthrow, both myself, with thee, my wife, and you, my sweet babes, shall miserably come to ruin, except (the which yet I see not) some way of escape can be found, whereby we may be delivered."[61]

Thus begins the immortal *Pilgrim's Progress,* written by that famous tinker of Bedford, John Bunyan. This book was printed in well over three hundred separate editions, in over 112 languages, and has been sold and read in countless millions of copies. Author and scholar Herbert Lockyer writes that although Bunyan has been dead for hundreds of years now, "he still speaks in his unique writings, the most renowned of which is the *Pilgrim's Progress,* a spiritual classic raising its author to the heights of the immortals."[62] Our native Anglo-Saxon comes forth with its greatest power in *Pilgrim's Progress.* It is a book that changed the face of England and has been used by God to transform millions of lives. It is one of the great tragedies of our time that so many people have never perused its pages. If you have not, let me exhort you to get *Pilgrim's Progress* and read it.

John Bunyan (1628–1688) was a tinker who mended pots and pans, which used to be a rather common occupation. He was also a very poor man. He had very little education. He learned to read and write only about as well as other poor people of the day, which is amazing, since he wrote one of the greatest, most famous writings of all times!

The three most famous works of Bunyan are *Pilgrim's Progress,* describing the pilgrimage of a Christian through this world from the City of Destruction to the Celestial City above; *Holy War,* which is an allegory describing the fall of man's soul into the hands of Diabolos, the devil, and its recapture by Emmanuel, the Son of God (a marvelous work); and his autobiography, *Grace Abounding to the Chief of Sinners.*

John Bunyan grew up, according to his testimony, as a very ungodly young man. But he became aware that he was a sinner and that the justice of God demanded the punishment of sin. Even though Bunyan participated in church-related activities, he became convicted of his sin—he knew he was a hypocrite. He delighted to hear others speak well of him as if he were pious, but everything he did, he did just so others would praise him for his outward righteousness.

He felt that there was no hope for him. But reading the Scripture, he came to the sixth chapter of John. He read verse 37, which says, "All that the Father giveth me shall come to me; and him that cometh to me I will in no wise cast out" (KJV). Ah, how blessed did John 6 seem to

John Bunyan! "Him that cometh to me I will in no wise cast out." God used this verse to open his spiritual eyes and convert him.

At this time he also described his own experience, which is what *Pilgrim's Progress* really is, an allegorical biography of John Bunyan. You will recall that Christian, the main character in that novel, leaves the City of Destruction to find salvation, but all the while, he has a burden of sin, like a heavy knapsack on his back. This burden weighs him down and makes virtually every step painful, yet he can find no way to remove it. But when he finally comes to the hill of Calvary, where he finds the three crosses, he at last comes to Jesus. It was there that Christian knelt before the center cross and suddenly his burden burst loose from his back and rolled down that hill into a tomb, never to be seen again. Bunyan was describing his own life. He had come to know that he had eternal life! He had experienced the grace of God.

In *Pilgrim's Progress* he describes how anyone who desires the pilgrim way may find that assurance, and the certain dangers along the way. In this allegory Bunyan takes human character traits and breathes life into them; suddenly they rise up from the page, walk on two legs, and speak—they swagger and they boast, they cry and they moan. Those marvelous characters! Who can forget these characters? They included Pliable; Obstinate; Mr. Worldly Wiseman, who has such sage advice for this foolish young Christian; Mr. Goodwill; Simple; Presumption; Formality; Hypocrisy; Talkative; Judge Hate-Good; Apollyon; Giant Despair; Mr. Legality, who would have him follow the Law to be saved (an impossible supposition). Indeed, there are many characters Pilgrim meets on his way—characters known to virtually all of us who tread the pilgrim way. Many of them lead to false starts and stops. Only by following God's straight and narrow way, through the guidance of the Evangelists (the Gospels) does he make it through.

Although the book is now more than three hundred years old, *Pilgrim's Progress* still retains its freshness and spiritual clarity. Because of the intense secularism of our age, the book is not as well known in our culture as in previous generations. J. D. Douglas writes that it was read in "virtually every Victorian home."[63] To this day it remains a bestseller! Without the Bible, there could never have been the great masterpiece, *Pilgrim's Progress*.

┇ THE BIBLE AND DOSTOEVSKY

Fyodor Dostoevsky (1821–1881), one of the most insightful novelists ever, was a committed Christian. According to Professor Roger Cox, "Among the post-Renaissance writers, one stands out from the rest as a possible successor to Shakespeare as the great practitioner of Christian tragedy—Fyodor Dostoevsky."[64] Dostoevsky was reared in what was initially a godly home; Dostoevsky biographer Geir Kjetsaa writes, "The Bible was, naturally, the most important text in this very religious household."[65] However, it was not surprising that he fell away from faith, for his father, a medical doctor, eventually became a miserly drunkard. He so mistreated his serfs that they actually murdered him.

As a young man, while attending a military engineering school in St. Petersburg, Russia, Dostoevsky began to meet on a regular basis with a group that was dedicated to studying French socialist theories. Because of his association with this group, he was arrested and convicted for political crimes. Shortly after being imprisoned at the Peter-and-Paul fortress in Saint Petersburg, Dostoevsky wrote to his brother Mikhail and asked of him: "You want to send me historical works? That would be fine. But it would be even better if you sent me the Bible (both Testaments). *I need it.*"[66] He received the New Testament, which he read and reread, and Dostoevsky was converted to Jesus Christ.

Shortly thereafter he was sentenced to death by firing squad. With death all but certain, he turned to one of the men he was to be killed alongside and is quoted by Kjetsaa as saying, "We will be with Christ."[67] But the sentence was not executed. In his final moments Dostoevsky received a pardon and was sentenced to hard labor in Siberia, in addition to service in the ranks as an ordinary soldier. Dostoevsky offered yet another glimpse of the effects the Bible had on him while serving his sentence in a labor camp in Omsk. According to Kjetsaa, there were very few pleasant people in the prison. But Dostoevsky found a friend— "Ali, whom Dostoevsky taught to read from his New Testament."[68] Years later, in responding to a mother's question about the rearing of her child, Dostoevsky wrote in a letter this advice:

> Your child is 3 years old; acquaint him with the Gospels, teach him to believe in God, strictly, as prescribed by the law. This is a *sine qua non*, because, without that, he cannot become a good man but will, at the best, turn into a *sufferer* and, at worst, into an indifferent *fat man*, or something even worse. There is no way of improving on Christ, believe me.[69]

He retained this respect for the Bible and Christ to his dying day. But, more important for our purposes here, the Bible had a great influence on his fiction.

His classic novel *Crime and Punishment* illustrates this. Referring to Sonia, the novel's spiritual voice, Alba Amoia expresses: "Dostoevsky brings out the innate skill of the unschooled, uneducated, and unso-phisticated Sonia in arousing the sensitivity of the educated man to the wonders of speech."[70] Amoia continues: "Mediated through Sonia's evangelical spirit, the Gospel—the expressed mind and will of God—turns Raskolnikov toward Christ."[71] In the novel's conclusion, Sonia gives Raskolnikov a New Testament, which he was reluctant to read. Yet Dostoevsky implies that he not only reads it, but that it transforms him. The novel closes with this paragraph:

> But that is the beginning of a new story—the story of the gradual renewal of a man, the story of his gradual regeneration, of his passing from one world into another, of his initiation into a new unknown life. That might be the subject of a new story, but our present story is ended.[72]

The subject of this beautiful novel embraces Christianity at the very end of the book.

In Dostoevsky's *The Idiot* we likewise see the profound impact of the Bible. In his book *Fyodor Dostoevsky: A Writer's Life*, Geir Kjetsaa explains the dynamics involved in *The Idiot*. He says that Dostoevsky wanted to create a character who was an "absolutely good person," but that he was fully aware that the only such figure was Christ.[73] So how was Dostoevsky to "transpose a Christ-inspired figure to an earthly, everyday existence"?[74] In a letter to his niece, Dostoevsky explained:

> The novel's central idea is to portray the absolutely good person. There is nothing more difficult than this in the whole world, especially in our time. . . . In the whole world there is only one absolutely good person: Christ, and consequently the very existence of this one infinitely good being is in itself an ineffable miracle. The entire Gospel according to St. John came into being over this thought: it sees the whole miracle in the appearance of the good, in the incarnation of the perfect flesh and blood.[75]

Kjetsaa believes Dostoevsky was successful: "If we are now to com-pare Dostoevsky's vision of Christ with the portrait we are given of Prince Myshkin [the 'absolutely good person'], we can hardly fail to observe the similarities."[76]

In the novel *The Devils* (often referred to as *The Possessed*) we read about a conversion similar to the transformation Raskolnikov experi-enced in *Crime and Punishment*. Alba Amoia writes, "Likewise in *The*

Devils, a Gospel reading enables Stephan Verkhovensky to surmount a lifelong 'stumbling block' to his belief in God."[77]

Dostoevsky's most important novel is *The Brothers Karamazov*. Here too the Bible plays a clear role. Roger Cox, author of *Between Earth and Heaven: Shakespeare, Dostoevsky, and the Meaning of Christian Tragedy*, writes: "Indeed, *The Brothers Karamazov* testifies more brilliantly than perhaps any other work of literature to the 'victory of the incarnation.' . . . The logic of human experience, faithfully and fully represented in the book, is what renders meaningful Alyosha's final declaration to the boys—'Certainly we shall all rise again.'"[78]

The book is considered to be his best novel, and it is heavily autobiographical. Konstantin Mochulsky, in commenting on Dostoevsky and *The Brothers Karamazov,* wrote, "Everything that he experienced, thought, and created finds its place in this vast synthesis."[79] Mochulsky later adds, "*The Brothers Karamazov* is not only a synthesis of Dostoevsky's creative work, but also a culmination of his life. . . . The novel . . . opens before us as its author's *spiritual biography* and his *artistic confession*."[80]

The novel focuses on the "tragic struggle [that] takes place between the father and his children."[81] This struggle results in the death of Fyodor Karamazov. The book shows striking differences between the Karamazov brothers, especially where they stand on the Christian faith. A fair reading of the novel shows that the believing brother, Alyosha, is more the hero of the novel, in contrast with the unbelieving brother, Ivan. Roger Cox points out, "In *The Brothers Karamazov* we can hardly overlook the fact that Ivan's atheism is identified specifically as a rebellion against the authority of God and that the murder of old Karamazov is the direct result of this rebellion."[82]

In Dostoevsky's own introduction to *The Brothers Karamazov*, he begins with John 12:24: "Verily, verily, I say unto you, except a corn of wheat fall into the ground and die, it abideth alone: but if it die, it bringeth forth much fruit."[83] Opening the novel with a quote from Scripture certainly sets its tone. In the opinion of Robert L. Belknap of Columbia University, the biblical content we find in this novel could have come from the respect Dostoevsky learned for the Sacred Volume when he was growing up:

Dostoevsky's first recorded reading was a book of Bible stories, which he may have already known from his deeply religious mother or the churches where she took him. In book 6, chapter 2, part *b* of *The Brothers Karamazov,* Father Zossima recollects such a book, "a sacred history, with beautiful pictures entitled *A Hundred and Four Sacred*

Stories from the Old and New Testaments," as the text he learned to read from.[84]

One positive character in the book is Father Zossima, a helpful man with good character, and a dedicated Christian. He stands in contrast with another monk or two who are cantankerous and ill-willed. Here's a brief description about Father Zossima and his love of the Bible:

> Father Zossima, in speaking with some visitors just prior to his death, is recorded as saying, "With my memories of home I count, too, my memories of the Bible, which . . . I was very eager to read at home." Later, when speaking of Job, he says, "Good heavens, what a book it is, and what lessons are in it! What a book the Bible is, what a miracle, what strength is given with it to man."[85]

We know what the author intended to communicate through this particular character. In a letter to N. A. Lyubinov, Dostoevsky writes of Father Zossima (sometimes translated as "the Elder Zossima"), "*I will force them to admit* that a pure and ideal Christian is not an abstraction but a tangible, real possibility that can be contemplated with our own eyes."[86]

Whatever personal flaws Dostoevsky had—including, at one point in his life, a gambling problem—his life and writings are replete with references that point to the influence of the Bible. Without the Bible we would not have the wealth of psychologically deep dramas that Dostoevsky left for the enrichment of the world.

THE INFLUENCE OF THE BIBLE IN THE LITERATURE OF SELECT AUTHORS

Let's also consider several other authors and the Bible's influence on their work.

Miguel De Cervantes

Miguel De Cervantes (1547–1616) created one of literature's most fascinating characters in his classic, *Don Quixote*. Harold Bloom of Yale describes Cervantes as "one of those few Western writers who cannot be surpassed."[87] A word has even been coined based on the novel, *quixotic,* meaning a naive, but noble, enterprise.

In an essay on *Don Quixote*, American linguist and philosopher Leo Spitzer says, "It is not the language, the gesture, the costume, or the body that matter to him, but the meaning behind all the exterior manifestations: the soul."[88] Professor Juan Bautista Avalle-Arce writes that Cervantes "gives his protagonist various names. . . . This changing of personal names, has its roots in the Judeo-Christian tradition, and we know that Israel is the name given in the Old Testament to Jacob after he wrestled the angel of the Lord. In the New Testament, Saul of Tarsus was a bitter Christian-hater, but after the vision on the road to Damascus and his conversion, he came to call himself Paul."[89]

Historians Will and Ariel Durant explain that by "making his picture of manners Cervantes established the modern novel and . . . raised the new form to philosophy by making it reveal and illuminate the moral gamut of mankind."[90] They also observe that in his own "quixotic way," Cervantes predicted that his book would sell thirty million copies, and it did indeed![91]

In *Don Quixote*, the entire journey is provoked by the title character's readings of many books. So obsessed with the reading of literature, he is said to have "sold many acres of arable land to purchase books of knight-errantry."[92] Later we read, "He so immersed himself in those romances that he spent whole days and nights over his books; and thus . . . he lost the use of his reason."[93] Here Cervantes parallels the biblical point that "of making many books there is no end, and much study is wearisome to the flesh" (Eccl. 12:12).

Another interesting point is that Don Quixote chose to travel, in imitation of Jesus, in a humble fashion. The don travels via an emaciated horse named Rozinante, parallel to the humble donkey Christ rode on the first Palm Sunday. Also interesting is the loyalty, submission, and Christian traits of his servant Sancho. Durant describes him as "good-hearted and charitable, wise without letters, and faithful to his master."[94]

The following short quotes from the novel reflect the influence of the Bible:

- "'There is no reason to take vengeance on anybody,' answered Sancho, 'for a good Christian never takes it for wrongs, and besides, I'll make my ass submit his wrong to my good will, and that means to live at peace as long as Heaven grants me life.'"[95]
- "'Since that is so,' said he of the Wood, 'let us give up going in search of adventures, and since we have loaves, don't let us go looking for tarts, but return to our cots, for there God will find us if it be His will.'"[96]

- "At length Don Quixote's last day came, after he had received all the sacraments, and expressed his abhorrence of books of knight-errantry. The notary, who was present, said that he had never read of any knight who ever died in his bed so peacefully and like a good Christian as Don Quixote."[97]

John Donne

John Donne (1572–1631) was, in the words of the Durants, "the finest poet of the age . . . as no other poet could match, in that amazing age, but Shakespeare himself."[98] Though his early works represent the writings of a man who has clearly lost his moorings, those of his later years display a man who has discovered the fear of God. Donne experienced a full and intense life, and this translated into the words he wrote—words that expressed a sensitive and caring countenance reflective of his faith.[99]

Donne wrote beautiful Christian poetry. He personified death in the following poem. Having a biblical worldview, Donne knew that death was not final for the Christian:

Death, be not proud, though some have called thee
Mighty and dreadful, for thou are not so;
For those whom thou think'st thou dost overthrow
Die not, poor Death, nor yet canst thou kill me. . . .
One short sleep past, we wake eternally,
And death shall be no more. Death, thou shalt die.[100]

In 1623, recovering from a serious illness, he wrote in his diary some famous lines: "Any man's death diminishes me, because I am involved in mankind; and therefore never send to know for whom the bell tolls; it tolls for thee."[101] Furthermore, Donne was a preacher in the Church of England, and published versions of his sermons are still in print.[102] Above all, John Donne was a great writer whose work was imbued with biblical themes.

Jonathan Swift

Another writer whose work reflects the Bible's influence, albeit in an indirect way, is Reverend Jonathan Swift (1667–1745), the author of *Gulliver's Travels*. A native of Ireland, Swift was a clergyman, writer, and satirist. He had an embittered life and a biting wit, traits displayed in much of his work. One of his earliest books was the highly satirical

Tale of a Tub. It deals with three men in a tub, engaged in a pedantic religious dispute. Many questioned his orthodoxy because of this work.

Of course, Jonathan Swift is best known for his masterpiece, *The Travels of Lemuel Gulliver*, better known as *Gulliver's Travels*, which he first published anonymously. Ironically, Swift wrote this novel to satirize politics in England. Instead, it became a children's classic! Terry Glaspey, in *The Great Books of the Christian Tradition*, points out that *Gulliver's Travels* demonstrates Swift's "disbelief in the perfectibility of human nature."[103] The Bible cautions us to not put our trust in man; as the Scripture says, "Cursed is the man who trusts in man and makes flesh his strength" (Jer. 17:5). In his own humorous way, Swift liked to underscore the foibles of humankind.

Charles Dickens

Charles Dickens (1812–1870) is perhaps best known for his classic— *A Christmas Carol*, a parable of a Christian conversion. His novels, from *Oliver Twist* to *David Copperfield*, from *Pickwick Papers* to *Hard Times*, arouse sympathy for the underdog in a heartless world. In this way he could prick the conscience of a smug Christian society, in the early decades of the Industrial Revolution, to understand that it wasn't meeting its own ethical standard toward the down-and-out. In Peter Ackroyd's biography, Dickens says of his own work: "One of my most constant and most earnest endeavors has been to exhibit in all my good people some faint reflections of the teachings of our great Master. . . . All my strongest illustrations are derived from the New Testament; all my social abuses are shown as departures from its spirit.'"[104] Ackroyd explains that Dickens "goes on explicitly to link his Christmas Books with that Testament: 'In every one of those books there is an express text preached on, and that text is always taken from the lips of Christ.'"[105]

In the well-known passage from Dickens's *A Christmas Carol*, the miserly Scrooge is visited by the ghost of his late former business partner, fellow miser Jacob Marley. Marley's spirit, whose spectral body is wrapped up in heavy chains, has no rest and is doomed to walk to and fro on the earth. There is no rest for the wicked. "Woe is me," declares Marley, borrowing a line from Scripture. Here's part of their dialogue:

"You are fettered," said Scrooge, trembling. "Tell me why?" "I wear the chain I forged in life," replied the Ghost. "I made it link by link, and yard by yard; I girded it on of my own free will, and of my own free will I wore it. Is its pattern strange to you?"[106]

While the specifics of Jacob's punishment (being condemned to roam the earth as a ghost in chains) is not necessarily biblical, the point—that those who have wealth in this world and withhold help from those in need will be judged—is definitely in the Bible. (For example, see the Lord's parable of Lazarus and the rich man in Luke 16.) So also is the point that we reap what we sow (Gal. 6:7). Marley says to Scrooge:

> "Oh! Captive, bound, and double-ironed," cried the phantom, "not to know that ages of incessant labor, by immortal creatures, for this earth must pass into eternity before the good of which it is susceptible is all developed! Not to know that any Christian spirit working kindly in its little sphere, whatever it may be, will find its mortal life too short for its vast means of usefulness!"[107]

In Dickens's immortal novel *A Tale of Two Cities,* which exposes the horrors of the godless French Revolution, he opens up with this well-known passage: "It was the best of times, it was the worst of times, it was the age of wisdom, it was the age of foolishness, it was the epoch of belief, it was the epoch of incredulity, it was the season of Light, it was the season of Darkness. . . . It was the year of Our Lord one thousand seven hundred and seventy-five."[108] In describing a room full of people (largely what appears to be degenerates), Dickens writes: "Projectors who had discovered every kind of remedy for the little evils . . . except the remedy of setting to work in earnest to root out a single sin, poured out their distracting babble into any ears they could lay hold of. . . . Unbelieving Philosophers who were remodeling the world with words, and making card-towers of Babel to scale the skies."[109]

At the end of the story, one of the main characters, Sidney Carton, sacrificially takes upon himself the death sentence that was to be meted out to another character. Although Carton was no Christ, the act itself points to the Christian theme, "Greater love has no one than this, than to lay down one's life for his friends" (John 15:13). As he is marched off to the guillotine, he comforts a young girl who is also to be executed; he encourages her with the thought of going to heaven. Dickens quotes Jesus' promise, which comforted both Carton and the girl: "I am the resurrection and the life, saith the Lord: he that believeth in me, though he were dead, yet he shall live: and whosoever liveth and believeth in me, shall never die!"[110]

The last book Dickens published was entitled *The Life of Our Lord.* He wrote this to tell his children the all-important story of Jesus. The writings of Dickens show once again that the impact of Scripture is found in many of our greatest classics.

C. S. Lewis

C. S. Lewis (1898–1963) was one of the most creative writers of the twentieth century, and the greatest Christian author of his time. An atheist early in his life, he became a Christian around the age of thirty. Christian literature—in particular that of G. K. Chesterton and George MacDonald—played an enormous role in his conversion. He said that MacDonald's *Phantastes* "baptized his imagination."[111]

Lewis served as a professor of English literature at Oxford University, and later in the same capacity at Cambridge. He is well known for his apologetics, such as *Mere Christianity, Miracles,* and *The Problem of Pain.* He also wrote wonderful works of fiction, including the popular *Chronicles of Narnia.* In the series there is a lion named Aslan, an allegorical figure for Jesus, who is "the Lion of Judah" (Rev. 5:5). Lewis also wrote a clever series of letters from a senior devil (Uncle Screwtape) to a junior devil (his nephew, Wormwood), which instruct Wormwood on how to sidetrack a Christian convert from practicing his newfound faith. These clever instructions comprise Lewis's *The Screwtape Letters.* C. S. Lewis also wrote a space trilogy (*Out of the Silent Planet, Perelandra,* and *That Hideous Strength*). These captivating novels creatively communicate great spiritual truths.

In both his fiction and nonfiction, Lewis was always very clever in restating the well-known in a fresh way or communicating a profound truth with simplicity. In one of the books in the *Chronicles of Narnia,* a character sums up the incarnation this way: "In our world too, a Stable once had something inside it that was bigger than our whole world."[112] On our need to die to self that we may be born again, Lewis wrote, "Die before you die. There is no chance after."[113] And on the issue of conversion, he penned, "It costs God nothing, so far as we know, to create nice things; but to convert rebellious wills cost Him crucifixion."[114]

The works of C. S. Lewis are widely read today, and they are thoroughly influenced by the Bible.

Flannery O'Connor

The American short-story writer Flannery O'Connor (1925–1964) provides another example of the Bible's influence in literature. O'Connor wrote two novels and two books of short stories. She was a committed Catholic whose stories are heavily influenced by her faith. Ironically, though, she had a "preoccupation with the grotesque,"[115] which is the natural by-product of man rejecting God. Her stories focus on "man's spiritual deformity" and "man's vain attempts to escape" from God.[116]

Her writings are not sugar-coated. Faith often shines forth in a somewhat uncomfortable setting, which is often true to life.

In an essay titled "Novelist and Unbeliever," O'Connor shows how she breaks with the twentieth-century tradition of skeptic writers:

> What I say here would be much more in line with the spirit of our times if I could speak to you about the experience of such novelists as Hemingway and Kafka and Gide and Camus, but all my own experience has been that of the writer who believes, again in Pascal's words, in the "God of Abraham, Isaac, and Jacob and not of the philosophers and scholars." This is an unlimited God and one who has revealed himself specifically. It is one who became man and rose from the dead. It is one who confounds the senses and the sensibilities, one known early on as a stumbling block. There is no way to gloss over this specification or to make it more acceptable to modern thought. This God is the object of ultimate concern and he has a name.[117]

In the same essay she writes: "Our salvation is a Drama played out with the devil, a devil who is not simply generalized evil, but an evil intelligence determined on its own supremacy."[118]

Here's an example of the Bible's influence in her fiction. In the story *The River*, there is a scene where two characters, Mrs. Connin and Bevel, come across a young preacher who is standing in a stream. In addressing the people on the bank (shades of John the Baptist), he said, "Listen to what I got to say, you people! There ain't but one river and that's the River of Life, made out of Jesus' Blood. That's the river you have to lay your pain in, in the River of Faith, in the River of Life, in the River of Love, in the rich red river of Jesus' Blood, you people!"[119] Later, O'Connor writes, "'Listen,' he sang, 'I read in Mark about an unclean man, I read in Luke about a blind man, I read in John about a dead man! . . . You people with trouble,' he cried, 'lay it in that River of Blood, lay it in that River of Pain, and watch it move away toward the Kingdom of Christ.'"[120]

Though her stories are often filled with unattractive characters with serious spiritual flaws, Flannery O'Connor was definitely influenced by the Book of books.

MORE BIBLICAL INFLUENCE ON LITERATURE

Because of obvious space limitations, I can't highlight how the Bible influenced every major fiction writer. Whole books have been written on the subject.[121] But many great writers whose works reflect the Scriptures merit a brief mention here:

- Nathaniel Hawthorne, nineteenth-century American author, shows great insight into the effects of sin and human depravity. While *The Scarlet Letter* provides a rebuke to puritanical self-righteousness, *The Celestial Railroad* provides a stirring rebuke to the anti-Bible modernism of his day.[122]
- Leo Tolstoy, nineteenth-century Russian novelist, wrote *Anna Karenina* and *War and Peace*, both of which are imbued with biblical themes. Although he rejected orthodox doctrine, he wrote sympathetically of Christian ideals.
- G. K. Chesterton, nineteenth- and twentieth-century British writer, penned creative works of fiction and nonfiction. He created one of the most endearing detectives, Father Brown, a pudgy, little, bumbling Catholic priest who would seem least likely to solve a mystery but catches his man (or woman) every time.
- T. S. Eliot, twentieth-century American author and poet (who settled in England), wrote *The Waste Land*, a searing look at the devastation of World War I. Eliot was an "Anglo-Catholic Christian," who also penned *Murder in the Cathedral* (about the martyrdom of Thomas Becket), *Ash Wednesday*, and the poem *Journey of the Magi*.
- James Weldon Johnson, twentieth-century African American poet, wrote "Lift Every Voice and Sing," which became the unofficial black anthem. Johnson is probably best remembered for his book of Christian poetry, *God's Trombones,* which includes "The Creation" and the quite moving funeral sermon, "Go Down, Death."
- Dorothy L. Sayers, twentieth-century British writer and mystery novelist, wrote a series of radio dramas based on the life of Christ that were performed on the BBC and later put together into book form, entitled *The Man Born to Be King*. She also translated Dante's *The Divine Comedy* from Latin.
- J. R. R. Tolkien, twentieth-century British author, wrote *The Hobbit* and The Lord of the Ring series, stories that reflect a biblical worldview. These popular novels deal with "a cosmic war between good and evil."[123] Tolkien was a friend of C. S. Lewis. With some other Christian writers, they had fellowship to improve each other's literary works.

In an amazing publication entitled *A Dictionary of Biblical Tradition in English Literature,* an index has been provided that displays some noteworthy authors whose literary works were clearly impacted by the Bible in one way or another. Here is a portion of that list, not counting the authors mentioned above: Samuel Beckett; William Blake; Lord Byron; Geoffrey Chaucer; Joseph Conrad; Stephen Crane; Emily Dickinson; William Faulkner; Robert Frost; Ernest Hemingway; Edgar Allan Poe; John Steinbeck; Alfred Lord Tennyson; Mark Twain; and Walt Whitman.[124] In fact, David Lyle Jeffrey, general editor of that book, points out that despite the secularism of our age, the Bible still influences twentieth-century literature: "It is no less widely recognized now than a century ago that for literature in the English-speaking world no text has continued to exert a more formative influence than the Bible."[125]

GREAT TRUTH INSPIRES GREAT LITERATURE

It is simply astonishing that the Bible is much maligned today by those who are considered the intelligentsia. The Bible, the same collection of books that inspired the likes of Dostoevsky and Shakespeare, is said to be the document of a group of simpletons and dolts. There can be no more convoluted logic than this. That such a Book, with its eternal consequences and earthly repercussions, is dismissed as myth and folklore exemplifies just how far those who hold lofty agendas will go to rationalize their behavior. (No wonder they would substitute soap operas for Shakespeare!)

How can it be that at one moment a person is extolling the genius of either Dante or Milton, while simultaneously dismissing the Bible as ancient intellectual fodder? The Bible is indeed *the* Book of books!

CHAPTER 9

THE BIBLE AND MISSIONS

"All authority has been given to Me in heaven and on earth. Go therefore and make disciples of all the nations, baptizing them in the name of the Father and of the Son and of the Holy Spirit, teaching them to observe all things that I have commanded you; and lo, I am with you always, even to the end of the age."

—Matthew 28:18–20

Coauthor Jerry Newcombe once had a friendly conversation with a Hindu on a bus ride in India. The subject got around to religion. The Hindu boasted of a great "holy man" who lived near the bus route. This mystic spent all of his time meditating. He let his hair and fingernails grow. Every once in a while, he would show up at the windowsill of his home and peer down to his admirers, to give encouragement and inspiration just by letting them see him. Jerry meekly replied that Christians have a different view of our holy people. "Our holy people," he commented, "are much more like Mother Teresa, who roll up their sleeves and help people in need to show them the love of Christ." His comments seemed to make an impression on the man.

Any discussion of what the Bible leads Christians to *do* must include the efforts of missionaries over the past two millennia. Where the Bible has had a significant role, missionary activity has usually been that much more intense.

THE BIRTH OF THE CHURCH— THE BIRTH OF MISSIONS

In the history of the world, "only three religions have been always and essentially missionary—Buddhism, Christianity, and Islam," writes Stephen Neill, author of *A History of Christian Missions*.[1] Of the three,

Christianity has made the greatest inroads. More people from more cultures in more nations voluntarily embrace the Christian faith than any other. Christian missions succeed. Missions are as old as the faith, though the Church has seen stagnant periods followed by productive periods. When the faith is vibrant, missions blossom. Neill writes: "Missionary activity is always a sign of vitality in the Church."[2] It's important to recognize that Christianity was missions-minded from its very birth.

Pentecost was the birthday of the Church, and on that day believers began carrying out the command to make disciples. Our age is the time for the gathering in of the Gentiles. Jesus said, "And Jerusalem will be trampled by Gentiles until the times of the Gentiles are fulfilled" (Luke 21:24). Furthermore, "This gospel of the kingdom will be preached in all the world as a witness to all the nations, and then the end will come" (Matt. 24:14).

The prophet Isaiah said the Messiah should be "a light to the Gentiles." When Jesus was circumcised, Simeon repeated this prophesy: "For my eyes have seen Your salvation which You have prepared before the face of all peoples, a light to bring revelation to the Gentiles, and the glory of Your people Israel" (Luke 2:30–32).

God always intended for the nations to be brought into the kingdom, but this first became clearly articulated to His people in the book of Acts. Peter said to the Roman Cornelius, "In truth I perceive that God shows no partiality. But in every nation whoever fears Him and works righteousness is accepted by Him" (Acts 10:34–35). God declared to Ananias about Paul, "He is a chosen vessel of Mine to bear My name before Gentiles, kings, and the children of Israel" (Acts 9:15). And so the message of the kingdom spread in Jerusalem, Judea, and (in our time) to the uttermost parts of the earth.

Without the Bible, the gospel would be heard by mouth only, and the oral tradition would be neither complete nor accurate. Through the writing of the New Testament, in the universal language of *Koine* Greek, the good news spread quickly and effectively.

Jesus is called the Light of the World, the True Light, the Light of Men, the Everlasting Light, and the Dayspring—which means the Sunrising of God. The world needed that light. Things that today we take for granted were completely unknown at that time. It was a time of ignorance—particularly the ignorance of God. Man was so blinded by sin that his knowledge of the true God was almost nonexistent, and most of what he thought he knew was wrong.

For example, suppose you found yourself on some dusty road in the Roman Empire two thousand years ago where you encountered a Roman or a Greek. Suppose you said to him, "Excuse me, sir, I'm taking a religious survey. I wonder if you would mind answering this question: Do you love God?" Today, the vast majority of people in America (whether they fully understand this or not) would answer yes. But not so then.

He would say, "Do I love God? Are you joshing, man, or are you mad? No one has ever loved a god. What is there about gods that one can love? Certainly gods do nothing for us. Oh, we fear them. I candidly admit that I fear them, because they are very powerful and very dangerous. We spend much of our time wondering how we may escape their wrath. They wake up with a headache and start throwing thunderbolts around. They're very dangerous, treacherous, and totally unreliable. Oh, yes, we may try to placate them or propitiate them, even by sacrifice, but *love*? *Love* a *god*? I've never heard of anything so absurd in all of my life! No man has ever loved a god, and furthermore, what god ever loved me? You tell me that. Why, then, should I love a god?"

Then Christ comes, and in that marvelous New Testament revelation of Him, we see those three single-syllable words, so simple that they can be read by almost any child, and yet filled with depths so profound that the greatest philosopher cannot plumb entirely those depths—three little words that changed the whole thinking of the world. If the Bible had done nothing more than simply bring this revelation to us, it would have drastically changed the attitude of mankind.

What were those three words? *God is love.* Astonishing! Today the concept is commonplace, but that was one of the bright beams Christ brought into our world. We have not first loved Him, but He first loved us and gave Himself for us. Not only was God love, but "God so loved the world that He gave His only begotten Son, that whoever believes in Him should not perish but have everlasting life" (John 3:16). What an incredible revelation!

THE EARLY SPREAD OF THE GOSPEL

The gospel spread with incredible speed at first. Even the eleven apostles (the twelve minus Judas) helped bring the Christian message to many different parts of the known world. According to the traditional accounts, summarized well in *Foxe's Book of Martyrs*,[3] the apostles brought the gospel into Egypt, Persia (modern Iran), and India. Thomas, the man who once doubted the Lord's resurrection, made up for lost time on the mission field! Here's what Foxe says of him: "Thomas preached to the Parthians, Medes and Persians, also to the Carmanians, Hyrcanians,

Bactrians and Magians. He was martyred in Calamina, a city of India, being slain with a dart."[4] All those different people groups (Parthians to Magians) lived in what is now Iran. Matthew took the gospel to Egypt and was martyred. Paul went north and west with the gospel, while Thomas and others went east and south with the good news.

Despite the full fury and might of the Roman Empire against the fledgling new faith, Christianity prevailed. This is all the more amazing when you consider that Rome was, in the words of Will Durant, "the strongest state that history has ever known."[5]

THE ONSLAUGHT OF THE BARBARIANS

Later came the Dark Ages, roughly the period from 500 (technically 476 when the western half of the Roman Empire fell) to 1000. An important turning point occurred on December 31, 406: the Rhine River froze. Consequently, tens of thousands of Germanic barbarians, illiterate and much poorer than their southern neighbors, walked over into the Roman Empire. The Roman soldiers couldn't stop them; there were too many places they could cross. The Vandals, one of these Germanic tribes, lost twenty thousand men that day at the hands of Roman soldiers, but still the barbarians kept coming. They overwhelmed the outnumbered soldiers.[6] The have-nots, often barefoot and hairy, roamed the streets of the haves, looting as they went. This feast of looting climaxed a few years later, in 410, with the sacking of Rome. The western half of the empire never recovered.[7]

Some modernists suggest that this period is called the Dark Ages because the Church had ascendancy. The truth is that the barbarians who sacked Rome brought on the dismal time. As these tribes were converted over the centuries, changes for the better followed. The Church was not a force of societal disintegration; it was a mitigating force at a time when the nation–state was deteriorating into feudalism.

Missionary work was sporadic in these tumultuous years. Courageous missionaries went among the fierce Germanic tribes, spreading the faith. The work was slow-going. Many of these missionaries became martyrs. But they persisted until, over the centuries, Christianity began to spread to one place and then another.

THE CRITICAL ROLE OF IRELAND

Historian Tom Cahill recently wrote a book about a critically important group of Irish missionaries. The name of the book is *How the Irish*

Saved Civilization: The Untold Story of Ireland's Heroic Role from the Fall of Rome to the Rise of Medieval Europe. Cahill calls this a "cultural cliffhanger,"[8] in that the barbarians could have destroyed *all* of what we know of antiquity had not the Irish worked to preserve our Judeo-Christian and Greco-Roman heritages. Cahill writes:

> Ireland, a little island at the edge of Europe that has known neither Renaissance nor Enlightenment—in some ways, a Third World country with, as John Bejeman claimed, a Stone Age culture—had one moment of unblemished glory. For, as the Roman Empire fell, as all through Europe matted, unwashed barbarians descended on the Roman cities, looting artifacts and burning books, the Irish, who were just learning to read and write, took up the great labor of copying all of Western literature—everything they could lay their hands on. These scribes then served as conduits through which the Greco-Roman and Judeo-Christian cultures were transmitted to the tribes of Europe, newly settled amid the rubble and ruined vineyards of the civilization they had overwhelmed. Without this Service of the Scribes, everything that happened subsequently would have been unthinkable. Without the Mission of the Irish Monks, who single-handedly refounded European civilization throughout the continent in the bays and valleys of their exile, the world that came after then would have been an entirely different one—a world without books. And our own world would never have come to be.[9]

St. Patrick

St. Patrick was the missionary who brought Christianity to Ireland. A native of Britain, he was reared a nominal Christian. As a teenager he was captured by a band of marauding pirates. He was bound, taken to Ireland, and sold as a slave to a Druid chieftain in Ireland. Cahill writes that Patrick's two companions then were hunger and nakedness.[10] So he prayed day and night; it was his only comfort. He remembered the faith of his youth, his soul was revived, and his relationship with Christ was rekindled.

After six years Patrick escaped. He vowed revenge—the noble revenge of sharing the gospel with the people who held him captive. He believed that he had been called by God to return to the land of his slavery. He spent time in preparation and learning (akin to seminary for a missionary of today). Patrick returned to Ireland as a missionary.

Because of his groundbreaking work, Ireland was converted to Christianity. In the history of missions, Patrick must be recognized as one of

the Church's most successful missionaries. A. Guggenberger, author of
A General History of the Christian Church, writes:

> Everywhere rose churches, monasteries and convents and schools,
> mostly of humble materials, but not the less centres of civilization for
> Ireland, and nurseries of missionaries for the newly established Teu-
> tonic kingdoms. . . . The conversion of Ireland was completed during
> the lifetime of St. Patrick, not indeed without temporary and local
> reactions in favor of heathenism, but without persecution and blood-
> shed. St. Patrick died probably in 493. The warlike and impressionable
> people of Erin [Ireland] manifested towards him an impassioned ven-
> eration which thirteen centuries have not lessened.[11]

Patrick was a bold missionary. He said, "Every day I am ready to be
murdered, betrayed, enslaved—whatever may come my way. But I am
not afraid of any of these things, because of the promises of heaven; for
I have put myself in the hands of God Almighty."[12] Cahill points out:
"Patrick was really a first—the first missionary to barbarians beyond the
reach of Roman law."[13]

A debate has raged among missionaries through the centuries: Which
of the local customs should missionaries adopt while they are guests in a
foreign country? St. Patrick chose to adopt Irish customs. Guggenberger
writes, "St. Patrick's success is due in part to his eminent prudence in
dealing with Irish customs. He confirmed in the law of the Brehons [Irish
judges] whatever did not clash with Holy Writ, the laws of the Church
or the consciences of the believers."[14]

A beautiful statement of faith is attributed to Patrick, and, as Cahill
points out, even if it wasn't written by him (in its present form), "it surely
takes its inspiration from him."[15] This great prayer is entitled "St. Patrick's
Breastplate." Here is a portion of his bold statement of faith:

Christ to shield me today
Against poisoning, against burning,
Against drowning, against wounding,
So that there may come to me abundances of reward.
Christ with me, Christ before me, Christ behind me,
Christ in me, Christ beneath me, Christ above me,
Christ on my right, Christ on my left,
Christ when I lie down, Christ when I sit down, Christ when I arise,
Christ in the heart of every man who thinks of me,
Christ in the mouth of everyone who speaks of me,
Christ in every eye that sees me,
Christ in every ear that hears me.[16]

How is that for a picture of Christ-centered life? St. Patrick gives us the source of his success as a missionary. He was wholly committed to Christ and the furtherance of His kingdom. This commitment is a trait that we'll see in all the key missionary figures we look at in this chapter.

Irish Missionaries

Several Irish missionaries followed Patrick's example, and carried the light of the gospel to different parts of Europe. Their work went on for roughly three centuries—stopped by the devastating invasions of the Danish Vikings. Adam Loughridge writes, "Saints like Finnian of Clonard (d[ied] c. 589) and Comgall of Bangor at home, and Columba and Columbanus abroad, made famous the name of the Irish Church."[17] Columba (also known as Columkille, 521–597) was the "most illustrious Irish churchman of the sixth century."[18] He founded an important college on the Scottish coast, which was dedicated to training evangelists and missionaries, in particular for the conversion of the Picts (ancient Scots).[19] Columbanus (c. 543–615) did missionary work in what is today France, Switzerland, and Italy.

THE CONVERSIONS OF VARIOUS TRIBES

Slowly, Christianity began to spread to our European ancestors—but not without resistance. The message of the Bible spread to the barbarians who had overrun the civilized world. Slowly, they were converting and being changed. Writing mostly of Europe, Stephen Neill says: "Conversion had been a long, slow business, in which every kind of quality and action had played their part, from pure and heroic sanctity down to the basest chicanery and violence."[20]

It's interesting to note that Adolf Hitler, who hated God, regretted the day that Christian missionaries ever set foot in Germany. He would much rather have had the celebrated pagan deities remain the gods and goddesses of Germany. He loved Wagner's majestic operas, works that seemingly glorify these deities. Hitler once said, "Whoever wants to understand National Socialist Germany must know Wagner."[21] He even felt Fate calling him to rule Germany while attending one of these Wagner operas. His twelve-year rule did much to return Germany to paganism.

One of the great missionaries to Germany in the early centuries of Christianity was St. Boniface (c. 680–754). In the spirit of Elijah, who engaged the prophets of Baal on Mt. Carmel (1 Kings 18), Boniface felled a great oak tree, which was, to quote Neill, "the sacred oak of

Thor at Geismar in Hesse, the chief object of the superstitious reverence of the non-Christians and of the half-Christianized peoples of that area."[22] The pagans thought all manner of evil would come upon Boniface for doing this. Instead, bats resting in the tree flew out. The people took it as a sign that Boniface's God was greater than theirs, so many became Christians. Wood from the tree was later used to build a church in honor of St. Peter. Boniface, like many missionaries down through the centuries, was later martyred for the faith.

Over the centuries Christianity spread to various tribes and countries throughout Europe, despite challenges from the rise of Islam, which took over much of Christendom, forcing thousands of Christians to convert or die. For instance, in the last half of the seventh century, there was a huge falling away of Christians to Islam in Egypt.[23] Throughout North Africa, "large numbers of Christians [were] annihilated" by the Muslims.[24] In fact, Dr. David Barrett, one of the greatest Church statisticians and historians alive, says that by about A.D. 949, "fifty percent of all former Christendom" had been "captured by Islam, including nomadic Berbers of Mauritania."[25]

Meanwhile, Christianity had to contend with splits within its own ranks. The first major split came between the Roman Catholic and the Eastern Orthodox Churches in 1054. One key conflict was the use of icons and sacred images, which some Catholics said bordered on idolatry; another important controversy occurred over papal authority. These two churches are officially separate to this day.[26]

In 1517 began the split between Roman Catholics and Protestants, which most readers of this book know as the Reformation. When Martin Luther discovered the glorious biblical truth that "the just shall live by faith" (Rom. 1:17), the light of the gospel burst forth in ways that continue today. However, it would take about two and a half centuries for the Protestant missionary movement to begin in earnest.

During the first eight hundred years of this millennium, there was a vigorous missionary program carried on by the Roman Catholic Church. This was, in the words of Stephen Neill, "a time of great and notable enterprises."[27] Within a century of St. Francis of Assisi founding the Franciscans, the monastic order had spread to "the ends of the known earth"![28] Around 1300, the Dominicans founded "the company of brethren dwelling in foreign parts among the heathen for the sake of Christ."[29] Catholic missionaries got as far as Japan and China, although ruthless persecution in both places wiped out much of their work.[30]

One of the most significant of the Catholic missionaries was Francis Xavier. Xavier is viewed as "the inspiration of modern Catholic missions."[31]

He worked briefly in India, then in Japan, and then back in India. His work in Japan caused him to rethink an important assumption. Neill writes:

> In earlier years he had been inclined to accept uncritically the doctrine of the *tabula rasa*—the view that in non-Christian life and systems there is nothing on which the missionary can build, and that everything must simply be leveled to the ground before anything Christian can be built up. This was the general view of the Spanish missionaries in Latin America and the West Indies; in his dealings with the simple and illiterate fishers in South India, Xavier had seen no reason to modify it. But now that he was confronted by a civilization with so many elements of nobility in it, he saw that, while the Gospel must transform and refine and recreate, it need not necessarily reject as worthless everything that has come before.[32]

Interestingly, the initial slowness of Protestant missionary activity was used as a criticism against it by the end of the 1500s. Robert Bellarmine, a sixteenth-century Roman Catholic defender of the faith, wrote up eighteen marks of "the true Church," one of which was missionary activity. As of that time, no significant Protestant missionary work was under way.[33] However, at that particular time, the Reformed movement was fighting for its survival. The first main Protestant missions were carried out by the Moravians.[34] The Moravians were a small Christian group started in 1722 in Bohemia. Count Zinzendorf, a generous noble who gave away much of his considerable fortune for missions, helped fund much of the Moravian work. Among other places, the Moravians founded Bethlehem, Pennsylvania. Moravian missionaries were on board the ship on that fateful day when John Wesley almost perished at sea; their courage in the face of death was instrumental in his conversion. In 1792 the modern missionary movement was begun with William Carey, a humble cobbler from England.

The modern missionary movement spread Christianity throughout the world at a new and unprecedented rate. Most of the rest of this chapter will look in depth at three great pioneer missionaries: William Carey, David Livingstone, and Hudson Taylor.

WILLIAM CAREY

The year, 1792; the place Nottingham, England—a name that conjures up memories of legends. In Nottinghamshire we find the famous Sherwood Forest where Robin Hood supposedly took from the rich and gave to the poor. On a particular day in May a far more significant event was to take place in Nottingham. Unfortunately, in the chronicles of the history of that town, this event is not generally recorded. But in the chronicles of heaven it was a tremendously significant day. Another young man came forth to take, not steal, the freely offered riches of heaven and to make an innumerable host of poor and benighted men and women infinitely and eternally wealthy. This young cobbler stood before a small group of ministers on that day and opened the Scriptures to the fifty-fourth chapter of Isaiah, and there he expounded on those great words of the evangelical prophet: "Enlarge the place of your tent, and let them stretch out the curtains of your habitations; do not spare; lengthen your cords; and strengthen your stakes. For you shall expand to the right and to the left, and your descendants will inherit the nations." And there, this young man gave what has been called the first and greatest missionary sermon of all time. The complete text of his message was not preserved, but we do know the two key principles he laid down: "Attempt great things for God; expect great things from God."[35]

William Carey (1761–1834) was used by God that day to awaken the slumbering Church to the needs of the world. He called upon these men to take the gospel to the world. The inquiry that he gave suggested this: "Whether the Command given to the Apostles to teach all the nations [referring to the Great Commission] was not binding on all succeeding ministers to the end of the world seeing that the accompanying promise ['Lo, I am with you always'] was of equal extent."

What was the result of his moving plea? We are told that the elder John Ryland stood and said, "Young man, sit down. When God pleases to convert the heathen, he will do it without your aid or mine!"[36] But Carey, a true visionary, disagreed.

Carey's view prevailed. A motion carried at the next meeting of those ministers that they would form a missionary society. And so in 1792, the first foreign missionary society began, dedicated to take the gospel to the whole world.

Carey's philosophy, again, was "Attempt great things for God; expect great things from God." But what was he to do? There was still no missionary to go, yet there was at least now a missionary society, and they had collected sixty-seven dollars—not a very auspicious beginning. But Carey felt growing in his soul the realization that God was calling him into the mission field. Finally, convinced of that, he volunteered to be the first missionary to go on behalf of the society—to India.

Sadly, the reaction to his decision was more rejection. His father said that he had lost his mind. His wife said that she would have nothing to do with such an idea. But with great heaviness of heart and weeping, they finally decided that Carey would take his oldest son, Felix, and set sail for India, leaving his wife and other children behind. Though he spent six weeks imploring her, she refused to go. He set sail on the *Earl of Oxford* from London, after having raised money for the journey, and got as far as Portsmouth, where the ship was stopped and held for six weeks. Finally Carey was told that he would not be allowed to enter India. It seemed that the East Indian Company, which controlled most of India at that time, was opposed to the evangelization of the Indians. The company feared that if the Indians converted, they might not be as easy for the British to govern. Carey was refused a visa to enter India.

He returned to London and finally found passage on a Danish ship. Before setting sail he made one more trip home, to implore his wife to come with him. To her credit, one more day's urging changed her mind to take the children and go with him. William Carey was thirty-two years old when he set sail for the part of India known as Bengal, famous for its tigers and crocodiles. During the first year that Carey worked there, twenty-five men were carried away by Bengal tigers.

Throughout his life, William Carey demonstrated certain virtues: patience in trying circumstances, tenacity of purpose, the ability to live simply, the courage to follow the deepest convictions that God had given him, and faith in the goodness of God. He had a passion for mastering languages, a devotion to the Word of God, and a passion for the immortal souls of men.

At fourteen, William Carey had discovered Latin. He was so enthralled with the language that he learned it by himself. One day after becoming a Christian, he read a commentary that included Greek words. Likewise thrilled at the discovery of Greek, he mastered it too. He then discovered Hebrew; it presented more of a challenge, but he learned it also. Then, of course, there was French, and Dutch. At less than twenty years of age, he had mastered all of these languages. God had given him a gift for languages, which He would enable him to use in a wonderful way.

William Carey had a tremendous determination of purpose. When he believed something should be done he plodded and plodded until he accomplished it. Carey was not brilliant—he was a plodder. He kept on and on and on until he succeeded.

Another great quality about William Carey was his love for the souls of men. When he arrived at Serampore and established the Serampore Mission, the first of the teachings of this mission stated in the form of agreement was to assert that the human soul is of infinite worth and that everything they did would be to prevent unconverted souls from slipping into eternal punishment.

William Carey preached every day to the natives in India. The result: for seven years, not a single convert among the Indians. Finally Krishna Pal, in 1800, became the first convert of the modern missionary movement. Soon there were hundreds, thousands, and tens of thousands, and millions who followed.

Carey and his fellow missionaries wrote up in 1805 an agreement that they would use to spread the gospel:

> [A]nother part of our work is the forming of our native brethren to usefullness, fostering every kind of genius, and cherishing every gift and grace in them: in this respect we can scarcely be too lavish of our attention to their improvement. It is only by means of native preachers we can hope for the universal spread of the Gospel through this immense continent.[37]

Carey said that perhaps the greatest break in the conversion of the heathen is the translation of the Scriptures into their language. During his ministry in India he mastered and translated at least a portion of Scripture, if not all, into the following languages: Hindi, Bengalis, Sanskrit, Oriya, Marathi, Punjabi, Bolochi, Mewari, Telugu, Konkani, Pashto, Assamese, Lahnda, Gujerati, Bikaneri, Awadhi, Kashmirir, Nepali, Bagheli, Marawari, Bhatneri, Magahi, Malvi, Braj Brasha, Garwhali, Manipuri, Palpa, and Khasi—thirty-four different Indian languages. He was clearly a linguistic genius!

One historian says that in no country in the world, in no period in the history of Christianity, had anyone devoted such energy to the translation of the sacred Scriptures into other tongues, as was displayed by a handful of consecrated men in Calcutta and Serampore.

Among his other accomplishments while in India, Carey published the first newspaper in an oriental language; he opened a savings bank for Christians that they might be good stewards; he desired and promoted agrarian horticultural experiments, became a famous horticulturist, and was inducted into the Linnean Society; and succeeded in doing away with infanticide in India and was personally responsible for the abolition of suttee, the horrible practice of widow burning. When a Hindu husband died, it was the cultural norm that his widow be burned on her husband's funeral pyre. She either did it voluntarily or it was forced upon her! For twenty-five years Carey labored against that horrible practice, finally succeeding in having it abolished by law.

In the thirty-five years after Carey went to India, dozens and dozens of missionary societies sprang up all over Great Britain, Europe, and America. The result was an outpouring of missionary activity and labor and zeal such as had not been seen since the first century. And all of this was sparked by a plodding cobbler. Carey had seen that there were 731 million people in the world, of which only 174 million were Christians. That burden lay upon his heart. Due in large part to the impetus given by his ministry, today there have been added to that 174 million, more than 1.6 billion additional professing Christians! God indeed made him the father of modern missions.

Carey was an ordinary man who accomplished extraordinary things because he had an extraordinary God. The late Yale historian Kenneth Scott Latourette said William Carey's career was "one of the most notable in the entire history of the expansion of Christianity."[38]

DAVID LIVINGSTONE

Jesus demands our utmost commitment to Him: "He who loves father or mother more than Me is not worthy of Me. And he who loves son or daughter more than Me is not worthy of Me" (Matt. 10:37). "And everyone who has left houses or brothers or sisters or father or mother or wife or children or lands, for My name's sake, shall receive a hundredfold [in this life and in the life to come], and inherit eternal life" (Matt. 19:29). I believe that when we examine the life of David Livingstone (1813–1873), we see a beautiful example of true commitment to Christ.

What was the secret of his strength and perseverance amid unbearable trials? Livingstone himself will tell you. After sixteen years in Africa, he returned to England for the first time. No white man had ever penetrated the interior of the "dark continent" before. To his astonishment he learned he was an international celebrity, but that meant nothing to David Livingstone.

He was invited to speak at the University of Glasgow, in his native Scotland. If he could have seen what was ahead for him he might have declined the invitation. (Yet knowing Livingstone, I'm sure he would have gone, regardless of what was waiting.) It was the custom of undergraduates in that day to heckle visiting speakers. So they were ready for this preacher with toy trumpets, whistles, rattles, and all manner of noisemakers. They even had pea shooters.

Livingstone came to the platform with the tread of a man who had already walked eleven thousand miles. His left arm hung almost uselessly at his side, his shoulder having been crushed by a huge lion. His body was emaciated, his skin a dark brown from sixteen years in the African sun. His face bore innumerable wrinkles from the ravages of the African fevers that had racked his body. He was half deaf from rheumatic fever, and half blind from a branch that had slapped him in the eyes. He described himself as a "ruckle of bones."

The students stared in disbelief. Their noisemakers were silent as a vast hush spread over the assemblage. They *knew* that here was a life that was sacrificed for God and fellow man. They listened while Livingstone told them about his incredible adventures; he told them about the extraordinary needs of the natives of Africa.

He said to them, "Shall I tell you what sustained me in the midst of all of these toils and hardships and incredible loneliness? It was a promise, the promise of a gentleman of the most sacred honor; it was this promise, 'Lo, I am with you always, even unto the end of the world'" (Matt. 28:20). That was the promise, that was his text, that was the secret of Livingstone's commitment. It was the presence of Jesus Christ with him everywhere, all of the time.

When I was in seminary, I read a great deal about Livingstone's life. Except for Jesus Christ, no other person has had such an impact upon me. There are parts of his life that I can barely read without breaking down. Whenever I think I have accomplished something noteworthy, his example slaps me right in the face and I say, "You slob, Kennedy, you haven't done a cotton pickin' thing." Livingstone has a way of humbling any man.

Livingstone's Background

Livingstone was born in 1813 in Blantyre, Scotland, to godly but very poor parents. His father, a saintly Sunday school teacher in the Presbyterian Church of Scotland, loved missionaries and mission stories. Every week he would sit young David down on a large hassock in front of an easy chair in the living room and tell his son wonderful stories about pioneer missionaries that had gone to exotic places to share the gospel. David loved these stories.

His favorite story was about Charles Gutzlaff, a missionary to China who became David's boyhood hero. As he grew older, he discovered that Gutzlaff himself had a hero, who was the supernatural Son of God; He was a divine Redeemer. So Livingstone accepted the same Savior for himself, and his life was changed. He decided he was going to the mission field.

The family was so poor that when Livingstone was ten years old, he went to work in a cotton mill from six o'clock in the morning until eight o'clock at night, six days a week. Yet he managed to gain an education, even while working. Finally, when he was twenty, he went to school and studied Greek. He had great felicity with language. He studied theology, and he went to Glasgow University, graduating with a degree in medicine.

As he prepared for the mission field, the door slammed in his face. The field was closed. War had broken out and Livingstone couldn't go.

God seemed to be saying to him, "David, it is not My purpose to send you to China," which is where Livingstone had planned to serve. In His great providence, God used the Opium War in China to accomplish His own purpose of sending David Livingstone to Africa.

No white man had entered the interior of Africa, though some were ministering on the coast. One was Robert Moffat, who came on furlough to Blantyre, Scotland, and told about Africa. He made a comment that grasped the heart of Livingstone for the rest of his life. Moffat said, "Often, as I have looked to the vast plains of the north [from the southern tip of Africa] I have sometimes in the morning sun seen the smoke of a thousand villages where no missionary has ever been."[39]

A thousand villages! thought Livingstone. *No missionary! No gospel! No Christ! No salvation! No life! No light! Nothing but sin and death and darkness! I will go to Africa.*

Pioneer Minister in Africa

As the pioneer minister to Africa, Livingstone faced many burdens, but he also discovered the sustaining power of Christ. One day a huge lion leaped upon him and clamped his teeth on his shoulder and crushed it. But one of his helpers killed the lion and saved him.

God used even that as a blessing. Livingstone was taken back to the coast, and was nursed to health at Moffat's mission station. Moffat's daughter Mary was there: for her and David it was love at first sight. Soon they married. She shared his zeal to take the gospel to the interior of Africa. As the years passed, they had five children.

While crossing one of the vast plains of Africa, one of their children died. After this incident, they concluded that it would be safer for his wife and children to go back to Scotland. The decision was the most difficult of his life, Livingstone said. Mary and the children said a fond farewell and left. For five years Livingstone did not see the faces of his wife and children. The loneliness weighed upon him.

But as difficult as this separation was, even more difficult to take was the criticism that came back to him. It was reported to him that people were saying the reason he had left his wife and children and had gone off "to ramble about in Africa" was that he didn't love them. If only his detractors could have read his own words. He wrote of his family (quoting Lord Tennyson from memory):

I shall look into your faces
And listen to what you say
And be often very near you
When you think I'm far away.[40]

But Livingstone pressed on, deeper and deeper into Africa, alone but never alone. By God's grace Livingstone was unstoppable.

Reunited with His Family

Years later the day came for Livingstone to return home. He rejoiced in anticipation. He would see his beloved wife, Mary, his children, and his mother and father. He would sit on that old hassock and tell his father about lives subdued to the Savior, about light shining in darkness.

He burst into his old home in Blantyre, Scotland, only to find it empty. His family had just buried his father. Livingstone looked at the old, worn hassock, fell on his knees, and wept. This man had faced ferocious beasts and wild savages with spears prepared, and never blinked; now he wept like a child. Yet Mary was there, and God sustained him.

So they fellowshipped and love was sweet. Yet his dreams were haunted by the specter of a thousand villages in the morning sun. At length, he told his wife he had to return to Africa. They parted again. More years passed, and finally he received a letter that caused his heart to leap. Mary was coming to Africa! The children were old enough now that she could leave them. She would join him, and spend the rest of her life reaching the lost souls of Africa.

For months she traveled across oceans and up steamy African streams and rivers, until finally she was in the arms of her husband. Yet Mary had barely arrived when she was struck down by an African fever. Dr. David Livingstone devoted every ounce of his medical skill to her care. Night after night he wiped her brow and ministered to her body as best he could. Finally, she breathed her last.

He buried his wife under a huge African baobab tree. When he placed a marker, he fell on that mound of dirt and again wept like a child. Burdens, tribulations, discouragements—Livingstone endured enough to crush a thousand men, but was he overwhelmed? Here is what he wrote in his diary: "My Jesus, my King, my life, my all; I again dedicate my whole self to Thee. I shall place no value on anything I possess or on anything I may do, except in relation to the Kingdom of Christ."[41] Through it all, Christ sustained him with His presence.

Deeper into the jungle he went until he came to Ujiji, and there natives stole his food, goats, and worst of all, his chest of quinine and other medicines he used to fight the terrible African fevers. For Livingstone, losing the medicine was a sentence of death, and he fell again to his knees and said, "O God, I can't go on without the medicine."

Livingstone hadn't seen a white man in five years, but now in the middle of Africa, he lifted up his eyes and looked into the face of a white man walking down the trail toward him! An instant answer to his prayers. Behind this white man was a huge caravan, and above them all was a flag unfurled and flying in the breeze. It was the United States flag! The man approached Livingstone and uttered those unforgettable words, "Dr. Livingstone, I presume."[42]

It was, of course, Henry M. Stanley, a reporter who worked for the *New York Herald*. His publisher, James Gordon Bennett, had said, "Stanley, they say that Livingstone is dead. I don't believe it. I believe he is there in the midst of Africa, lost and ill and forsaken. Stanley, go out and find him. Bring him back to civilization. And don't count the cost."[43]

Stanley searched until he found the missionary. The reporter described himself as the biggest swaggering atheist that ever lived. Stanley, who lived in the same little hut with Livingstone for four months, said that the missionary was apparently not an angel. He was a man, and yet he could find no fault in his life. His compassion, his earnestness, the quietness with which he went about his work, the sympathy that he showed to all about him, quickened the sympathy in his own heart. Stanley was converted to Christ through Livingstone.

Livingstone would not return to civilization with Stanley. He plunged deeper into Africa. He wrote in his diary, "Grant, O Gracious Father, that ere this year is gone I may finish my task."[44] He came to the place, at last, where he had taken up his belt three notches to ease the pangs of hunger. For months he had nothing to eat but maize. Gradually all his teeth loosened and fell out as he tried to chew the kernels. He now had boils and lacerations all over his feet. He could no longer even walk. Was he through? Not David Livingstone. He had his followers—and by this time there were only three left—make a stretcher and carry him onward. He had them prop him up in front of a tree in the villages, and he preached the gospel to all those with whom he came in contact.

Then came the day when not only could he not walk or stand, but he couldn't even be moved. His helpers built a hut there in the middle of Africa. It was pouring rain. Livingstone went to sleep on his cot. He died that night, although his companions did not learn that until the next day. Biographer Tim Jeal writes:

> To their amazement Livingstone was no longer in his bed. As he had felt death coming, with a final superhuman effort, he had somehow

managed to crawl from his bed into a kneeling position. For a moment Susi [one of the African men] thought he was praying. The men did not go in at once but waited for some movement. When they saw none, one went in and touched the kneeling man's cheek. It was almost cold. David Livingstone had been dead for several hours.[45]

David Livingstone has gone down in the annals of history as one of the greatest missionaries who ever lived. His complete commitment to Christ is evident in an entry to his journal:

I place no value on anything I have or may possess, except in relation to the kingdom of Christ. If anything will advance the interests of the kingdom, it shall be given away or kept, only as by giving or keeping it I shall promote the glory of Him to whom I owe all my hopes in time and eternity.[46]

Had the Bible never been penned, there never would have been a David Livingstone. Over time, his work was very effective. There were ten million Christians in Africa in 1900, a quarter century after his death; today there are over three hundred million Christians there![47]

HUDSON TAYLOR

Among the great pioneer missionaries stands the founder of the China Inland Mission, James Hudson Taylor (1832–1905). His philosophy and strategy of missions laid the foundation for much future work in missions. He stressed the importance of the personal beliefs and prayer life of his missionaries and urged them to focus on evangelism. Taylor was a medical doctor, and humanitarian needs were always a top priority; yet the proclamation of the gospel came first. Hudson Taylor was ahead of his time in utilizing women missionaries on the field. He believed strongly that God's work done God's way would not lack funds; thus the missionaries did not receive regular pay, but relied on God to provide their needs. As a rule, they adopted Chinese clothes and customs. J. C. Pollock, in his book *Hudson Taylor and Maria,* writes: "Behind the choice of trousers or gown, whiskers or pigtails, fork or chopsticks, lay the whole question whether Christianity should spread in China as a universal or a western religion."[48]

Born in Yorkshire, England, Hudson Taylor grew up in a Christian home. He heard talk of missions and faraway places. Even as a child he knew he wanted to go to China. His father, James Taylor, was a druggist with an apothecary where Hudson worked as an apprentice in his teens. He was frail and often sick, and through his life he had to deal with his weak constitution and asthma.

As a teenager he rejected the faith, but his mother prayed for him with great intensity. One Saturday afternoon he read a Bible tract and came upon the words, "It is finished." The redemptive work of Christ was brought back to him with such a force and clarity that he returned to Jesus. He knew in an instant that he had to go to China! We should never underestimate a mother's prayers. He found that not only had his mother been praying for him, but his sister had been in daily prayer for his salvation as well.

Hudson Taylor began to train for the mission field. He rid himself of creature comforts and exercised to toughen himself up. He knew that a geographical move was not going to make him a soul-winner, so he started various ministries. He moved to Hull and became an assistant to a kind and busy doctor, Dr. Hardey. He chose to live in the working-class slums to strengthen his spiritual muscles. The good doctor was often neglectful in paying his young assistant. It was then that Hudson Taylor learned to rely on God to supply his needs. He went to London to further his studies. He nearly died from touching an infectious cadaver, but he made an amazing recovery.

In September of 1853, he left for China, sent by the Chinese Evangelization society. He sailed alone to Shanghai on March 1, 1854. He received no instruction or support from his mission organization; again he had to rely on God, who provided for his every need. He would later always tell new missionaries, "Depend upon it; God's work, done in God's way, will never lack for supplies."[49] He learned the language, and he developed such a burden to go inland where no foreigners ever went. He made his way and started preaching. His heart was with the Chinese people. He saw their terrible need, and he found his place of ministry in the inland of China.

As he labored in China, he learned how low the value of human life was there. Their story of creation sheds light on why. A former Taoist priest who converted to Christianity explained it like this:

Panku brought the world out of chaos. He forms the heavens and the earth with his hammer and chisel. He used 1800 years for this work. At his death creation started. Of his breath the winds were created; of his voice, the thunder. His right eye becomes the moon, and his left, the sun. Of his sweat the rain is brought forth, and from his blood, all the rivers are flowing. His flesh becomes the earth, and his hair becomes plants and trees. The fleas and tics on his body become human beings.[50]

If man is likened to parasites, then no wonder life was so cheap in China! What a contrast with the biblical view of man, where the psalmist writes with wonder: "You have made him a little lower than the angels, and You have crowned him with glory and honor" (Ps. 8:5).

During his six first years in China, Hudson Taylor met and fell in love with Maria Dyer, who was a missionary working at Miss Aldersey's school for Chinese girls. The missionary community was against their marriage, but they married nevertheless on January 20, 1858. They had a daughter the next year, and named her Grace. The six years in China took their toll on the already frail missionary; his health was deteriorating and he went back to London with Maria and Grace.

The next years the Taylors lived in poverty in London's East End. Hudson Taylor continued his medical studies and translated the Bible into the Ningpo language. Yet he longed to be back in China.

During those years in London, his wife helped him immensely. Dr. Taylor had the greater intellect, she the better education. She was born a "lady" at a time when people put great stock in status. She polished and helped him in every way, and he grew comfortable in any social circle. Most of all, she loved him through his depressions and melancholy. Taylor's son and biographer, Dr. Howard Taylor, writes, "Her hand wrote for him, her faith strengthened his own, her prayers undergirded the whole work, and her practical experience and loving heart made her the Mother of the Mission."[51]

In June of 1865 a great insight came to Dr. Taylor on the beach in Brighton. There he realized God's total care for him and the ministry. He had been so reluctant to lead a mission, for the burden of caring for the missionaries' spiritual and physical needs seemed too great. He understood now that all the missionaries going to China would go in obedience to God, and not to him. If they were going in obedience to God, they were God's responsibility; He would take care of them, and meet their every need. This discovery is known as "Hudson Taylor's Spiritual Secret."

By faith Hudson Taylor asked God for twenty-four willing and skilled laborers—one for each of the different districts of China. God answered his prayers and soon raised up twenty-two such missionaries! Together, they formed the China Inland Mission (CIM) in 1866. That same year, the Taylors and the others sailed for China.

The new missionaries had many trials and disappointments—one of those trials being the voyage itself, because of several typhoons. Yet in spite of the difficult journey, no lives were lost, and most of the crew was converted! The first inland settlement for the mission was in Hangchow.

The Word of God went forth, and their labor bore fruit. But in the midst of their blessings were hardships; the Taylors' daughter, Grace, died of disease in 1867. Despite riots and false accusations against the missionaries, new converts came to faith, and new missionaries answered the call to China.

Hudson Taylor traveled back and forth from China to the West, pleading on behalf of the Chinese people. Charles Spurgeon said, "China, China, China, is now ringing in our ears in that special peculiar musical, forcible, unique way in which Mr. Taylor utters it."[52] Taylor spoke about the missionary effort in China in Germany, Australia, New Zealand, Norway, and Sweden. One day he was preaching in the drawing room of Lady Beauchamp's home in Norfolk. The local gentry attended, as did her little boy Montague, who sat on a small stool near Mr. Taylor. The lad was fascinated by the Chinese dress, the chopsticks, and the Buddhist idols. Some years later he became one of the "Cambridge Seven." This group of young aristocrats made quite a stir when they joined the CIM, arriving in China in 1885. One of the other young men, C. T. Studd, received a large inheritance, and he gave it away to missions. He "gave £5,000 to D. L. Moody to build Moody Bible Institute, and 5,000 to General William Booth to send 50 Salvation Army missionaries to India."[53]

Hudson Taylor continued to claim China for Christ. When he began there were 380 million Chinese who had never heard the name of Jesus. At the end of his life, thirteen thousand were baptized; several hundred Chinese worked among 750 CIM missionaries. About $400 million came into the mission, unsolicited. One surprising donor was George Mueller of Bristol, England. This penniless orphanage director requested the names of all the new CIM converts and prayed for them. He also managed to send the equivalent of about ten thousand dollars annually to the China Inland Mission. (God provided the money, and Mueller forwarded it to CIM!)

The father of the mission was a humble man. He said, "I often think that God must have been looking for someone small enough and weak enough for him to use. . . . He found me."[54]

Christianity in China experienced a major setback in 1948 with the rise of the Communists. Mao-Tse Tung butchered tens of millions of people, including every Christian he could get his hands on. Yet in the last decade or so, the Chinese Church has enjoyed incredible growth. Dr. David Barrett estimates that there are easily as many as eighty million Christians in that country![55] That number contrasts greatly with the 1949 figure (of Protestants only) of less than one million![56] After Mao's death in 1976, the persecution of Christians in China was somewhat relaxed until 1994, when it began again in earnest. Despite the intense persecution of Christians in China, some estimates say twenty-five thousand Chinese become Christians each day!

FROM DARKNESS TO LIGHT

The apostle Paul, St. Patrick, William Carey, David Livingstone, Hudson Taylor, and many other lesser-known Christian missionaries for two millennia took God's elect from darkness to light. In the last century, A. W. Milne visited a part of New Guinea inhabited by cannibals. Darkness was thick in the air. Through his intrepid preaching, one after another of these fearsome cannibals became humble servants of Jesus Christ. When finally he ended his ministry and was buried in their midst, they placed a marker on his grave with this inscription:

Here lies the remains of A. W. Milne,
When he came to us there was no light,
When he died there was no darkness.[57]

What a glorious career. And wonder of wonders, every one of us as a Christian—whether as a missionary abroad or here in America—should be a beacon of light. Jesus said He was the Light of the World, and that we also are lights in a dark world. We can reflect His glory to others.

MISSIONS TODAY

We have only scratched the surface of what God has done through missions, particularly in the last two centuries. There are thousands of missionaries today in every corner of the globe. They provide food, education, health care, development, and relief to people who wouldn't have these needs met by anyone else. Above all, they share the message of the Bible: Jesus died for the forgiveness of sins and rose from the dead. Millions are coming into the kingdom of Christ today like never before. Billy Graham has brought tens of thousands of people into the kingdom of Christ; his work continues under the leadership of his son, Franklin Graham. The gospel is going forth in earnest in our time. Dr. David Barrett, editor of the massive *World Christian Encyclopedia,* reports that on average, every twenty-four hours, some 106,000 people around the world become professing Christians![58]

The message of the Bible now goes to places where it has never been heard before. Modern technology plays a critical role in this achievement.

I know of a Christian man from Iran who is a convert from Islam. His conversion alone could cost him his life. But this man broadcasts the gospel into Iran through shortwave radio. He has received all sorts of letters from Iranian Christians who are secretly worshiping the Lord— reminding me of the early Christian converts who met in the catacombs! The authorities know of his work and have placed a bounty on his head! But God has preserved him for years. Through his radio ministry, the message of the Bible is able to reach into places where it has been barred for centuries. Christian broadcasting, particularly shortwave radio broadcasting, is having an incredible impact on the spread of the gospel. I don't believe we'll know the full extent of it until we get to heaven. But just to give you an idea, consider this point from Ron Cline, the president of HCJB—a shortwave radio ministry situated in Quito, Ecuador, that has the potential of reaching 80 percent of the world's population. He said that before the collapse of the Soviet Union, they estimated that some 38,000 house churches were meeting there, huddled around listening to the gospel on the shortwave radio on Sunday mornings. God has opened windows for His Word that no tyrannical government can shut! Even as the government attempts to once again shut out evangelism, there are means God will use to make His Word known.

On the Internet millions of people can be exposed to the gospel. *TIME* magazine recently put an image of Christ on the cover with the title "Jesus Online."[59] The article was appropriately titled because Christians are extensively using this incredible communications tool to spread the gospel—again, in places where tyrannical governments would like to shut it out. In the privacy of their own homes, people with computers in Saudi Arabia, Japan, and Western Europe can read the message of the Bible. One recent study found that there were more than five thousand Christian ministries, churches, or agencies using the Internet for evangelism and discipleship. By comparison, 650 Jewish groups use the Internet to spread Judaism. Islamic groups with sites on the Internet numbered around two hundred.[60] So Christians are indeed on the cutting edge of this particular mission field, and that's exciting.

"WHO HAS BEEN HIDING THE BOOK?"

We can thank God for what missionaries have accomplished, yet we must remember that the task is unfinished. Pay close attention to this haunting question of a convert from India. May it motivate us to actively pray, to actively give, and perhaps—for some readers—to even go to the mission field:

> A colporteur missionary [one who distributes Christian books] told the Christmas story to a group of people in a village in North India. Then he read the story from the Scriptures. "How long ago was this great day when God's Son was born?" one person asked. "About two thousand years ago," replied the missionary. "Then why has the news been so long in reaching us?" asked the villager in surprise. "Who has been hiding the Book all this time?"[61]

We must no longer hide the Book! We must not rest until the whole world learns its great truths.

CHAPTER 10

THE BIBLE AND EXPLORATION

"Declare His glory among the nations,
His wonders among all peoples."

—Psalm 96:3

For centuries, the people in the interior of the western end of the island of New Guinea, now called Irian Jaya, were sealed from the rest of the world. They lived as cannibals, as warring tribes, as illiterates with no knowledge of other civilizations. They were closed off from the outside world by daunting cliffs and crocodile-infested swamps that naturally prevented easy access. But in the twentieth century, brave missionaries managed to penetrate the region. Why? To proclaim the message of the Bible. Today, many decendants of the cannibals live as Christians. Those missionaries have opened up this region to the rest of the globe.

Throughout the centuries, many parts of the world were similarly cut off from civilization until some brave Christian risked life and limb to go there. In the past five centuries, one place after another has opened up to the rest of the world, so that now some use the term *global village*. Most often missionaries, or Christian laymen, were the first to explore such places.

"To boldly go where no man has gone before" was part of the mission statement of the starship *Enterprise* in the classic television series *Star Trek*. In truth, throughout the centuries, the Bible has inspired some important death-defying voyages and explorations. Because of the importance of Columbus's discovery, we will examine his life and work in greater depth than any other explorer.

LEIF ERICKSON

For centuries it was widely held that Columbus was the first to sail to America, but then came evidence that perhaps a brave Norsemen named Leif Erickson accomplished that feat. We certainly know that after Columbus, knowledge of the New World spread through Europe, which was not true in the case of Erickson's voyage. But from a Christian perspective, it's fascinating to consider that the spread of the faith served as the impetus for both voyages. In the book *Who Was Who in World Exploration,* the story of Erickson's voyage is told:

> King Olaf commissioned Erickson to introduce Christianity to the Norse colonists on Greenland. In about the year 1000, Erickson supposedly sailed west from Norway, intending to reach Greenland, but was blown off course to the coast of North America. The party went ashore at a site on the eastern seaboard, somewhere between Nova Scotia and Chesapeake Bay.[1]

Archaeological digs in the twentieth century have confirmed that they landed and temporarily settled in Nova Scotia. When he and his crew set sail east again to Greenland, they came across a trading vessel that was shipwrecked, with the crew still alive. The men on the wrecked ship rewarded him with the rich cargo still intact, and he received the nickname "Leif the Lucky." Upon arriving in Greenland, he fulfilled his task. One encyclopedia states, "After he reached Greenland, he carried out his commission to bring Christianity to the settlers. One of his converts was his mother, Thjodhild, who is said to have built Greenland's first Christian church at Brattahlid."[2] Explorer Robin Hanbury-Tenison points out that Erickson was "probably the first European to set forth on America in about the year 1000."[3] Whether it was Columbus or Erickson, it was the intention of these men to spread the Word of God. And so they did, opening a new world and new possibilities.

A WORD ON SPANISH AND PORTUGUESE EXPLORERS

Before we discuss the significance of the Spanish and Portuguese explorers, it is important that we clarify a few things. The Spanish and Portuguese explorers of the fifteenth and sixteenth centuries are sometimes hard to recognize as good men. The Portuguese introduced slavery to the Western world, in tandem with Muslim traders and African chieftains (generally enslaving rival tribesmen). The Spanish conquistadores who explored the Americas were guilty of many heinous crimes, as in the region of Peru where the conquistadores forced the Indians to mine gold. Thousands died in the process.

The mistake the politically correct crowd makes is to present the Europeans (Christians) always as the bad guys—exploitative, oppressive—and to present the native Americans always as the good guys—peace-loving, in harmony with nature. Historian John Eidsmoe describes what Hernando Cortez and his men found when they entered the Aztec temples in Mexico:

> As they entered the temples they discovered that everything Diaz and Gomara have described in other parts of Mexico was here in the city: the stone altars, the obsidian knives, the black-robed priests with long matted hair, the fiendish-looking idols complete with basins in which to place sacrificed human hearts, the walls and steps coated with blood and human gore, the enormous piles of skulls and bones, and there was more. Gomara described an ossuary or theater made of skulls and mortar: "Andreas de Tapia, who described it to me, and Gonzalo de Umbria counted them one day and found them to number 136,000 skulls, including those on the poles and steps. Those in the towers could not be numbered." There were pits of beasts and poisonous snakes; sometimes the bodies of sacrificed victims were cast into these pits after people had eaten the arms and legs. And one very large idol was made out of seeds, ground and kneaded with the blood of babies and virgins who had been sacrificed.[4]

If that isn't horrifying enough, let's read more about the degradation the Spaniards found in the New World *prior to any Christian influence.* Caution: the following description is not for the faint of heart. Ripley's Believe It or Not, in their *Wonder Book of Strange Facts,* describe "a carved circular stone about seven feet across" found in the National Museum in Mexico City. Ripley's says of this stone:

> It is the bloodiest spot on earth.
>
>   It is the sacrificial stone of the Aztecs, and on it more than a million human beings have had their hearts cut out. Although the ancient Aztecs were a comparatively mild and peaceful people with a sense of brotherly love and charity, and attained a high degree of civilization, they believed in human sacrifice.
>
>   On great occasions, such as the crowning of a king or the dedication of a temple, men were slaughtered by the thousands. Six years before Columbus came to America the temple of the War God was consecrated. The prisoners, who for several years had been held in reserve for this festival, were ranged in files forming a procession nearly two miles long. This long line slowly walked to their death marking time to the shrieks of the dying as they were bent naked on

this stone and their hearts torn from their bodies. It required four days to finish the slaughter.[5]

As Paul Harvey likes to say, "It is *not* one world." Amen!

In today's politically correct milieu, we are reminded *ad nauseam* of the terrible misdeeds (some real and some imagined) of the Europeans who settled the New World. We often hear about the mistreatment of the Indians at the hands of the Europeans. Seldom do you hear of the low value placed on human life by many of these Indians. You rarely hear about the cannibalism, savagery, and even human sacrifice often found in America prior to any form of Christianity coming. We cannot justify the exploitation some explorers were guilty of; yet we realize that they introduced Christianity to the New World and thus sowed the seeds for positive change.

Samuel Huntington, a professor at Harvard and director of the John M. Olin Institute for Strategic Studies, wrote recently, "When Westerners went out to conquer the world in the sixteenth century, they did so for God as well as gold."[6] Above all, the important point to grasp here is that had there been no Bible, had there been no Christianity, then the fearless men who zigzagged the globe—going where no man had gone before—would very likely never have made their dangerous journeys. Or if they had, it could have been only for gold, looting, and plunder—like the Vikings in the ninth and tenth centuries.

THE CIRCUMNAVIGATION OF THE GLOBE

One of the most important accomplishments in the history of the world was sailing around the globe. The first man credited with that achievement died before the voyage was complete, but his men finished the task and made history. Few men have displayed as much courage and faith as Ferdinand Magellan (1480–1521). Antonio Pigafetta, who accompanied Magellan on his classic voyage, kept copious notes on his travels. Pigafetta wrote of Magellan:

Magellan's main virtues were courage and perseverance, in even the most difficult situations; for example, he bore hunger and fatigue better than all the rest of us. He was a magnificent practical seaman, who understood navigation better than all his pilots. The best proof of his genius is that he circumnavigated the world, none having preceded him.[7]

And Magellan, who was a man of God, was interested in spreading the gospel wherever he was. In Magellan's will we read these words:

> In the name of the Most High and Mighty God our Lord . . . believing firmly and truly in the Holy Trinity, the Father, Son and Holy Ghost—three persons and only one true God, as every faithful Christian holds and believes . . . being willing and desirous of placing my soul in the surest and most certain path that I can discern for its salvation . . . commend my soul to God our Lord, who made and created it, and redeemed me with His precious blood.[8]

Ian Cameron recounts a story that happened on January 11, 1520. He writes that Magellan's fleet "found to their delight a broad reach of water . . . as far as the eye could see." They dropped anchor, and Magellan called a conference aboard the flagship. They were now, he told his captain and pilots, approaching seas no Christian man had ever sailed in: "on the threshold of a great discovery."[9] Magellan was "the first European to cross the Pacific Ocean and the first person to circumnavigate the globe."[10] The world would never be quite the same.

In his many encounters with the natives on his journeys, Magellan shared his Christian faith. In his book *Magellan*, Tim Joyner says that in one encounter with natives with whom Magellan wanted to trade, this exchange occurred: "When Magellan queried them about family relationships in their society, they said that 'when fathers and mothers grew old, they received no further honor, but their children commanded them.' Shocked, Magellan told them that the Christian God 'had commanded us to honor our fathers and mothers, and that whoever did otherwise was condemned to eternal fire; that we are all descended from Adam and Eve, our first parents.'"[11] Another such account was recorded by Pigafetta: "The Captain-General warned them against adopting Christianity either from fear or in the hope of pleasing him [that is, Magellan]. If they really wished to become Christians, he said, they must do so for the love of God. . . . They then declared, as with one voice, that they wished to become Christians of their own free will. The Captain-General then embraced them with tears in his eyes."[12]

Desmond Wilcox, in his book *Ten Who Dared* (taken from the BBC television series by the same name), wrote:

> They [Magellan and crew] crossed the Pacific and arrived, as had Vasco de Gama sailing from the other direction, in the known waters of its western shores and archipelagos. But Magellan was killed in a squabble with the inhabitants of the Philippines, and the *Victoria* came

with her load of cloves, sailing wide of the Portuguese lanes. It was a momentous feat. In the space of 30 years, Africa had been defined, the two Americas had been discovered and Magellan had proved that all the seas were one, that the sea was a single body in which the continents stood.[13]

Here we see another important milestone accomplished "for the glory of God and advancement of the Christian faith."[14]

VASCO NUNEZ DE BALBOA

Vasco de Balboa (1475–1519) was one of many great figures of exploration. He has been called the "discoverer of the Pacific Ocean."[15] Carl Waldman and Alan Wexler write of Balboa in their book *Who Was Who in World Exploration:*

[Balboa] was the first European to see the Pacific Ocean from the western coast of the Americas. His exploit had a profound influence on subsequent explorers, encouraging hopes that the new-found continent was narrow enough to provide an all-water route to the Pacific. His explorations also revealed that the riches of the Far East lay much farther west of the American landmass than previously believed. Balboa established the first overland trail across the Americas, which subsequently provided the Spanish with a direct route to the west coast of South America.[16]

Vasco de Balboa (also called Vasco Nunez) had a real "mountaintop" experience when he saw, perhaps as the first white man ever, the Pacific Ocean. *The Oxford Book of Exploration* describes the situation:

Captain Vasco Nunez, having gone ahead of his company, climbed a hill with a bare summit, and from the top of this hill saw the South Sea. Of all the Christians in his company, he was the first to see it. He turned back toward his people, full of joy, lifting his hands and his eyes to Heaven, praising Jesus Christ and His glorious Mother the Virgin, Our Lady. Then he fell upon his knees on the ground and gave great thanks to God for the mercy He had shown him, in allowing him to discover the sea, and thereby to render so great a service to God.[17]

To this, the book *Great Adventures That Changed Our World* adds, "After planting a great cross on the top of the hill, Balboa 'commanded that the names of all the men who were there with him should be written down so that the memory should remain of him and of them, because they were the first Christians who saw that sea.' The little ceremony ended with all hands joining in a 'Te Deum,' a pious hymn of praise."[18] Here again we see that Christ and the Bible had a part in changing the world.

CHRISTOPHER COLUMBUS

Of all the Spanish and Portuguese explorers of note, Christopher Columbus was the most significant. He was a man influenced by the Bible far more than most people know.

At about eight o'clock on the morning of October 12, 1492, Christopher Columbus struggled out of the surf onto the Western Hemisphere, and thus a new world was born. Desmond Wilcox, author of *Ten Who Dared,* writes this of Columbus:

> The voyage of Columbus . . . was conceptually breathtaking. It had long been known that the world was a sphere, but sailing around it was a startling idea that only a few years earlier would have been unthinkable. Columbus was an inspired purveyor of ideas as well as a splendid seaman, and he readily synthesized all the information at hand into a pattern that established that China lay some 3,000 miles due west of Europe. If he had known that the distance was really 12,000 miles, perhaps he would never have set sail; certainly his crew wouldn't have gone.[19]

Until a hundred years ago, there was worldwide adulation for this feat. All of Europe and the Americas held the discoverer of the New World in the highest esteem. There are more cities and lakes and parks and other places in this country (and the Americas) named after Columbus than for any other human being.

"Columbus Got Mugged"

But nowadays, something is different. Columnist Gary Wills put it this way:

> A funny thing happened on the way to the quincentennial observation of America's discovery: Columbus got mugged. This time the Indians were waiting for him. He comes now with an apologetic air—but not, for some, sufficiently apologetic. He comes to be dishonored.[20]

Why the attack? Who has not read articles, seen TV docudramas or motion pictures that have trashed Columbus in every conceivable way? For example, Russell Means, a Native American activist wrote:

"Columbus makes Hitler look like a juvenile delinquent. He was a racist, a mass murderer, a slave trader, a rapist, and a plunderer."[21] What has happened in the last hundred years that we have gone from adulation and honor to disrespect and slander?

John Eidsmoe, in his outstanding book on Columbus, *Columbus and Cortez,* says, "Some are determined to remake America into a secular or pagan society. To do so, they must move this nation away from its Christian foundations."[22]

In the past hundred years, we have seen the rise of atheism, skepticism, communism, fascism, socialism, and every other kind of "ism" opposed to the Word of God—whose proponents hate God and Christ and Christianity. These people are determined to refashion America in *their* image—in their unbelieving, ungodly, or pagan image. But to do so, they have to move this nation off its Christian foundations.

Keep in mind that Columbus was not an angel; he was not a sinless human being or saint, in the common understanding of the meaning of that word. He was a man of flesh and blood. He was a sinner like all of us. He was a man who made mistakes. Yet he cannot be blamed for the things the modern critics would like to dump upon him.

If he brought disease to the Western world, which the sailors and the settlers did, we must realize that the people living at that time had no understanding of the germ theory of disease. By the way, it is never mentioned that the explorers also carried back to Europe New World diseases that decimated Europe. Eidsmoe adds that if Columbus is to be blamed for the shortcomings of Western culture, then he also must be given some of the credit for its achievements.

He writes:

Let us credit [the Europeans] for their achievements and contributions: art, music, architecture, ethics, liberty, law, government, a Constitution that has served as a model across the world, an economic system that has produced the greatest good for the greatest number and the highest level of prosperity the world has ever known, and a spirit of ingenuity and achievement that led to unparalleled medical and technological advances.[23]

For these things Columbus and the rest of the European explorers are not given credit; they are merely blamed for the bad things.

We are told that innocent natives were slaughtered. Columbus never slaughtered any native. He not only never committed genocide, he didn't kill *anyone.* In fact, he was very kindly toward the natives. Furthermore, as we have already seen, the natives were not all the simple, idyllic, gracious people that the defenders of the multicultural view would have us to believe. Some of the Indians, however, were honorable people.

What Kind of Man Was Columbus?

Given the current attitude toward Columbus, it's natural to wonder what kind of man he really was. His son tells us that with his family he was a gracious and loving man. He so attended to the reading of the Scriptures, prayers, and fasts of the worship services that he could have been mistaken as a member of a holy order.

Consider what he did when he landed in the Western Hemisphere. When he staggered up out of the ocean, what did he say? His very first words were:

> Blessed be the light of day,
> And the Holy Cross we say;
> And the Lord of Veritie
> And the Holy Trinity.[24]

In fact, at the beginning of each new day, this hymn had been sung daily on the ship during that fateful voyage.[25]

And he planted in the New World a cross—the cross of Jesus Christ. His name means "Christ-bearer." (*Pherein* means "to bear.") Christopher Columbus believed all of his life that it was his calling by God to carry Christ to distant lands, to the far isles of the sea.

Interestingly, the pilot of the *Nina*, one of the three ships made famous by Columbus, drew a map of the known world. At the top of the map is a drawing of St. Christopher carrying the Christ child across the Atlantic Ocean to the New World. The features of St. Christopher are unmistakably the features of Christopher Columbus, who, his son tells us, was a tall man with blonde hair and blue eyes. He was a gentle man who hated swearing and blasphemy and tried to live a godly life.

The word *Columbus*, coming from the Italian *colon*, means, "a member." Columbus liked to say he was a member of the body of Christ and would carry Christ to the New World.

Think about the places he named. The first place he landed he named San Salvador, which means "holy Savior." Then he landed at a place he named Vera Cruz, which means the "true cross"; then, at La Navidad, which means "the Nativity" or "Christmas." Then he came to an island with three hills on it, which he named Trinidad, meaning "the Trinity." In most of the textbooks in our schools today, there is virtually no mention of any spiritual or biblical or Christian motive or aspect to the life of Columbus at all. When these places are mentioned, the students are never even told what they mean.

Columbus's *Book of Prophecies*

Something of his own faith is seen in one of the two books that Columbus wrote. One is his log and the other is the *Book of Prophecies*, in which he quotes many of the prophecies of the Bible. He felt that he was called by God to fulfill those Scriptures, to take the gospel to the far islands of the sea. He says:

> The Holy Scriptures testify in the Old Testament, by the mouth of the prophets, and in the New [Testament], by our Savior Jesus Christ, that this world will come to an end: Matthew, Mark, and Luke have recorded the signs of the end of the age. . . . And I say that the sign which convinces me that our Lord is hastening the end of the world is the preaching of the Gospel recently in so many lands.[26]

Kay Brigham, a scholar who painstakingly produced a new translation of Columbus's *Book of Prophecies* for the five-hundredth anniversary of his voyage, writes:

> Without faith in God and his Word Columbus could not have overcome the obstacles that stood in the way to accomplish his great idea. . . . Faith liberated Columbus from the chains of human myopia, propelling him to the providential encounter with a vast territory and a multitude of peoples with their indigenous cultures up to that time unknown to Europeans.[27]

Luther's nailing of his Ninety-five Theses to the church door at Wittenberg was twenty-five years away when Columbus set sail from Palos in Spain, yet Columbus believed much of what the Reformers stood for. Of course, John Huss and John Wycliffe had done their work long before, and perhaps Columbus knew of them. He held his right to interpret the Scriptures for himself. Some of his favorite Scriptures were:

- "Surely the isles shall wait for me, and the ships of Tarshish first, to bring thy sons from far, their silver and their gold with them, unto the name of the LORD thy God, and to the Holy One of Israel, because he hath glorified thee" (Isa. 60:9 KJV).

- "I will also give thee for a light to the Gentiles, that thou mayest be my salvation unto the end of the earth" (Isa. 49:6 KJV).

He believed that God was calling him to be that light to the Gentiles. You can't read Columbus's *Book of Prophecies* without being impressed by his knowledge of Scripture. The entire book is mostly portions of the Word of God that Columbus wrote out in his own hand, interspersed with comments on why he undertook his voyage and how the Bible strengthened him for the task. Surely, Columbus writes, if it were not for the Lord and His Word, he would never have been able to pull off such an accomplishment! Here are Columbus's own words, found in a letter to King Ferdinand and Queen Isabelle that he reproduced in *Book of Prophecies:*

> At this time I have seen and put in study to look into all the Scriptures, cosmography, histories, chronicles and philosophy and other arts, which our Lord opened to my understanding (I could sense his hand upon me), so that it became clear to me that it was feasible to navigate from here to the Indies; and he unlocked within me the determination to execute the idea. And I came to your Highnesses with this ardor. All those who heard about my enterprise rejected it with laughter, scoffing at me. Neither the sciences which I mentioned above, nor the authoritative citations from them, were of any avail. In only your Highnesses remained faith and constancy. Who doubts that this illumination was from the Holy Spirit? I attest that he [the Spirit], with marvelous rays of light consoled me through the holy and sacred Scriptures, a strong and clear testimony with forty-four books of the Old Testament,[28] and four Gospels with twenty-three Epistles of those blessed Apostles encouraging me to proceed, and, continually, without ceasing for a moment, they inflame me with a great sense of urgency.[29]

Columbus goes on to talk about all the frustrating years he spent in the court arguing the matter over with "the experts" who didn't agree with the plan. But he argued to them that "the outcome will be fulfillment of what our Redeemer Jesus Christ said, and had said beforehand by the mouth of his Holy Prophets."[30]

"It Was the Lord Who Put It into My Mind"

We have heard that Columbus sailed for "gold and glory." But hear again what Christopher Columbus said himself:

It was the Lord who put it into my mind to sail to the Indies. . . . The fact that [the] gospel must still be preached to so many lands in such a short time—that is what convinces me.[31]

Columbus made his voyage for the sake of the gospel. Yet you never read that information in your school textbook. Nor did you see that motivation portrayed in any of the recent docudramas.

As far as gold is concerned, Columbus was interested in discovering it because of another matter of great concern. Besides the evangelization of the world, he was concerned about delivering the Holy Sepulchre of Christ and the holy city of Jerusalem out of the hands of the Mohammedan infidels. His great desire was to find gold to finance a final crusade. And Isabella agreed that the gold that would be raised would be used for the purpose of freeing the holy Sepulchre of Christ. Listen to Columbus's own words:

I must repeat: for the execution of the enterprise to the Indies, neither reason, nor mathematics, nor cartography were of profit to me in the manner that the prophesies of Scripture were. This is what I have to report concerning the liberation of Jerusalem. . . . At the time I was motivated by the Scriptures to go to discover the Indies, I went to the royal court with the intention of entreating our Sovereigns to specify revenues that they might accrue to be spent on the reconquest of Jerusalem.[32]

George Grant has written a book on the matter, titled *The Last Crusader: The Untold Story of Christopher Columbus*.

His Treatment of the Indigenous People

The very first day he landed—when the critics would say he was interested in conquests and gold—this is what he wrote in his log:

I, in order that they [the natives] might develop a very friendly disposition towards us, because I knew that they were a people who could better be freed and converted to our Holy Faith by love than by force, gave to some of them red caps and to others glass beads, which they hung on their necks, and many others things. . . .[33]

He refused to allow his sailors to give them things of no value—they would accept anything—because he wanted nothing to interfere with these natives coming to Christ. He said: "I don't recognize in them any religion, and I believe that very promptly they would turn Christians."[34]

Columbus sought to win the worlds in the far isles of the sea to the Savior Jesus Christ. Had the Bible never been written, Columbus would never have made his voyage, a voyage that changed the world. It's not politically correct to praise Columbus for his revolutionary voyage, yet he changed the world. And no amount of politically correct denial, denigration, or historical revision can change that fact! His own writings show that the Scripture provided the key motivation for this major turning point in human history. Theodore Roosevelt said of Columbus: "He was first a Christian, second an adventurer, third a genius, fourth a visionary, fifth a real father, and finally a man of action. O that we had such men in our own time."[35]

MARQUETTE AND JOLIET

It was many a person's hope that the Mississippi River emptied into the Pacific.[36] So in 1673, Father Jacques Marquette (1637–1675) and Louis Joliet (1645–1700) set out to discover the endpoint of this river. As we know, and much to their chagrin, the Mississippi led them to the Gulf of Mexico. Waldman and Wexler write in *Who Was Who in World Exploration:*

> The Joliet–Marquette expedition descended the Mississippi to the mouth of the Arkansas River, midway between present-day Memphis, Tennessee, and Vicksburg, Mississippi. Quapaw Indians warned them that they faced monsters and hostile tribes if they ventured farther southward. Using his navigational skills, Joliet determined that the river had taken them to a point far enough south that it must drain into the Gulf of Mexico.[37]

Both were men of God. If there would be problems along the way, God would take care of them. Marquette was an ordained missionary priest who worked among the Indians in the French portion of Canada. In 1667, Louis Joliet left the priesthood and eventually met up with Father Jacques Marquette, close to Niagara Falls.[38] Their pioneering work played an important role in opening up the interior of North America. Christianity was at the heart of their mission.

JAMES COOK

When we think of seafarers and explorers, the name Captain Cook is legendary. In the book *Ten Who Dared,* Desmond Wilcox writes of the accomplishments of Captain James Cook (1728–1779), who was from Great Britain:

He was the greatest navigator of his time, and his three-year circumnavigation of the world in the round-bottomed *Endeavour* was a land-
mark voyage in naval annals. He explored the reaches of the Pacific
Ocean from Alaska to Antarctica. His extraordinarily accurate charts
could still be used for navigation today.[39]

Captain Cook was also a man of God. He believed in honoring God on
the Lord's Day. In fact, he himself led the services. Wilcox writes:

On Sundays, Cook's usual captain's inspection was always followed
by a religious service. Cook appeared on deck and the drum beat the
retreat. Men fetched stools from below and brought chairs for the officers. The bell was tolled and the church pendant was hoisted at the
gaff. Cook conducted the service on the quarterdeck, with a Bible and
a prayer book in front of him, placed on a cloth draped over the compass box. A lesson was read, a hymn sung.[40]

The Bible has similarly given strength, encouragement, and comfort for
the journey to millions through the centuries.

DAVID LIVINGSTONE AND HENRY MORTON STANLEY

We've already dealt at length with Dr. Livingstone. Now we'll consider a major by-product of his work—opening Africa to the rest of the
world. David Livingstone's objective was to spread the gospel, but
because of the "tribalism and all its traditions," he felt the only way to
have them "accept the white man's God" would be to infuse British com-
merce to "shed their savage ways."[41] This led him to seek "a navigable
waterway connecting the African interior with either the Atlantic or the
Indian Oceans," so that it could be converted into a great avenue of
British trade.[42]

After his arrival in Africa in 1841, Livingstone set out to search for
the Nile's source.[43] *National Geographic* writes:

One major journey took Livingstone northwest from Linyanti across
well over a thousand miles of almost unknown country to Luanda on
the east coast, which he reached in May 1854. After recuperating, he
turned back the way he had come and proceeded east along the Zambezi River. Upon reaching Quelimane on the east coast, he became the
first European to cross Africa.[44]

Unfortunately, due to the rugged nature of the waterways "his repeated
attempts to establish a trade route on the Zambezi were thwarted by

miles of rapids, and Shire and Rovuma Rivers proved little better."[45] Down but not defeated, Livingstone carried on: Combining exploration with God's work, he could also check on the Arab slave trade.[46] In 1866, as proposed by the Royal Geographical Society, Livingstone went on a long search for the source of the Nile River.

Livingstone was also "the first European to see the great falls of the Zambezi."[47] Today we know this marvelous example of the handiwork of God as Victoria Falls. They are a sight to behold, reaching as high as 350 feet. Livingstone said of these towering shafts of water, "They are constantly running down, but never reach the bottom."[48]

Just before he died David Livingstone found some of the details on the Nile that he had been seeking for years. In the book *Great Adventures That Changed Our World, Reader's Digest* reports on his death this way: "Among his papers was one of the saddest documents ever penned: an announcement of the 'discovery' of the fountains of the Nile, with only the latitude and longitude left blank."[49] I can't agree with their perspective! What he had found was beneficial for the whole world, whether he received recognition for it in this life or not. Meanwhile, we can only imagine his great homecoming in heaven!

When, in 1869, journalist Henry Morton Stanley (1841–1904) was commissioned to search for the Scottish explorer, he not only became a Christian, but an explorer as well. Wilcox reports:

> What turned him into an explorer was the death of Livingstone. Stanley had found in Livingstone a wise and kind figure—something he had sought all his life. He heard about Livingstone's death when he arrived back in England. There and then he decided he must return to Africa to complete the exploration that Livingstone had left unfinished. Particularly, he wanted to solve the mystery of the River Lualaba in unexplored Central Africa, which Livingstone had reached and believed to be the headwaters of the Nile.[50]

Stanley then went on to lead "the first expedition along the Congo from east to west."[51] The Bible motivated Livingstone, who in turn motivated Stanley to complete the work. Had it not been for the Bible, the interior of Africa might never have been opened up to the rest of the globe.

OTHER NOTEWORTHY EXPLORERS

Other Christians throughout history have gone where civilization has not gone before. In a missionary spirit, and in order to advance the gospel, they have pioneered their ways—opening up that region to the rest of the world. Consider these other notable Christian explorers:

- Marco Polo, who spent seventeen years traveling in the East beginning in 1271. He wrote the classic *The Travels of Marco Polo*, which "helped fire the European hunger for trade with the East."[52] Polo was a Christian who sent back via his uncles (with whom he had journeyed to China) an important message from Kublai Khan, who asked for one hundred Christians to come to China in order to prove "to the learned of his dominions, by just and fair argument, that the faith professed by Christians is superior to and founded on more evident truth than any other."[53] Tragically, this request was barely acted upon. (Twenty years later, the pope sent two men, one of whom died on the way!)
- Jedidiah Smith, a successful nineteenth-century American commercial explorer who hunted beaver skins. His faith sustained him through the most difficult of travels. Desmond Wilcox says of Smith, whom he describes as a "pious, abstemious Methodist":

   His was as harrowing a journey as any in the history of exploration—across the burning Mojave Desert, where no man had ventured before, to California through hostile Indian territory. . . . In six years he covered more of the mountain region than any man before him. . . . He had opened up the Oregon Trail that later was to carry settlers in their thousands from St. Louis and Independence to the Pacific Coast.[54]

- Mary Slessor, a nineteenth-century missionary from Scotland into the African interior of Calabar. Although she was only about five feet tall, she showed tremendous courage and faith, working among fetish worshipers, headhunters, and cannibals. One after another they yielded their lives to Christ. One after another the horrible customs plaguing these people were abolished. She gave herself to Africa for forty years. Slessor, like Livingstone and Stanley before her, helped open a part of Africa because of her commitment to get the message of the Bible into people's lives.

A HIGH PRICE FOR THE SAKE OF THE GOSPEL

There are hundreds of missionaries who have done brave, pioneering work in order to reach isolated tribes and people groups with the gospel. What people don't realize is the incredible sacrifice such pioneers often underwent. It's easy to read about their adventures with our creature comforts well in place: air-conditioning, indoor plumbing, well-stocked refrigerators, microwave ovens, and the like. But consider the hardships undergone by such Christian pioneers. Consider the Pilgrims. We all know of their *Mayflower* voyage and settling of Plymouth. What we don't realize is the high price they paid. For example, they faced starvation just a couple of months after they landed in the New World. Read Governor William Bradford's eyewitness description in *Of Plymouth Plantation*—written in third-person narrative—of this terrible ordeal. It should give us an appreciation of the human cost to such brave explorations. Through the worst of it, the Bible sustained them:

> But that which was most sad and lamentable was, that in two or three months' time half of their company died, especially in January and February, being the depth of winter, and wanting houses and other comforts; being infected with the scurvy and other diseases which this long voyage and their inaccommodate condition had brought upon them. So as there died some times two or three of a day in the foresaid time, that of 100 and odd persons, scarce fifty remained. And of these, in the time of most distress, there was but six or seven sound persons who to their great commendations, be it spoken, spared no pains night nor day, but with abundance of toil and hazard of their own health, fetched them wood, made them fires, dressed them meat, made their beds, washed their loathsome clothes, clothed and unclothed them. In a word, did all the homely and necessary offices for them which dainty and queasy stomachs cannot endure to hear named; and all this willingly and cheerfully, without any grudging in the least, showing herein their true love unto their friends and brethren; a rare example and worthy to be remembered.[55]

This painful account of the realities of the hardships often faced by Christian explorers should give us all a deeper appreciation for their incredible accomplishments. Would it have happened if the Bible had never been written? I think not.

CHAPTER 11

THE BIBLE AND EVERYDAY THINGS

"The earth is the LORD's, and everything in it."
—Psalm 24:1 NIV

In a survey conducted nearly a decade ago, successful "business and education leaders" were asked which book "most affected their lives." One-quarter of them said the Bible. Four percent listed Charles Dickens's *A Tale of Two Cities,* and 2 percent named the Book of Mormon. "No other book was mentioned twice."[1]

This survey is just one of many examples of the Bible's influence on our culture, and on our everyday lives. We've seen how the Bible helped shape our civilization more than any other book in history. As we consider a Christian worldview, recall the cultural mandate in the first chapter of Genesis—in which God tells man to "fill the earth and subdue it"; to "have dominion over the fish of the sea, over the birds of the air, and over every living thing that moves on the earth" (Gen. 1:28). This means that all of man's life should be lived under God's control and for His glory. Man has dominion over all of the earth; he must take all the potential the earth offers and use it to bring out the best in himself, and offer it all to God. This includes politics, economics, literature and the arts, and science. For the Christian, *this is my Father's world.* This book deals with various activities and accomplishments in times past and present of many Christians holding such a worldview. Now, we want to focus on how the Bible has impacted everyday things.

FOOD

Food is universal, so let's begin with the Bible's impact on what we eat, including some of the common names associated with food. The word *breakfast* comes from the concept of breaking the fast. *Dictionary of Word Origins* says the word dates to the fifteenth century: "The word is first recorded in a text of 1463: 'Expenses in breakfast . . .' It is a lexicalization of the phrase 'break one's fast,' which itself seems to have originated in the 14th century."[2]

And speaking of breakfast, did you know that Kellogg's Corn Flakes have Christian origins in their own way? The corn flake was developed by Dr. Harvey Kellogg, a devout Seventh-day Adventist who is well known today for the brand of cereals named after him. Kellogg believed, writes professor and author Peter Gardella, "that eating cereals instead of meat and eggs would weaken the passions and reverse the effects of original sin."[3] Though viewed as an eccentric by some, Dr. Kellogg was ahead of his time in advocating various practices of good health. For example, several decades before they became widely accepted, Dr. Kellogg "advocated counting calories, warned against tobacco and praised yogurt and molasses."[4]

Another Christian, Mr. Welch, was looking for a way to develop a nonalcoholic drink made with grapes for Communion. Thus was born Welch's Grape Juice.[5]

The graham cracker was invented by a Christian minister, Reverend Sylvester Graham. His goal was to create a product that would curb one's desire for liquor; he was "convinced that a craving for whiskey could be cured by eating bread baked with bran."[6]

The pretzel is an everyday snack. Why is it twisted into that well-known shape? The pretzel was developed by a godly Christian monk in A.D. 610 to reward the young students who would say their prayers. He shaped the snack in such a way as to reflect the crossing of the arms for prayers. Many centuries later, its twisted shape still reflects its straight and narrow origins.[7]

Today, from Europe to Latin America, from Asia to Africa, from Australia to North America, *restaurant* is the universal word for an eating establishment, and its origin goes back to a Bible verse taken out of context. The "rest" in *restaurant* comes from Jesus' promise in Matthew 11:28: "Come to Me, all you who labor and are heavy laden, and I will give you rest." Prior to 1766, public places to eat were associated with inns or hotels. But in Paris, an entrepreneur and chef named Boulanger opened to the public an establishment dedicated only to eating. He placed in bold letters outside the eating place a paraphrase (and misquote, really) of Matthew: "Come unto me, all ye that are hungry and I shall restore you."[8] Robert Ripley writes: "From that word 'restore' (in French 'restaurai') the establishment became known as a 'Restaurant' and this name has since been applied to eateries the world over."[9]

THE CALENDAR

Why does our week consist of seven days? Why not make it a ten-day week? It might make things easier. In fact, during the French Revolution, they threw away any known Christian influence—including the way they measured time. Walter Grab, author of *The French Revolution,* writes: "At the suggestion of the deputy Romme, the Convention voted on 5 October 1793 to abolish the Christian calendar and introduce a republican calendar. . . . Weeks were replaced with periods of ten days (decades) so that the Christian Sunday would disappear."[10] The revolutionaries counted the years according to the establishment of their republic (beginning 1792) rather than the birth of Christ. (Napoleon restored the Christian calendar a dozen years later.) So why do we have seven days in a week and not ten, or a dozen, for that matter? The answer rests with our Judeo-Christian heritage. In the beginning God created the world in six days and He rested on the seventh, the Sabbath (Gen. 1). As *The Basic Everyday Encyclopedia* points out, "Our months were fixed by Caesar, but the 7-day week came in from Old Testament sources, under Christian influence."[11]

Why was the Sabbath changed from Saturday to Sunday? The answer is that Jesus rose from the dead on Sunday. The early Christians worshiped Him on that day and established the first day of the week as the Lord's Day. A few centuries later Constantine made it official for the whole Roman Empire. The monumental shift of the Sabbath from Saturday to Sunday is one example of the mounds of evidence that Jesus Christ rose from the dead.[12] Most countries in the world with a Christian heritage (North America, South America, Europe, Australia, and parts of Asia) treat Sunday as a special day. For many, it is the only day off—although, tragically, that's becoming less and less true in our culture. The special nature of Sunday as a day of rest is a direct result of Christianity. Those millions who sleep late on Sunday morning have Jesus and the Bible to thank for the day off!

Our calendar is the Gregorian calendar. It is essentially the Julian calendar (devised by Julius Caesar) and corrected by Pope Gregory XIII. The Julian calendar, unlike the Muslim or lunar calendar, is a solar calendar with 365 days plus six hours, requiring a leap year every four years. However, the actual time in a year is 365 days plus 5 hours, 48 minutes, and 46 seconds![13] Gregory devised a system to correct the error that had accumulated over several centuries; he demonstrated that by 1582, ten days had been lost since the implementation of the Julian calendar. He also "ordained skipping leap years in years ending in 00, unless they were divisible by 4."[14] This proved to be a "much closer approximation."[15]

The Gregorian calendar was finally applied in England in 1752. For that reason ten days were lost. (That's why, as an example, the date the pilgrims signed the Mayflower Compact is sometimes listed as November 11, 1620—which is what the document itself reads—or sometimes listed as November 21, 1620.)

Soon we will enter the twenty-first century. That designation obviously has a direct relation to the Bible, as it will be the twenty-first century after Christ's birth. (Technically, Jesus was born 4 B.C.—or four years Before Christ!—because the medieval monk, Dionysius Exiguus, who first divided history into "before Christ" and "anno Domini," was off by four years. That he erred by a few years is not the point; the point is that Jesus Christ is the focus of history.) If time were measured in any other way, the time we recognize as January 1, 2000, would be some other year, not at all related to Jesus. All the billions of people who will be ushering in the new century and the new millennium will be paying indirect homage to Christ and the Bible.

LANGUAGE AND WORD ORIGINS

The Bible has had a profound impact on language. Many of the world's languages were written down for the first time by Christian missionaries as they translated the Bible into an as-yet-unwritten tongue. In some cases, the translators even had to create an alphabet.[16] Yet there is far more to the story than that.

The great Christian reformer John Wycliffe (1320?–1384), translated the Bible into English, and in doing so became the father of English prose;[17] he is "remarkable as being the first distinguished English scholar."[18]

Similarly, we know that Martin Luther had a profound impact on the German language. Historian Will Durant says this of Luther's translation of both the Old and the New Testaments:

> Luther's supreme achievement as a writer was his translation of the Bible into German. . . . Despite their imperfect scholarship, these translations were epochal events. They inaugurated German literature and established *Neuhochdeautsch*—the New High German of Upper Saxony—as the literary language of Germany. . . . His translation had the same effect and prestige in Germany as the King James version in England a century later: it had endless and beneficent influence on the national speech, and is still the greatest prose work in the national literature.[19]

The very words on this page read as they do because of Christianity. Art historian H. W. Janson explains how the revival in art experienced under Charlemagne (a committed Christian who ruled France around A.D. 800) shaped even our lettering:

> For it is printed in letters whose shapes derive from the script in Carolingian[20] manuscripts. The fact that these letters are known today as Roman rather than Carolingian recalls another aspect of the cultural reforms sponsored by Charlemagne: the collecting and copying of ancient Roman literature.[21]

Had the Bible never been written, we of European stock might still be writing with simplistic runic marks,[22] as did our ancestors prior to the influence of Christianity.

Many common phrases, expressions, and words come right out of the pages of the Bible. You cannot be truly literate without reading the Bible. The following are numerous examples of famous expressions right from the pages of Holy Writ. While I list a Scripture reference, note that it is *a* Scripture reference. In some cases, the particular phrase appears in other verses as well. Many of these are everyday expressions that you should recognize. These phrases are so well known that many people may not be aware that they come from the Bible. This list is not exhaustive. (Note the profound influence of the King James Version of the Bible in these phrases.):

- "In the beginning" (Gen. 1:1 and John 1:1)
- "Let there be light" (Gen. 1:3)
- "Be fruitful and multiply" (Gen. 1:28)
- "Bone of my bones and flesh of my flesh" (Gen. 2:23)
- "My brother's keeper" (Gen. 4:9)
- "The mark of Cain" (based on Gen. 4:15)
- "The tower of Babel" (Gen. 11)
- "Thy neighbour's wife" (Ex. 20:17 KJV)
- "An eye for an eye, a tooth for a tooth" (Ex. 21:24)
- "The golden calf" (Ex. 32)
- "The day of atonement" (Lev. 16)
- "The year of Jubilee" (Lev. 25)
- "The scapegoat" (Lev. 16:26)
- "The promised land," which was "a land flowing with milk and honey" (Num. 13:27)
- "What hath God wrought" (Num. 23:23 KJV)
- "Sin in the camp" (Josh. 7)
- "David and Goliath" (1 Sam. 17)

- "Still small voice" (1 Kings 19:12–13)
- "Chariot of fire" (2 Kings 2:11)
- "Go in peace" (2 Kings 5:19)
- "The wheat and the chaff" (based on Ps. 1)
- "A rod of iron" (Ps. 2:9 KJV)
- "Out of the mouth of babes" (Ps. 8:2)
- "A little lower than the angels" (Ps. 8:5)
- "Beside the still waters" (Ps. 23:2)
- "The valley of the shadow of death" (Ps. 23:4)
- "My cup runneth over" (Ps. 23:5 KJV)
- "In the presence of mine enemies" (Ps. 23:5 KJV)
- "All the days of my life" (Ps. 23:6)
- "The shadow of the Almighty" (Ps. 91:1)
- "A new song" (Ps. 98:1)
- "Praise the Lord" (various places in the Bible, including Ps. 150)
- "Inherit the wind" (Prov. 11:29)
- "Spare the rod, spoil the child" (based on Prov. 13:24)
- "As a man thinketh in his heart, so is he" (based on Prov. 23:7 KJV)
- "Vanity of vanities" (Eccl. 1:2)
- "There is a time for everything under the sun" (based on Eccl. 3:1 — The well-known pop song of the 1960s "Turn, Turn, Turn" is completely based on Ecclesiastes 3:1–8.)
- "Evil under the sun" (Eccl. 6:1)
- "Cast your bread upon the waters" (Eccl. 11:1)
- "Come now, let us reason together" (Isa. 1:18)
- "They shall beat their swords into plowshares" (Isa. 2:4)[23]
- "Holy, holy, holy" (Isa. 6:3)
- "Prince of Peace" (Isa. 9:6)
- "The wolf shall dwell with the lamb . . . and a little child shall lead them" (Isa. 11:6)
- "A bruised reed" (Isa. 42:3)
- "'Peace, peace' when there is no peace" (Jer. 6:14)
- "Feet of clay" (based on Dan. 2:33)
- "The fiery furnace" (based on Dan. 3)
- "The handwriting on the wall" (based on Dan. 5)
- "In the lion's den" (based on Dan. 6)
- "The valley of decision" (Joel 3:14)
- "Tithes and offerings" (Mal. 3:8)

As we move into the New Testament, we find many more examples. Many of them come directly from our Lord:

- "A voice crying in the wilderness" (based on Matt. 3:3 and Isa. 40:3)
- "Baptism of fire" (based on Matt. 3:16 and other passages)
- "It is written" (Matt. 4:4)
- "Man does not live by bread alone" (based on Matt. 4:4)
- "Even the devil quotes Scripture" (based on Matt. 4:6)

Note how many familiar phrases come from the Sermon on the Mount:

- "The poor in spirit" (Matt. 5:3)
- "The meek shall inherit the earth" (based on Matt. 5:5)
- "Blessed are the peacemakers" (Matt. 5:9)
- "The salt of the earth" (Matt. 5:13)
- "A city on a hill" (based on Matt. 5:14)
- "Every jot and tittle" (based on Matt. 5:18)
- "Turn the other cheek" (based on Matt. 5:39)
- "Go the second mile" (based on Matt. 5:41)
- "Don't let your left hand know what your right hand is doing" (Matt. 6:3)
- "Our daily bread" (Matt. 6:11)
- "Lead us not into temptation" (Matt. 6:13 KJV)
- "No one can serve two masters" (Matt. 6:24)
- "God and mammon" (Matt. 6:24)
- "The lilies of the field" (Matt. 6:28)
- "O ye of little faith" (Matt. 6:30 KJV)
- "Do not judge or you will be judged" (based on Matt. 7:1)
- "Pearls before swine" (Matt. 7:6)
- "Seek and ye shall find" (Matt. 7:7 KJV)
- "The straight and narrow" path (based on Matt. 7:14)
- "Wolves in sheep's clothing" (based on Matt. 7:15)
- "Do unto others as you would have them do unto you" (based on Matt. 7:12)

Now, we continue beyond the Sermon on the Mount:

- "Say the word and I shall be healed" (based on Matt. 8:8)
- "Weeping and gnashing of teeth" (Matt. 8:12)
- "Arise and walk" (Matt. 9:5)
- "Your faith has made you whole" (Matt. 9:22 KJV)
- "According to your faith be it unto you" (Matt. 9:29 KJV)
- "Sheep without a shepherd" (based on Matt. 9:36)

- "Shake off the dust from your feet" (Matt. 10:14)
- "Be as wise as serpents and as innocent as doves" (Matt. 10:16)
- "Shout it from the housetops" (Matt. 10:27)
- "The very hairs of your head" (Matt. 10:30)
- To "take up your cross" (based on Matt. 10:38)
- "A house divided against itself cannot stand" (based on Matt. 12:25)[24]
- "A pearl of great price" (Matt. 13:46)
- "A prophet is without honor in his own hometown" (based on Matt. 13:57)
- To "walk on water" (based on Matt. 14:25)
- "The hem of His garment" (Matt. 14:36)
- "The blind leading the blind" (based on Matt. 15:14)
- "The signs of the times" (Matt. 16:3)
- "The gates of hell shall not prevail" (Matt. 16:18 KJV)
- "The keys of the kingdom" (Matt. 16:19)
- "Get thee behind me, Satan" (Matt. 16:23 KJV)
- "Take up your cross and follow Me" (Matt. 16:24)
- "Faith as small as a mustard seed" (based on Matt. 17:20)
- "Faith to move mountains" (based on Matt. 17:20)
- "The kings of the earth" (Matt. 17:25)
- "Suffer the little children" (Matt. 19:14 KJV)
- "With God all things are possible" (Matt. 19:26)
- "The last will be first, and the first last" (Matt. 20:16)
- "A den of thieves" (Matt. 21:13)
- "Many are called, but few are chosen" (Matt. 22:14)
- "Render therefore unto Caesar the things that are Caesar's" (Matt. 22:21 KJV)
- "Love your neighbor as yourself" (Matt. 22:39)
- "Do what they say, not what they do" (based on Matt. 23:3)
- "Blind guides" (Matt. 23:16)
- "Straining out a gnat but swallowing a camel" (based on Matt. 23:24)
- "Whitewashed tombs" (Matt. 23:27)
- "Rumors of wars" (Matt. 24:6)
- "Nation against nation," "kingdom against kingdom" (based on Matt. 24:7)
- "Well done, thou good and faithful servant" (Matt. 25:21 KJV)
- "The poor you always have with you" (based on Matt. 26:11)
- "The spirit is willing but the flesh is weak" (based on Matt. 26:41)
- "He who lives by the sword shall die by the sword" (based on Matt. 26:52)
- "Loaves and fishes" (based on Mark 6:41)

- "What will it profit a man if he gains the whole world, and loses his soul?" (Mark 8:36)
- "What therefore God hath joined together, let man not put asunder" (Mark 10:9 KJV)
- "And it came to pass" (Luke 2:1)
- "Glory to God in the highest" (Luke 2:14)
- "Peace on earth" (Luke 2:14)
- "Good Samaritan" (based on Luke 10:30–37)
- "Eat, drink, and be merry" (Luke 12:19)
- "Prodigal son" (based on Luke 15)
- "Fatted calf" (Luke 15:27)
- "Betrayed with a kiss" (based on Luke 22:48)
- "Father, forgive them; for they know not what they do" (Luke 23:34 KJV)
- "Children of God" (John 1:12)
- "Born again" (John 3:3)
- "Living water" (John 4:10)
- "Manna in the desert" (John 6:31)
- "The bread of life" (John 6:35)
- "Light of the world" (John 8:12)
- "The truth will set you free" (John 8:32 NIV)
- "Demon possessed" (based on John 8:49)
- "The good shepherd" (John 10:11)
- *"Ecce homo"* (Latin for "Behold the man"; in the NIV: "Here is the man!"; John 19:5)
- "Doubting Thomas" (based on John 20:24–29)
- "Break bread together" (based on Acts 2:46)
- "Damascus road conversion" or "Damascus road experience" (based on Paul's conversion, Acts 9)
- "It is more blessed to give than to receive" (Acts 20:35)
- "Against all hope" (Rom. 4:18 NIV)
- "The wages of sin" (Rom. 6:23)
- To be "all things to all people" (based on 1 Cor. 9:22)
- "Faith, hope, and love" (1 Cor. 13:13)
- "You reap what you sow" (based on Gal. 6:7)
- "Peace that passes all understanding" (based on Phil. 4:7)
- "A thief in the night" (1 Thess. 5:2)
- "Avoid even the appearance of evil" (based on 1 Thess. 5:22 KJV)
- "The love of money is a root of all kinds of evil" (1 Tim. 6:10)[25]
- "The widow and the orphan" (based on James 1:27 KJV)
- "The Alpha and the Omega" (Rev. 1:8)
- "The First and the Last" (Rev. 1:17)
- "The seventh seal" (Rev. 8:1)
- "King of kings and Lord of lords" (Rev. 19:16)
- "Streets of gold" (based on Rev. 21:21)

This is not to mention all sorts of common terms that come straight from the pages of God's book, such as *circumcised, uncircumcised, heaven, hell, angel, devil, demon, Satan, Lucifer, antichrist, Armageddon,* and so on. The list above demonstrates the need to understand the Bible if you really want to be literate in Western civilization. Now let's go beyond phrases; let's look at words whose origin is either directly from the Bible or its teaching.

Here are several words of either biblical or Church origin that need no explanation: *amen, angel, apocalypse, ark, babel, carol, Christian, church, evangelist, hallow, jubilee, mission, pagan, redeem, redemption, Sabbath, saint, shibboleth, testament, trinity, tutor, vicar, vigil, worship.*

Less obvious examples of words derived from the Bible and Christianity include *bedlam,* which is a contraction of Bethlehem. The Hospital of St. Mary of Bethlehem of London was established in 1247, and by the sixteenth century it was an institution for the insane. The *Dictionary of Word Origins* writes, "The word *bedlam* came to be used for any 'madhouse,' and by extension for a 'scene of noisy confusion,' in the seventeenth century."[26]

Have you ever wondered why the word *bye* is spelled the way it is? *Good-bye* means "God be with ye."[27] Again, let's hear from the *Dictionary of Word Origins:* "The expression is a contraction of *God be with you,* a form of farewell first recorded in the late sixteenth century."[28]

The word *sodomy* comes from the Judeo-Christian Scriptures. Sodom was one of two sister cities destroyed by God precisely because of what we now call sodomy (Gen. 19).

Messiah, from which we derive the term *messianic complex,* is biblical in origin. *Messiah* is a Hebrew word meaning "Anointed One." The Greek form of the word *Messiah* is *Christ. Christ* is not Jesus' last name, rather His title; Jesus Christ means "Jesus, the Messiah." Isn't it interesting that when nonbelievers use His name and title in profanity they are irreverently acknowledging that Jesus is the Messiah.

We are familiar with the Philistines in the Bible (a people found throughout the Old Testament). Today, the word *philistine* means "a person deficient in culture, and wanting in taste; a person of narrow views."[29]

There are several words related to the cross. These words include *crux, excruciating, crucial, crusade, crucifix,* and *crucible.*

The word *holiday,* often used now to secularize Christmas, also has Judeo-Christian roots. It means "holy day." "Happy holidays" means "Happy holy days." (But you better not tell that to the ACLU or Grinch-like school administrators!)

Of course, many common names come from the Bible. Think of all the names that have been derived from *Christ* alone — Christopher (Christ-bearer), Christian, Christy, Christine, and Chris. (You might see these same names spelled with a *K*. For example, coauthor Jerry Newcombe's wife, a native of Norway, has a name that means "Christian woman": Kirsti.) Think of all the people you know with such biblical names as Peter, Paul, and Mary. (Note that when Jesus gave Simon the name Peter, He was inventing the name. It didn't exist before then!) Think of all those you know named Matthew, Mark, Luke, John, James, Andrew, Timothy, Thomas, Philip, Stephen, Joseph, Rachel, Leah, Deborah, Caleb, Esther, Samuel, Daniel, Ruth, David, Joshua, Benjamin, Jonathan, and Sarah. In contrast, you never hear of anyone naming their child Judas, Baal, Lucifer, Ahab, Jezebel, Herod, or Pontius.[30] Names speak volumes about our values. At the outset of World War II, there were twenty-three Hitlers in the New York City phone book. By the end of the war, they had all changed their names or moved away! A name is very important. As Dale Carnegie once said, "A man's name is to him the sweetest and most important sound in any language."[31]

There are many less common names that come right from the pages of Scripture. In the black community, one can find many with names such as Moses, Isaiah, Ezekiel, or Hiram; in the Hispanic community, Jesus (pronounced HAY-soos) is common. The names Saul, Aaron, Reuben, and Solomon are common today, particularly among the Jews (but not exclusively). The Puritans were fond of giving their children biblical names, including Ichabod, Nathanael, and Jerusha.

In fact, did you know that until relatively recently, one's given first name (and middle name, if applicable) was known as his or her "Christian name"? That term, *Christian name,* had come about because of the widespread practice of child baptism — when the child was christened, his full name was used. Only in the last few decades have the words *Christian name* disappeared from our culture.[32]

NOAH WEBSTER

Another impact of the Bible on language, English in particular, is the person of Noah Webster. The way words are spelled in this book (and any twentieth-century book for that matter) has been directly impacted by another man of God, Noah Webster (1758–1843), famous for his Webster's dictionaries. The *Encyclopedia of American Biography* says, "Webster's American dictionary was a scholarly achievement of the first rank, winning critical acclaim at home and abroad."[33] History professor Richard J. Moss explains, "We know Webster, perhaps as well as any name from the early republic, because he wrote a dictionary."[34] He is the father of a crowning achievement in American history. And to this we owe the Bible.

Noah Webster wanted our young nation to distinguish its language from that of its progenitor, England. Harvard professor Oscar Handlin tells us, "The language of the new nation was not the same as that of England, and he would ultimately compile a dictionary to prove it."[35] Of this achievement Professor Handlin wrote, "His efforts . . . [had] the effect of standardizing the national language in written if not altogether in spoken form."[36]

Webster was a man who trusted in Christ and in the Holy Bible. There is no record that details his conversion in 1808, but Professor Moss believes that it may have been a result of associating "stability, order, and peace of mind with his childhood and his father's home in rural Connecticut."[37] In a letter written to Webster by his parents in 1782 we read these touching words: "I wish . . . you may live as to obtain the favor of Almighty God and his grace in this world and a Saving interest in the merits of Jesus Christ, without which no man can be happy."[38] Webster wrote these words about the moment he gave his life to Christ:

> My mind was suddenly arrested . . . fastened to the awakening and upon my own conduct. I closed my books, yielded to this the influence which could not be resisted or mistaken, and was led by a spontaneous impulse to repentance, prayer, and entire submission and surrender of myself to my Maker and Redeemer.[39]

It is this faith and conviction that gave birth to the *American Dictionary of the English Language* in 1828.

The Bible had much to do with Webster's codification of the American language. The essence of his theory on the genesis of language finds itself in the Bible. "For him," writes professor Moss, "language had supernatural roots."[40] Moss adds:

> The Bible stated that Adam and Eve replied to God when they asked for forgiveness for their sin, and on this evidence he [Webster] concluded that language, or at least speech, was "of divine origin" and that "all languages having sprung from one source," the original words from which they have been formed, must have been of equal antiquity.[41]

Moss then writes:

> For Webster, the multiplicity of languages on earth was also clearly explained in the Bible. The biblical Noah preserved not only animal life from the great flood, but language as well, and that language was

Chaldee. Noah's sons settled in on the plain of Shinar and spoke Chaldee until God, angered by the tower of Babel, "interposed and confounded their language, so they could not understand each other."[42]

Webster's dictionary was saturated with quotes from and references to the Bible. He used these quotes to effectively convey both the meaning of a particular word and the proper usage of it. Here are just a few of literally hundreds of examples.

- For the word *love* Webster quotes from Matthew: "Thou shalt *love* the Lord thy God with all thy heart."[43]
- For the word *follow* we can read a verse from 1 Kings, "If the Lord be God, *follow* him."[44]
- Concerning the word *rather*, a verse from Job is used: "My soul chooseth strangling and death *rather* than life."[45]

Aside from direct references to the Bible, Webster managed to squeeze in some thoughts of his own. For example, under the word *love* we find, "The christian [sic] *loves* his Bible. In short, we *love* whatever gives us pleasure and delight, whether animal or intellectual; and if our hearts are right, we *love* God above all things."[46]

The dictionary penned by Webster was a great gift to America. To this codification of our nation's language, we are in debt to the Bible. Professor Moss sums up quite well the Christian motivation that underlay Webster's achievement: "The quest for authority came to a climax when Webster found God and the idea of submission to the laws of the Bible. . . . Even his dictionaries and language theory reflected his new-found devotion to God."[47] To which Moss adds, "The dictionary that he published in 1828 was written by the light of the Bible."[48]

GEOGRAPHY

Geography has been impacted by the Bible. Look at all the names of cities in the United States. Well-known examples include Philadelphia (the city of brotherly love); Zion, Illinois; or Corpus Christi (Spanish for "the body of Christ"), Texas. Many cities throughout the country have been named after cities found in the Bible. Assorted examples include Bethesda, Maryland; Bethlehem, Pennsylvania; Lebanon, Indiana; Shiloh, Tennessee; Dothan, Alabama; and Nineveh, New York. There are also dozens of towns named Jerusalem across America. This is not to mention all the cities of California with names derived from Catholicism. These cities include Los Angeles ("the angels"), San Francisco (named after St. Francis of Assisi), and Sacramento (named after the Eucharist). Up and down the California coast, we find the names of Christian saints — Santa Barbara, San Bernardino, San Diego. There are about two dozen or so of these names. These city names reflect the fact that the state was founded by the Catholic missionary Father Junipero Serra. Christian heritage tour guide and author Catherine Millard writes:

> Junipero Serra, "The Apostle to California," as he is called, president of the Franciscans for many years, and the first person to bring the good news of salvation to the West Coast of America, was a giant among men, indeed. He founded nine missionary outposts, all of which later became major West Coast cities. They range over a 555-mile stretch from San Diego in the south to San Francisco in the north, and between them are San Juan Capistrano, San Gabriel, San Carlos, San Luis Obispo, Santa Clara, Santa Barbara, and Carmel. Although small in stature, he was great and godly in his life, work and outreach, bringing many Indians to the saving knowledge of our Lord and Savior Jesus Christ.[49]

Cities are not the only geographical entities affected by the Bible. The flags of many countries contain the cross of Jesus Christ, or its derivative. The Scandinavian flags (Norway, Sweden, Finland, Denmark, Greenland, and Iceland) directly bear the cross of Jesus Christ. When these flags are hung from the top down, the cross shows forth in all its glory. The cross of St. George (a derivation of the cross of Christ) is the focus of the British flag, and the same cross is found in the flags of Australia, New Zealand, and Fiji. Other countries with flags that contain the cross in one way or another include Greece, Dominica, the Dominican Republic, and Switzerland.

LEISURE AND RECREATION

When we think of leisure and recreation, the Bible doesn't usually leap to mind. Yet basketball was created by a Christian as a game for helping inner-city children at the YMCA in Springfield, Massachusetts, in 1891 by Dr. James Naismith. The game was born at a time when the "Y" was thoroughly evangelical. In fact, YMCA stands for "Young Men's Christian Association." The YMCA was "an organized body of young men determined to win their fellows to a saving faith in Christ."[50] Bible studies were then a regular part of the YMCA's program; they still are in some, but not most, of its chapters. Jess Stein writes that basketball is "the only major sport completely American in origin."[51] Basketball is one of the most-watched games in our country, and it began with a man who sought to expose young people to the Bible.

Organized camping was also given birth by the YMCA in the nineteenth century.[52] Perhaps this is why singing "Kum-ba-yah" and other Christian songs around the campfire is still a fairly common practice.

Another way the Bible has profoundly influenced our culture is in the area of retail and sales. What is the most profitable time of the year for most retailers? Christmastime! The wise men—or the "Magi" as the Bible calls them—brought gifts to Jesus when He was a child, and Christians have been giving gifts ever since. Although Christmas is so commercial these days and the original meaning is often crowded out, shoppers are nonetheless paying indirect homage to the Bible. Personally, I wouldn't be surprised if I found out that all the merchants got together on December 26, held hands, and sang, "What a Friend We Have in Jesus"!

Carnival derives its name from the Church. The *Dictionary of Word Origins* states: "Etymologically, *carnival* means 'raising flesh'—that is, the 'removal of meat' from the diet during Lent."[53] The word and the celebration before the Lenten fast come from Christian origins. Shrove Tuesday, the day before Ash Wednesday, is the day to "pig out" before the long fast of Lent—a fast based on the forty days of fasting Jesus suffered in the desert. Thus, this is the origin of Mardi Gras!

The Bible has had a profound impact on art and music.[54] Here is an observation from an unlikely source—Charlie Chaplin, one of the alltime great artists in the realm of the motion picture. Chaplin—who gave the world such classics as *The Kid, City Lights, Modern Times,* and *The Great Dictator* (his outstanding spoof of Adolf Hitler)—created a universally beloved character, "the tramp." One night, when he was a child, his mother told him the gospel story. He was captivated by what she said. Chaplin writes that "she gave the most luminous and appealing interpretation of Christ that I ever heard or seen."[55] Chaplin then recounts the various aspects of Christ's life that she revealed to him. He concludes:

> Mother had so carried me away that I wanted to die that very night and meet Jesus. But Mother was not so enthusiastic. "Jesus wants you to live first and fulfill your destiny here," she said. In that dark room in the basement at Oakley Street, Mother illuminated to me the kindliest light this world has ever known, which has endowed literature and the theatre with their greatest and richest themes: love, pity, and humanity.[56]

Although there's evidence that would imply Chaplin was not a Christian, this quote in and of itself shows the impact of Christ and the Bible on the world, including the arts.

Even some superstitious beliefs have been derived from the Bible (not that the Bible in any way encourages superstition; in fact, it condemns it). The superstition surrounding the unlucky number 13 has its origin with Christianity. Jesus and the twelve apostles comprised thirteen people, until Judas Iscariot who betrayed Christ killed himself. Judas was number 13, and 13 has been viewed as unlucky ever since.

So too is the occult influenced by the Bible. Occultists reject the Bible, and repeatedly desecrate all that is holy to Christians. Satanists have the cross upside down. They hold the "black mass." They use a chalice, in direct mockery of Christianity. The Antichrist, 666, and the beast of Revelation are exalted by many involved in the darker aspects of the occult. Much of rock music, especially heavy metal, is filled with anti-Christian references.[57]

Many people are seeking divine guidance in all the wrong places! Tarot cards, Ouija boards, psychics, and horoscopes should all be avoided like the plague. They are Satan's counterfeits to the divine guidance available to us in God's Word. The existence of these counterfeits points to the existence of the genuine. Thus, we see that the Bible has profoundly influenced our culture, even indirectly!

SELF-HELP

If you flip through catalogs of motivational tapes, you are inundated with New Age thoughts and images. Yet, the essence of so many self-help programs is to get the listener/viewer/seminar attendee to redirect their thinking, to renew their minds. The Bible took this approach centuries ago! Solomon said, "As [a man] thinketh in his heart, so is he" (Prov. 23:7 KJV). Paul talks about the need for us to "renew our minds" through the Holy Spirit (Rom. 12:2). Paul lays the framework for any real self-help program by telling us to forget the things that are past and to strive toward the goal (Phil. 3:13–14). Zig Ziglar acknowledges the biblical source of this profound thought. Ziglar, a master motivator and evangelical Christian, writes:

> An exciting new field of psychology has been developed which doesn't dig up all the old garbage of the past. It doesn't "saw sawdust" by harping on the problems of the past. Instead, it deals with the hope of the future. . . . Actually, this still puts man 2,000 years behind the advice the Apostle Paul gave us in the Holy Bible when he said,

"Forgetting those things which lie in the past I press forward toward the mark."[58]

Millions of people today have found themselves in the grip of addictions that they can't control. These addictions include alcoholism, drug addiction, gambling, and even the problem of overeating. But to help people come out of these addictions, self-help groups have popped up in all these areas—Alcoholics Anonymous, Narcotics Anonymous, Gamblers Anonymous, and Overeaters Anonymous. The grandfather of all these clubs is Alcoholics Anonymous, which began in a church in New York City. These programs are not directly Christian. For some Christians the 12-step formula is objectionable, since people can choose whatever "Higher Power" they wish, in violation of God's first and second commandments. On the other hand—and this is an important point—for many people, 12-step programs have proven to be a gateway for nonbelievers to end up in church. In any event, many are getting help for their addictions through these programs. And for that, we are grateful. I'm also aware of some Christian groups that use the 12-step approach and apply it in a directly Christian context.

Psychologist Jeffrey Satinover points out how the Christian view of sin is inscribed in part of AA's teaching:

> The first three steps in AA are:
> 1. We admitted that we were powerless over alcohol—that our lives had become unmanageable.
> 2. Came to believe that a Power greater than ourselves could restore us to sanity.
> 3. Made a decision to turn our will and our lives over to the care of God as we understood him.
> Replace the word "alcohol" above with the word "sin" and we have the essence of the Judeo-Christian view of man.[59]

Recently, it was reported that AA has become less effective because it's become increasingly secularized. Ann Rodgers-Melnick, writing for the *Pittsburgh Post-Gazette*, states:

> Alcoholics Anonymous and other 12-step recovery programs are losing effectiveness because they have slipped from their spiritual moorings, say disciples of the Episcopal priest on whose principles the 12 steps are reportedly based. . . . While the 12 steps have never been explicitly Christian, they are based on biblical principles. The ideas of sin, soul searching, repentance, forgiveness and good works contained in the 12 steps are common to most faiths.

But the steps assume a personal, powerful God outside oneself. In fact, the first premise of the 12 steps is the very Christian notion that human nature is so flawed that people cannot overcome their worst problems without help from a higher power.

"It was assumed in the beginning that the higher power was God," said the Rev. David Else, director of the Center for Spirituality in 12-Step Recovery in Pittsburgh and an Episcopal priest.

AA's basic text, the Big Book, has two references to the higher power but about 200 references to God, he said. "Bill Wilson felt that Bible study was a normal outcome of AA."[60]

Even with this increasing secularization of AA and its consequent reduction in effectiveness, think of the millions of people who have been freed from the scourge of alcoholism through AA; many of them have called upon Jesus Christ as their "Higher Power." Again, I'm not saying that all of the Anonymous groups and all that they teach are consistent with the Word of God. But I am saying that were it not for the Bible, such groups would never have existed.

Another example of the Bible helping to directly or indirectly give birth to self-help programs is in the case of Toastmasters International, a network of public speaking clubs. Hundreds of thousands of people through the years have profited (and still profit) from attending Toastmasters to develop poise and experience at the lectern. This worldwide organization was founded in a YMCA in the 1920s by Ralph Smedley. Smedley was the educational director of the "Y" in the Bloomington, Illinois, area. *The Toastmaster* magazine writes:

> Realizing that the older high school boys at the YMCA needed training in communication, he formed a weekly club in which members took turns making short speeches, evaluating them and presiding at the meetings. The group became "The Toastmasters Club," mainly because the meeting resembled banquets with toasts and after-dinner speakers.[61]

Now, more than seven decades later, Toastmasters has some eight thousand clubs worldwide and 170,000 members.[62] And it all began in a Christian organization that was dedicated to the spread of the Bible.

Some time-management writers have made the point that one of the first known instances of delegation comes from the pages of Holy Writ. In Exodus 18, Moses' father-in-law, Jethro, visits and observes Moses in action as the chief judge in Israel. But Moses was growing weary dealing with a variety of petty grievances. So Jethro suggests that Moses appoint other trustworthy men to deal with the lower cases. Meanwhile,

Moses would deal with the more difficult cases that worked their way from the "lower courts." Thus, Moses became, in a sense, the chief justice of the Supreme Court and not the only judge in the land. (In one sense, Moses simultaneously served as president, Speaker of the House, and chief justice of the Supreme Court!) Jethro's timeless advice to Moses to delegate is worthy of the busiest executive, whatever the endeavor. As Ted Engstrom and R. Alec MacKenzie write in *Managing Your Time:*

> The Bible has been quoted in numerous instances for its demonstration of management principles. One of the most outstanding examples is the instruction of Moses by Jethro some fifteen hundred years before the birth of Christ (Exodus 18:13–27).[63]

The Bible talks about redeeming the time, for the days are evil (Eph. 5:16). Through the centuries, the chimes of Christendom rang out a prayer. Note that we often hear this very melody on many American college campuses today. The bells are ringing out this prayer (known as the Westminster Chimes):

> Lord, through this hour, be Thou our guide,
> So by Thy power, no foot shall slide.[64]

Visit many a college campus in this country and you'll hear this melody playing most every hour. And to think, it's a Christian prayer!

A ONCE-GREAT CULTURE

Many aspects of our everyday lives have been positively impacted by the Bible. In some respects, today's Christian may well feel like an archaeologist digging around at what once was a great civilization. Our civilization has suffered from the influence of the modern barbarians who have overrun our educational system and taken over our cultural institutions. We feel like strangers in a strange land, even though it was the Bible that shaped our nation, our culture, and our institutions from the start. However, there is still much good that remains. What we need is national renewal. What we need as a culture is to get back to the Bible!

PART 2

HOW I KNOW
THE BIBLE
IS THE WORD
OF GOD

CHAPTER 12

THE RELIABILITY
OF THE BIBLE

*"All Scripture is given by inspiration of God, and is profitable for
doctrine, for reproof, for correction, for instruction in righteousness."*
—2 Timothy 3:16

The well-known children's hymn declares: "Jesus loves me, this I
know, for the Bible tells me so." But with all the doubts cast on the Word
of God by the critics of the Bible in the last two centuries or so, we might
sing, "Jesus loves me? I don't know. I wish someone could tell me so!"
Well, God Himself has told us so in a multitude of ways. In this chapter we will take a glimpse at some of the things we know about the Judeo-
Christian Scriptures that make their divine origin clear.

CAN WE TRUST THE BIBLE?

In today's world, whom can you trust? Stockbrokers don't always
pick winners. Doctors make mistakes. Psychiatrists sometimes can't get
to the root of a problem. Fortune-tellers are virtually never reliable (nor
should anyone ever go see one). So whose word is good? Doesn't everything contain an element of *risk* and an element of *reliability*?

What about the Bible? Can we trust it? Unfortunately, there is a host
of "authorities" in our culture today who say we *cannot* trust it. They
write books, they hold seminars, they appear on talk shows, their work
is given cover stories in major news magazines. These "Bible scholars"
denigrate the Scriptures in a variety of ways. A prominent example is
John Shelby Spong, an Episcopal bishop. Spong has even written a book
about the Bible, *Rescuing the Bible from Fundamentalism*. Spong says
that the Bible itself makes the case against taking the text literally. Bishop
Spong denies the virgin birth; he denies that Jesus rose from the dead
bodily. In his opinion, such antiquated beliefs retard progress in the

Church! Thus, the Bible is in danger, and Spong is a savior intending on rescuing it! He says:

> I could not believe that anyone who had read this book would be so foolish as to proclaim that the Bible in every literal word was the divinely inspired, inerrant word of God. Yet the claim continued to be made and continues to this day. Have these people simply not read the text? Are they hopelessly uninformed? Is there a different Bible? Are they blinded by a combination of ego needs and naivete?[1]

I've read the Bible many times. I've read it in the original languages. I've translated portions from the original Hebrew and Greek. In fact, I believe that serious study of the Scriptures shows an amazing text—a text not easily dismissed by a sneering modern cleric. The Bible contains many evidences, internal and external, that argue very much for its authenticity as the very Word of God. No, I couldn't disagree more with the likes of Bishop Spong—the Bible doesn't need to be "rescued" from fundamentalism. And it can certainly withstand attacks from modern unbelievers.[2] This bishop is not alone. There are many seminary professors who really don't believe the Bible is the Word of God, and they are spewing their unbelief to a new generation of students.

Another example of critics attempting to disprove the Bible's reliability is the Jesus Seminar. This group of "Bible scholars" (one of whom is a Hollywood producer, the creator of *Robocop*) sits in judgment on the sayings of Jesus, casting grave doubts on most of what He said.[3] In fact, they assert that Jesus said only 18 percent of the words attributed to Him! They don't make these judgments based on the text itself or historical criticism. They make them based on their own anti-supernatural prejudices. Of the Lord's Prayer, the only phrase that survived their criticism was "Our Father"![4] They wrote a book titled *The Five Gospels*[5] because they give the "Gospel of Thomas," which has never been recognized by the Church as part of Scripture, the same authority as Matthew, Mark, Luke, and John.[6]

What should you think of such "Bible scholars"? One of my seminary professors, Dr. William Childs Robinson, said that you *choose* your scholars. There are scholars that say everything! The scholars you choose to believe will determine your conclusion. This principle is worth saying again and emphasizing: *You choose your scholars. There are scholars that say everything. The scholars you believe will determine your conclusion.* Some liberal Bible scholars deny some or many tenets of the faith, yet there are just as many—perhaps more—scholars who hold to a much more conservative position. For instance, there is a much larger group of biblical scholars than those seventy-four or so of the Jesus Seminar who believe Jesus said everything attributed to Him in the four Gospels. But those conservative scholars are not going to make the cover of the news magazines. There is an obvious anti-Christian bias in the media. In fact, major portions of one of our previous books reveal this—*The Gates of Hell Shall Not Prevail*.[7] But apart from any type of numerical comparison of the types of scholars (believing vs. unbelieving), I think that any honest, open-minded person who looks into the type of evidence that I will explore momentarily will conclude that the Bible is indeed the very Word of God.

IS THE BIBLE THE WORD OF GOD?

We know the Bible is God's Word because God Himself says so. Beginning with Moses and the Ten Commandments, He spoke to all the Old Testament prophets and commanded them to write down His Words. "Thus saith the Lord" or "God spake these words" appears over two thousand times in the Old Testament. In the book of Exodus, with forty chapters, "God spake all these words" appears 160 times. Moses closed his ministry with this command to the children of Israel:

Set your hearts on all the words which I testify among you today, which you shall command your children to be careful to observe—all the words of this law. For it is not a futile thing for you, because it is your life, and by this word you shall prolong your days in the land which you cross over the Jordan to possess. (Deut. 32:46–47)

Proverbs 30:5 tells us: "Every word of God is pure; He is a shield to those who put their trust in Him."

JESUS AND THE BIBLE

Jesus believed the Scriptures to be the Word of God. When the devil came to tempt Him to abandon His mission and to seek personal power and glory, Jesus quoted Scripture (Matt. 4:1–10). One passage He quoted speaks directly about His total reliance upon Scripture: "Man shall not live by bread alone, but by every word that proceeds from the mouth of God" (v. 4). After He rose from the dead, Jesus confirmed that Moses was the writer of the first books of the Law, and that the prophets spoke for God. "And beginning at Moses and all the Prophets, He expounded to them in all the Scriptures the things concerning Himself" (Luke 24:27).

In John 10:35, Jesus declared that "the Scripture cannot be broken." In Luke 16:17, He stated, "It is easier for heaven and earth to pass away than for one tittle of the law to fail."

Jesus believed every word of the Old Testament, even the miracles. In Luke 17:29, He talked about the supernatural judgment on Sodom and Gomorrah, when Lot's wife was turned into a pillar of salt. In John 6:32, He spoke of the miracle of the manna from heaven, which fed the Israelites for forty years in the wilderness. In John 3:14 he recalled how those who had been bitten by snakes were cured instantly when they looked on Moses' brass serpent. In Matthew 12:39–40, He likened His death and resurrection to the miracle of Jonah being swallowed by a big fish for three days.

Theologian and author John R. W. Stott says Jesus' view of Scripture is the ultimate apologetic for its veracity. He writes:

> The overriding reason for accepting the divine inspiration and authority of Scripture is plain loyalty to Jesus. . . . If Jesus endorsed the Old Testament, setting upon it the stamp of his own approval, he also foresaw the writing of the Scriptures of the New Testament, parallel to the Scriptures of the Old Testament. Indeed, he not only foresaw it, he actually intended it, and he deliberately made provision for it by appointing and authorizing his apostles.[8]

Stott's argument is not circular, but linear.[9] He begins by assuming nothing. As he reads the historical, first-century, eyewitness accounts of Jesus, he sees that Jesus held the Old Testament to be the Word of God, and that He clearly predicted and made provision for the New Testament.

THE APOSTLES AND THE SCRIPTURES

The apostles also proclaimed their belief in Scripture. Paul described the Scriptures as the "oracles of God" (Rom. 3:2). Hebrews 4:12 speaks of Scripture as a powerful weapon: "For the word of God is living and powerful, and sharper than any two-edged sword, piercing even to the division of soul and spirit, and of joints and marrow, and is a discerner of the thoughts and intents of the heart." Writing to Timothy, Paul gave the clearest and most comprehensive definition of Scripture found in the Bible: "All Scripture is given by inspiration of God [meaning it is "God-breathed"], and is profitable for doctrine, for reproof, for correction, for instruction in righteousness, that the man of God may be complete, thoroughly equipped for every good work" (2 Tim. 3:16–17).

The early Church held the apostles in such high esteem that no book found its way into the canon of Scripture unless it was penned by an apostle (including Paul, who was called late in the process) or was the direct by-product of an apostle's input (such as Mark, which is widely believed to have received tremendous input from Peter). In A.D. 200 or thereabout, the North African Christian Tertullian wrote, "We Christians are forbidden to introduce anything on our own authority, or to choose what someone else introduces on his own authority. Our authorities are the Lord's apostles, and they in their turn choose to introduce nothing on their own authority. They faithfully passed on to the nations the teaching which they had received from Christ."[10]

THE BIBLE'S FULFILLED PROPHECIES

In Deuteronomy 18:22, God tells us how we may know if a prophet is sent from Him: "When a prophet speaks in the name of the LORD, if the thing does not happen or come to pass, that is the thing which the LORD has not spoken; the prophet has spoken it presumptuously; you shall not be afraid of him."

The Scriptures are unique in that in the Old Testament alone, there are over two thousand prophecies that have already come to pass. You will look in vain for anything as reliable as this in the world. If we consider all the other religions of the world, there are twenty-six books that the followers of these religions claim to be divinely inspired—the books themselves make no such claim—and the books contain no specific prophecies.

Of the more than two thousand prophecies found in the Bible, 333 deal with the coming of the Messiah. There is no other individual in the history of mankind whose entire life has been so prophetically and predictively detailed.

Frederich Meldau points out that as few as five simple points of identification can single out any individual from all of the nearly six billion other people that live on this planet, and yet with Christ we have 333 points of identification! For example, suppose your name is Lester B. Smith and somewhere in the world an envelope with that name and the address 4143 W. Madison Avenue, Chicago, Illinois, U.S.A., is mailed. It doesn't matter in what country that letter is mailed, it will ultimately come to you because it has the five key points of identification: the country, the state, the city, the street, and your name.

The 333 prophecies concerning Jesus Christ give us the exact date when He would come into the world (Dan. 9); the exact place: Bethlehem Ephrathah (Mic. 5:2); that He would be born of a virgin (Isa. 7:14). Furthermore, they set forth many of the details of His ministry: His character, His betrayal for thirty pieces of silver, His crucifixion, the piercing of His hands and His feet, His burial in the grave of a rich man, His resurrection from the dead, His ascension into heaven, His proclamation to the Gentiles, and scores of other particulars.

Lee Strobel, a former skeptic, likes to say that the Old Testament gives us a thumbprint: "It says when you find the person that fits this thumbprint, that's the Messiah. That's the Son of God, and throughout history, only Jesus Christ has had that thumbprint."[11] Strobel—who earned a law degree at Yale—used to be an award-winning legal affairs journalist for the *Chicago Tribune* until he was confronted with the claims of Christ. He decided to apply all of his journalistic skills toward Christianity so that he could show how historically incorrect it was. But the skeptic became a believer when he studied the facts.

As Strobel studied the prophecies that Jesus fulfilled, he found they weren't easily dismissed. He writes, "The more I studied them, the more difficulty I had in trying to explain them away."[12] As he looked at the odds of any one person fulfilling these prophecies, he was stunned at the scientific evidence that Jesus was the Messiah. Strobel was shocked by the work of mathematician Peter Stoner,[13] who proved that the chance of any one person fulfilling even eight of these Old Testament prophecies was one in 10^{17}—that's 1 with seventeen zeroes after it! Strobel began to grapple with the implications of those formidable odds:

> To try to comprehend that enormous number, I did some calculations. I imagined the entire world being covered with white tile that was one-and-a-half inches square—every bit of dry land on the planet—with the bottom of just one tile painted red.
>
> Then I pictured a person being allowed to wander for a lifetime around all seven continents. He would be permitted to bend down only one time and pick up a single piece of tile. What are the odds it would be the one tile whose reverse side was painted red? The odds would be the same as just eight of the Old Testament prophecies coming true in any one person throughout history![14]

If that didn't boggle Strobel's mind enough, Stoner demonstrated that the chances of anyone fulfilling forty-eight prophecies were 10^{157}![15] Strobel realized the incredible implications of that as well. It would be like finding "a single predetermined atom among all the atoms in a *trillion*

trillion trillion trillion billion universes the size of our universe!"[16] Lee Strobel finally did the intellectually honest thing—he recognized Jesus as the Messiah. Today he serves as a pastor of the popular Willow Creek Community Church in the suburbs of Chicago.

That Jesus of Nazareth fulfilled the messianic prophecies provides compelling evidence for the divine inspiration of the holy Scriptures. The other 1,700 or so prophecies of the Old Testament deal mostly with the cities and nations that were in or near the land of Israel. Their future is outlined in those prophecies. The major emphasis of Scripture itself is on those thousands of specific prophecies.

THE BIBLE'S INDESTRUCTIBILITY

The indestructibility of Scripture is another proof that it is divinely inspired. For 2,600 years all the powers of this world have combined to destroy this book and yet it still remains.

One person has said the indestructibility of the Bible is like the Irishman's wall. One Irishman built a wall four feet high and five feet thick around his farm. Someone asked him why he made it so thick. He replied, "If anyone knocks it over, it will be higher than it was before." Now this does not prove the Bible was written by an Irishman (as sad as that may seem for a Kennedy) but it does show the remarkable hand of God.[17]

King Manassah of Judah, born in 697 B.C., was such a violent, ungodly pagan man that he was determined to destroy all the copies of the Mosaic Law because they denounced the sins he was guilty of—all manner of abominations, even the sacrifice of children to the pagan god Molech. He destroyed all of the copies of the books of Moses—except the one copy hidden in the wall of the temple.

Twenty years after his death, his grandson Josiah ascended to the throne. He discovered that copy of the Law, which had almost been forgotten. He proclaimed that all of Israel should gather together to hear the reading of the Law of God. The result was a tremendous revival among the Israelites.[18]

During the period between Malachi and Matthew, Antiochus Epiphanes, the wicked Syrian tyrant, conquered Israel. He offered a pig on the altar of the temple, and murdered all of those who owned a copy of Scripture. His actions led to the Maccabean revolt. No sooner was Antiochus in his grave than there was a great revival of interest in the Scripture and numerous copies were made. The annual celebration of Hanukkah commemorates the successful revolt of the Maccabees over the Syrians.

In A.D. 303, Emperor Diocletian, one of the last great persecutors of the Church, saw that the Bible was the source of courage for Christians who opposed his paganism. He ordered the confiscation of all Christian property and the destruction and burning of all Scriptures. Only ten years passed before Diocletian was dead and Constantine the Great had risen in his stead to sit upon the throne of Rome. He professed to trust in Christ as his Savior. He ordered the writing of many copies of the Scripture, and encouraged everyone in the Roman Empire to read the Bible!

In the Middle Ages, sometimes even the clergy placed the Bible on a list of banned books. The Synod of Toulouse forbade anyone to possess a copy of the Scriptures. Men such as John Tyndale, who tried to translate it into the vernacular of the people, were burned alive. John Huss, who proclaimed that the Bible was the final authority, was burned alive. John Wycliffe, who translated the Scripture into English, couldn't be burned because he died too soon; but his bones were exhumed and burned and his ashes scattered into the river.

Mary, queen of England, also known as Bloody Mary, ordered that anyone possessing a copy of the Bible would be burned. Five years after her edict, she was dead. Queen Elizabeth I ascended to the throne of England. During her time as queen, she ordered no less than 130 editions of the Bible to be published.

ARCHAEOLOGY
CONFIRMS INSPIRATION

One of the wonders of our time is the confirmation of Scripture by archaeology. For the last 150 years, archaeologists have excavated thousands of sites in the Near East, many times working with great animosity toward Scripture, attempting to disprove it. Yet every time they turned over their spades, they discovered another confirmation of the Bible.

Let's look at one example, the list of kings. The Old Testament lists all the kings of Israel and Judah, and additionally mentions forty-seven other kings in the Gentile world of Egypt, or Babylon, or Syria, or Greece—such countries as these. Not a single history book mentioned even one of them. But when the archaeologists began to dig, they found the names of every one of those forty-seven kings exactly in the places that the Bible said they had reigned.

A major best-selling book (with more than ten million copies in print) appeared several decades ago, which made known the fact that the Bible was right after all. The book was by a German, Werner Keller, and it was titled *The Bible as History*. The writer spent an exhaustive amount of time poring through the various archaeological finds related to the Scriptures. He sifted through material hitherto seen only by archaeologists. As he did his research, he saw over and over that the Bible was right! Keller writes:

> In view of the overwhelming mass of authentic and well-attested evidence now available, as I thought of the skeptical criticism which from the eighteenth century onward would fain have demolished the Bible altogether, there kept hammering in my brain this one sentence: "The Bible is right after all."[19]

Every once in a while, we'll hear about some archaeological finding that opposes the Bible. But give it time. The Scriptures will be vindicated. Nelson Glueck, a famous archaeologist, said it can be categorically stated that not one single archaeological discovery has ever controverted a biblical text.[20] The more we learn about the people and the times that the Bible describes, the more we see how accurate it is. Now, I'm not saying that archaeology *proves* the Bible—that it could never do—but I am saying archaeology *confirms* the Bible.

HAS THE BIBLE CHANGED?

The Bible, in particular the New Testament, is *the* most reputable book of antiquity. When writing was first done on scrolls, the copies deteriorated with time. However, a copy was made from the original scroll. When we compare the reliability of those copies and the earliest appearance, we see the New Testament stands alone among the books of antiquity. Dr. Ravi Zacharias says, "If you compare any other literature from that time . . . the writings of Caesar, the writings of Homer . . . there is nothing that stacks up to the original dating and the nearest extant copies."[21] Indeed, the number of manuscript copies weighs heavily in favor of the New Testament. For example, we have ten copies of *Caesar's Gallic Wars*, seven copies of Plato's *Tetralogies*, and 643 copies of Homer's *Iliad*. Yet we have 5,366 copies of ancient Greek New Testament manuscripts! Furthermore, the New Testament is *far* superior to other ancient writings when it comes to the time lapse between the original manuscript (or autographa) and the earliest extant copy. For example, *Caesar's Gallic Wars* dates back to circa 60 B.C., yet the earliest extant copy is from A.D. 900, a span of nearly one thousand years. Plato's *Tetralogies* dates back to circa 400 B.C., but the earliest manuscript copy known is from A.D. 900, a span of roughly 1,300 years. And Homer's *Iliad* was written circa 900 B.C. The earliest manuscript copy is from 400 B.C., five hundred years later. In contrast, while the New Testament was written during the first century, no later than A.D. 100, the earliest known manuscript that contains most of the New Testament dates to A.D. 200, and there are fragments dating back as early as A.D. 125, hence, a gap of only twenty-five years![22] Sir Frederic Kenyon, a great scholar and author of *The Bible and Archaeology*, sums up the significance of this evidence:

> The interval then between the dates of original composition and the earliest extant evidence becomes so small as to be in fact negligible, and the last foundation for any doubt that the Scriptures have come down to us substantially as they were written has now been removed. Both the *authenticity* and the *general integrity* of the books of the New Testament may be regarded as finally established.[23]

As in the example of archaeology, this reliability does not prove the divine nature of the Bible, but it does confirm it. Evidence is also abundant for the authenticity of the Old Testament, as we'll see shortly.

Over time, the Bible has become the most widely published book in the world. Since it has been translated and retranslated so many times, some people question if it is the same book: Does it match the ancient manuscripts? This question was completely settled with a resounding yes when the Dead Sea Scrolls were discovered in 1947. The story of how this discovery was made is absolutely fascinating.

In the winter of 1947, outside the community of Qumran near the Dead Sea, some Bedouin shepherds were tending their flocks. One shepherd was throwing rocks at the cliffs, which contained caves. His rock sailed into an opening and he heard the sound of an earthen jar shattering. Another shepherd lowered himself into the cave and found ten tall jars lining the walls. In two of the jars, they found three manuscripts and decided to sell them to an antiquities dealer in Bethlehem. They did some more searching and found another cave with five more scrolls, which they sold to another dealer in Bethlehem. These scrolls contained the complete book of Isaiah, a commentary on Habakkuk, the Genesis Apocryphon (an Aramaic paraphrase of Genesis), and two scrolls making up a manual of discipline used by an ancient religious community.

During Holy Week of 1947, St. Mark's Syrian Orthodox Monastery in Bethlehem bought the scrolls. One year later, a monk who was trying to catalog all of the monastery's rare books came across them and could not figure out what they were, so he asked for help. That is when the world found out about them.

Soon archaeologists got into the picture. Several hundred caves were explored, and eleven of them contained manuscripts. The most exciting discovery was a cave that contained forty thousand fragments of four hundred different manuscripts, one hundred of which were biblical. Every book of the Old Testament except Esther was represented.

Scholars determined that the manuscripts dated back to between 200 B.C. and A.D. 200, making them the oldest in the world. When scholars compared the manuscripts they had been using (which dated from the eighth century) with the Dead Sea Scrolls, they were almost an exact match, meaning that the inspired Word of God has been faithfully preserved and transmitted through the ages to this present day!

All the implications of the Dead Sea Scrolls have not been fully unraveled, but these finds definitely show the incredible accuracy of the Old Testament. In his book *Secrets of the Dead Sea Scrolls,* Dr. Randall Price points out:

> Before the Dead Sea Scrolls were found, the biblical text of the Old Testament was known only from a text dating to the Middle Ages. The earliest known complete Hebrew manuscript of the Old Testament was the Ben Asher Codex . . . dating to about A.D. 1008, which was still more than 1,000 years removed from the last book composed by an Old Testament writer (circa 325 B.C.). . . . This left us with nagging questions about the integrity and reliability of the traditional text of the Old Testament (the Masoretic Text). These doubts were settled forever with one of the first Scrolls discovered, which was a copy of the entire book of Isaiah (later fragments representing another 21 copies were found). . . . Once a comparison was made between the text of *Isaiah Scroll* and the Masoretic Text, it was evident that, except for minor details (such as spelling) that do not affect the meaning of the text, the two were almost identical.[24]

Thus, God has preserved His Word down through the centuries.

THE LIVING PROOF OF INSPIRATION

The ultimate proof of divine inspiration is in the human heart. When the Holy Spirit takes up residence there, people know the Bible is indeed the living Word of God. I don't know of a single atheist who would even claim to have been improved as a human being by their atheism. But I know of millions of Christians who claim that their lives have been greatly improved by the Bible. Dennis Praeger, a Jewish radio talk show host, once made a brilliant point about the transforming power of the Bible in people's lives. In a debate with a skeptic, he described this scenario (summarized here by Ravi Zacharias):

> If you were stranded on a street alone at night, your car had broken down, say at 2:00 A.M. on a lonely street in Los Angeles . . . pitch black darkness, and you get out of your car and suddenly, you see ten big burley men coming out of a house and walking toward you, would it or would it not be comforting for you if you knew they were just coming out of a Bible study?[25]

What a brilliant point, and so true to life!

Many years ago there was a young man who became converted after a profligate life. He had shown no interest in the things of the Lord and even had a Christian friend who never opened his mouth about the gospel because he wrote that man off as too worldly to be converted. I was the young man who had been written off as beyond the grace of God! But as I invited Christ to come into my life when I heard the Word of His glorious grace, He changed my life and transformed me from the inside out. A person who had no interest in the Scriptures, I was suddenly hungry for all I could get. Down through the centuries, hundreds of millions of people can attest the same thing — people saved from a variety of backgrounds and all manner of evil.

THE BIBLE TELLS ME SO

God's Word is 100 percent inspired, reliable, and unchanging. We can count on it at all times. If we follow it, we will not be disappointed, defrauded, or destroyed. And so we can say with confidence:

> Jesus loves me, this I know.
> For the Bible tells me so.

I close with what the Bible says about itself. These words come from Peter's second epistle. He's writing about prophecy, but what he says here applies to the whole Bible:

> Above all, you must understand that no prophecy of Scripture came about by the prophet's own interpretation. For prophecy never had its origin in the will of man, but men spoke from God as they were carried along by the Holy Spirit. (2 Peter 1:20–21 NIV)

CHAPTER 13

THE CENTRAL MESSAGE OF THE BIBLE

"For God so loved the world that He gave His only begotten Son, that whoever believes in Him should not perish but have everlasting life."
—John 3:16

The Bible was written between 1500 B.C. and A.D. 90. A golden thread runs throughout it, in spite of the differences in culture and time among the men who penned it. The unity of the Bible from Genesis to Revelation is a strong witness to the inspiration of the Holy Spirit.

The message of the Bible is creation, fall, and redemption. Our heavenly Father created a sinless world, where the first two people lived in freedom and joy. The Fall introduced sin, and death followed. But God reached down to a rebellious world, and restored a portion of humanity to Himself through the sacrifice of His Son.

THE BIBLE IN ONE VERSE

Through modern technology, man has been able to reproduce the entire Bible in a small square of microfiche. Yet in a very real way, the Scriptures have already been reduced to miniature form in John 3:16, perhaps the best known verse of the Bible: "For God so loved the world that He gave His only begotten Son, that whoever believes in Him should not perish but have everlasting life." That one sentence summarizes the central message of the Bible.

JESUS CHRIST—THE CENTRAL FIGURE OF THE BIBLE

In the central message there is a central figure—Jesus Christ! The whole Scripture is the Word of God, but Jesus is the personification of God. The apostle John explains it like this: "In the beginning was the Word, and the Word was with God, and the Word was God. . . . The Word became flesh and made his dwelling among us" (John 1:1, 14 NIV).

Jesus is more than the central figure of the Bible: He's the central figure of all time. Charles Spurgeon once said this:

> Christ is the central fact in the world's history. To him everything looks forward or backward. All the lines of history converge upon him. All the great purposes of God culminate in him. The greatest and most momentous fact which the history of the world records is the fact of his birth.[1]

The purpose of searching the Bible is to find the Lord revealed in its pages. C. S. Lewis writes: "It is Christ Himself, not the Bible who is the true word of God. The Bible, read in the right spirit and with the guidance of good teachers, will bring us to Him."[2] When Jesus encountered the religious leaders of His time, they didn't recognize Him as their Messiah; they were blind to His true identity. He rebuked them, saying: "You diligently study the Scriptures because you think that by them you possess eternal life. These are the Scriptures that testify about me" (John 5:39 NIV). It is through Jesus, as He is found in the Bible, that we receive eternal life.

BRIEF OVERVIEW OF THE MESSAGE OF THE BIBLE

The Bible begins with the creation of all things, matter and energy, animals and men. God placed Adam and Eve in a beautiful and perfect garden. They had all they needed or could ever want. They were sinless; they were in harmony with God and each other.

In the garden was the Tree of Knowledge of Good and Evil. Adam and Eve could eat from any tree in the Garden, except this tree. Satan tempted Eve and, through her, Adam, with the lie that God kept something good from them. They believed the devil. The light turned to darkness, the happiness to gloom. The king and the queen of the world became a farmer and his wife. With sin came guilt and sickness, fear and shame. Worst of all, sin introduced spiritual and physical death.

Sin and death are the consequences of disobedience. So God pronounced His judgment in the form of a curse, as we saw in Chapter 7.

Adam, the first man, represented the whole race. When he sinned, man departed from God—the fountain of every blessing—and was banished from the Garden. A fierce angel with a flaming sword now guards the Tree of Life, and man wanders the hostile earth. Why are there hurricanes, tornadoes, earthquakes? Why is there suffering in the world? Because of man's rebellion against God. John Wenham, author of *The Goodness of God*, writes:

> The Bible begins with a paradise lost and ends with a paradise regained. In Genesis 3 disobedience is followed not only by pain, but by shame, fear, toil and death. In Revelation 21 there is the promise that God will be with his people in the New Jerusalem and that "he will wipe away every tear from their eyes, and death shall be no more, neither shall there be mourning nor crying nor pain any more." It is probably right to infer that on [sic] the biblical view all suffering is ultimately caused by sin of some sort, and that in an unfallen world there would not even be illness, old age and accident such as we experience.[3]

THE PROTO-EVANGELICA

Even as God pronounced the curse as punishment for Adam and Eve's sin, there was yet a glimmer of hope. He said to the snake (Satan), "He [the seed of the woman, the coming Messiah] will crush your head, and you will strike his heel" (Gen. 3:15 NIV). This statement is the *proto-evangelica*, the first promise of the Messiah, who would one day destroy the work of the devil. (When Jesus died, His heel was struck by the devil, but at the same time, He destroyed Satan's head.) The Law and the Prophets repeat the promise of the Messiah many times.

Here's an early prophecy from the reluctant Balaam, circa 1200 B.C.:

I see him, but not now
   I behold him, but not near.
A star will come out of Jacob;
   a scepter will rise out of Israel. (Num. 24:17 NIV)

Here's a prophecy about Jesus from the prophet Zechariah, some seven hundred years later:

Rejoice greatly, O daughter of Zion!
Shout, O daughter of Jerusalem!

Behold, your King is coming to you;
He is just and having salvation,
Lowly and riding on a donkey,
A colt, the foal of a donkey. (Zech. 9:9)

Jesus (whose name means "Savior") is the promised Christ (Messiah). Jesus took away the physical and the spiritual effects of the curse. The Bible tells us clearly that Christ was made a curse for us. All of our sin and guilt was imputed to Him. As our first parents were banished from the Garden, so He was banished from the earth itself. Between earth and heaven, He hung upon that lonely cross. As Adam and Eve were separated from God, and all mankind with them, so was Jesus, as He cried: "My God, my God, why hast thou forsaken me?" (Ps. 22:1; Matt. 27:46 KJV). The wrath of God—just condemnation for our rebellion— fell upon Christ as He endured the anguish, pain, suffering, and sorrow that man deserved.

THE CLOTHING OF RIGHTEOUSNESS

"The clothing of righteousness" is another theme we find throughout the Scriptures. After Adam and Eve sinned they were ashamed of their nakedness and covered themselves with fig leaves. But God Himself made clothes for them from the skin of an animal. Here is a picture— the very first in Scripture—of the gospel. An animal had to die for Adam and Eve's sake, pointing to the ritual sacrifices instituted by Moses, and ultimately to the sacrifice of Jesus on the cross. Adam and Eve's fig leaves were a picture of our efforts to make ourselves right with God; the fur coats God made them were a picture of God's righteousness in Christ Jesus, which He provided by the death of His Son.

Job said, "I put on righteousness, and it clothed me" (Job 29:14), and in Psalm 132, we read: "I will also clothe [Zion's] priests with salvation" (v. 16). The prophet Isaiah took up this thread in chapter 61, verse 10: "For He has clothed me with the garments of salvation, He has covered me with the robe of righteousness."

Jesus tells the parable of the Wedding Feast (Matt. 22:1–14). The king (God) invited his people (the Jews) to his son's wedding (the Wedding Feast of the Lamb, Rev. 19). The people invited first wouldn't come, so the invitation went out to anyone the king's servants could find (the Gentiles), until the "house was full." God invites us to the Great Wedding Feast of the Lamb, and He provides proper attire for us as well. Just as Adam and Eve's fig leaves weren't sufficient to cover their nakedness, so nothing we could find to wear would be holy enough for heaven. Our clothes would appear as "filthy rags" (Isa. 64:6). When we see our own clothes as stained and dirty, we turn in repentance and faith to Jesus. God then clothes us in the white robes of the righteousness of Christ. In Christ, all the filth of sin can be cleaned away; all can be restored and forgiven.

THE WHITE ROBE OF RIGHTEOUSNESS

There are two things you must have to stand before the Almighty. First, you must have a record of perfect obedience to every commandment of God. Second, you must have a record of no sin whatsoever! Unless you have no sin and perfect obedience, I assure you on the basis of God's Word you will never enter that city of gold.

I want to tell you that I have that. I have a robe of perfect whiteness, perfect obedience. But let me hasten to add that I didn't live it, and I didn't earn it. It was lived and earned by Jesus Christ, paid for by His shed blood upon the cross. Paul says further:

> The righteousness of God apart from the law is revealed, being witnessed by the Law and the Prophets, even the righteousness of God, through faith in Jesus Christ, to all and on all who believe. For there is no difference; for all have sinned and fall short of the glory of God, being justified freely by His grace through the redemption that is in Christ Jesus. (Rom. 3:21–24)

In the book of Revelation we meet the white-robed multitude of tribes and nations, languages and peoples, standing before the throne of God. They are restored, now in heaven, perfect in will, mind, and body. How did they arrive in God's paradise? They have "washed their robes and made them white in the blood of the Lamb" (Rev. 7:14).

Johnny Hart, the world-famous cartoonist (creator of *B.C.* and *The Wizard of Id*), is now a born-again Christian. Thankfully, my television broadcasts played a part in his conversion. In a panel of one of his comic strips, he had a poem entitled "T'.e Suffering Prince" that sums up well the relationship between Christ's sacrifice for our sins and the white robe of righteousness:

> Picture yourself tied to a tree,
> Condemned [for] the sins of eternity.
> Then picture a spear parting the air,

Seeking your heart to end your despair.
Suddenly—a knight, in armor of white,
Stands in the gap betwixt you and its flight,
And shedding his "armor of God" for you—
Bears the lance that runs him through.
His heart has been pierced that yours may beat,
And the blood of his corpse washes your feet.
Picture yourself in raiment white,
Cleansed by the blood of the lifeless knight,
Never to mourn the Prince who was downed,
For He is not lost! It is you who are found.[4]

We've heard the phrase "dress for success." There was a best-seller a few years back by that title. Well, the ultimate example of dressing for success is donning the white robe of righteousness that Christ gives to those who come to Him. Worldly success in this life without making it to heaven is the ultimate failure.

THE SHEDDING OF INNOCENT BLOOD FOR THE FORGIVENESS OF SIN

The theme of blood sacrifice is another aspect of the central message of the Bible. There is a direct parallel between the sacrifices God instituted through Moses, and the death of Christ, which was the "once and for all" sacrifice.

From the earliest times, man has known that somehow it is not enough to tell God, "Sorry." We see that Abel sacrificed to God, as did Abraham. With Moses, God instituted the daily ritual sacrifices. Abraham said these prophetic words: "My son, God will provide for Himself the lamb" (Gen. 22:8). God provided a lamb for Abraham and his son, and God provided Himself as the final sacrifice—through Jesus, who became a sacrifice upon the cross. Jesus is called the Lamb of God (John 1:36).

The Old Testament clearly states that without shedding blood there is no remission of sin. Leviticus 17:11 proclaims, "It is the blood that makes atonement for the soul." The New Testament repeats this idea: "Without the shedding of blood there is no forgiveness" (Heb. 9:22 NIV).

When God gave Moses the tablets of the Law, He also gave him the specific regulations for the sacrificial system. Where the Law revealed sin, there also was the lamb or bull slain for the sinner's guilt. All of the sacrifices of the Old Testament were foreshadowing the one true sacrifice of the Lamb of God.

In Exodus chapter 12 we see the institution of the Passover. Every household of the people of God was to take a lamb "without blemish" (v. 5). They were told to smear the blood from that lamb on the two sides and top of the doorway. As some of the blood would drip down from the top, the blood on the doorway would make the shape of a cross! The angel of the Lord would then pass over that household.

The children of Israel would eat the Passover lamb with bitter herbs and unleavened bread. The leaven, a symbol of sin, would be removed from the household. The lamb would be roasted by fire, and eaten without breaking any bones (Ex.12:9). In Psalm 34:20 we read, "He protects all his bones, not one of them will be broken" (NIV). This prophecy had its fulfillment in Christ, when the soldiers refrained from breaking His legs after His death on the cross (John 19:33, 36).

The daily sacrifices of bulls and goats and lambs were a daily reminder of just how serious sin is. As the high priest had to go into the Holy of Holies to atone for the sins of the people, so Christ went into heaven itself with His own blood to atone for the sins of mankind. "For it is not possible that the blood of bulls and goats could take away sins" (Heb. 10:4). These sacrifices were a symbol of the real sacrifice that was to come. Only Jesus was the perfect, sinless Lamb of God, who could take away the sin of the world. And just as God passed over the houses of the Israelites where the blood was painted on the doorposts, so will God's judgment pass over those who are covered by the blood of the Lamb.

Jesus is the Lamb of God who takes away the sins of the world. The apostle Peter says, "You were not redeemed with corruptible things, like silver or gold, from your aimless conduct received by tradition from your fathers, but with the precious blood of Christ, as of a lamb without blemish and without spot" (1 Peter 1:18–19). The blood that Jesus shed on the cross is the only blood in the universe that can take away sin. In the book of Revelation, Jesus is referred to as "the Lamb" who was "slain from the foundation of the world" (13:8). Before He created the world, God knew man would fall and that He would provide the Savior.

This is the "Greatest Story Ever Told"—the story of Jesus and His love. It was love alone that kept Him on that cross. He could have come down at any moment and swept into hell all of those who mocked Him. But love held Him—not those great and bloody spikes.

FAITH AND REPENTANCE

Faith is more than knowledge. It is resting upon Christ. It is trusting Him and Him alone for our salvation. Many people trust good works to get them to heaven. They wonder how many good works are good enough to get there, and they hope they have enough to suffice. I used to think that, until I came to understand there's only one Savior. On that day, I realized I needed to get out of the savior business and let Jesus save my soul. How? I turned from my sins. I confessed them and asked His forgiveness. Above all, I asked Jesus Christ to come into my heart and cleanse me and make me a new person—the person He had intended me to be. I made that decision more than forty years ago, and I can honestly tell you that was the most important decision I've ever made in my entire life!

Furthermore, the Bible tells us that we can *know* that we have eternal life. We can receive the assurance of our salvation. Listen to what the Scriptures say on this all-important topic:

> And this is the testimony: that God has given us eternal life, and this life is in His Son. He who has the Son has life; he who does not have the Son of God does not have life. These things I have written to you who believe in the name of the Son of God, that you may know that you have eternal life. (1 John 5:11–13)

I am happy to say that I *know* that I have eternal life. I know that if I die today, I will be with Christ forever. I have not always known that. When I was a young man, about two years after college, I heard the gospel and I came to know that assurance. Recently, I took a plane north for a speaking engagement. Shortly after takeoff, the pilot said they would have to return to the airport because it seemed the landing gear was down, and they didn't know whether or not it was locked in place. Then he announced, "We're going in on crash-landing mode." People started weeping and crying and wailing. It was very interesting. There was a Christian lady I knew sitting right across from me, and I was trying to talk to her about how thankful I was for the assurance of salvation. I spoke loud enough so that other people could be encouraged. The man next to me couldn't understand it. He asked, "How can you talk like that?" "Well," I said, "if the plane goes down, I go up!"

If you have never turned your life over to Jesus Christ and received Him into your heart as your Savior and Lord, I urge you to do so right now. You could say a prayer like this to God:

> Lord Jesus, I need to get right with You. I acknowledge that I have sinned, and that I am wrong in Your sight. I have been on the wrong road, I have sought to justify myself by my own deeds. But now my excuses are gone. I cast myself before You and seek Your mercy. I ask that You clothe me with the perfect white robe of Your righteousness so that I might stand pure before Your throne. In Your holy name, I pray with thanksgiving. Amen.

If you sincerely prayed that prayer or one like it, you have taken the first step in the most important journey of your life.

I have prepared a book for you if you are just now coming to know Jesus' forgiveness and new life. I'd like to send it to you free of charge. Just write to me and ask for *Beginning Again*.[5] This book will teach you how to live the Christian life. It will introduce to you some of the basics you need to know to grow spiritually.

Meanwhile, here are a few key basics to growth in Christ. These are steps you can take:

- Read your Bible. Read at least a chapter a day. Memorize key Bible verses. Get study aids that will help you study the whole book.[6] If you need to get a more modern translation to help you understand the Bible better, I recommend the New King James Version (Nashville: Thomas Nelson Publishers). Read at least a chapter a day. I suggest you begin reading in the book of John, the fourth book of the New Testament. Romans 10 says, "Faith comes by hearing, and hearing by the word of God" (v. 17). Nothing will build your faith so much as reading, studying, and meditating on the Word of God.
- Join a Bible-believing church. It is crucial for believers to be a part of the local body of Christ. He never intended for us to "go it alone." There's really no such thing as a "lone ranger Christian." Choose carefully where you go to worship.[7] Note especially the Church's attitude toward the inerrant Word of God. It is a critical issue. Also look for a church that is active in its outreach to non-Christians.
- Tell people about your decision to live for Christ. Talk with your friends and family. Get involved in the church you choose to attend. Too many Christians have become like ponds. They receive input at one end, but they never give at the other. They spiritually take, take, take, but they never give back to others. When you share with others the gospel of Christ, you share the greatest story ever told. It is a privilege to be partners with the Lord in spreading His message.[8]

KING OF KINGS

The Bible centers around Jesus Christ. Someone once put it well, saying that if any great man were to come into the room, we would rise to greet him. But if Jesus Christ were to enter, we would get on our knees to greet Him! He is the One before whom everyone will give an account. He is the King of kings and Lord of lords!

CHAPTER 14

THE VITAL IMPORTANCE OF THE BIBLE

"For the word of God is living and active. Sharper than any double-edged sword, it penetrates even to dividing soul and spirit, joints and marrow; it judges the thoughts and attitudes of the heart."

—Hebrews 4:12 NIV

If you had to leave your home in haste, not knowing if you would ever return, and you could only bring *one* thing, what would it be? Virtually all Christians would give the same answer: the Bible. Why is the Bible so important to us?

Because the Bible is the Word of God. God spoke during the centuries when the Bible was being written, and He speaks to us today through the Bible. As Francis Schaeffer once said: "He is there and He is not Silent." Verses written 2,500 years ago for the people of Israel speak to me today. Take for example Isaiah 41:10: "So do not fear, for I am with you; do not be dismayed, for I am your God. I will strengthen you and help you; I will uphold you with my righteous right hand" (NIV). Millions of believers around the world take comfort from verses such as these. The Swedish theologian Bå Giertz said:

> When God spoke to Israel twenty-five or thirty centuries past, He also had the coming millennia in mind. He wove in a picture of Christ, not only in the prophecies, but also in what is told about Israel's kings and high priests. He wove in a picture of the new Israel, Christ's Church, in what is told about the people of Israel. He spoke also to us and to all coming generations. Therefore, so often we'll find a double meaning in the words. What is said about Israel, God's elect, who were chosen to convey the message of salvation to the whole world, was also said

about Christ. Sometimes it was a word about His Church or to His Church. . . . The Word of God is not just eternal truths, but spiritual Power.[1]

The Bible is living because the Holy Spirit is present as the individual reads the Scriptures. That is how a passage can have different meanings to us at different times. Not because the Word changes, but because we change and because the Holy Spirit knows us intimately.

Because God Himself is present in the Word, it is spiritual food. Jesus said: "I am the living bread, which came down from heaven. If anyone eats of this bread, he will live forever" (John 6:51). In Psalm 119:50, we read, "For Your word has given me life." God declares, "Man does not live on bread alone but on every word that comes from the mouth of the LORD" (Deut. 8:3 NIV). It was also the creative power of God's Word that spoke the world into existence.

WHY WE READ THE BIBLE

We Christians read the Word of God because we love Him, and because the Scriptures demonstrate His love for us. God's Word is a love letter that should be scrutinized; to ignore it demonstrates a lack of love for Jesus. We cannot say that we love God and ignore His Word. The Bible is God's "will" to us, and apart from the reading and claiming of the provisions of that will, we do not inherit the promises. When Israel entered the promised land, God said that everywhere they walked, He had already given them. But they had to walk there and claim it for their own.

So it is with the Word of God. There are thousands of promises in that Word. So it behooves us to study His Word and learn those promises. Yet there are many professing Christians who rarely pick up the Good Book. That's a problem. Let me make an analogy.

Imagine visiting the wife of a friend of yours during the Vietnam War. John had gone overseas to fight that war. He was slugging his way through the jungles of Vietnam, fighting the Viet Cong and the mosquitoes—perhaps seriously wounded, perhaps killed in combat. So you ask, "Mary, how is John doing? What do you hear from him?"

She says, "Oh, I'm so glad you mentioned John. You know, I love John more than anything in this world. He is the very apple of my eye, the delight of my life. He fills my heart. He is my all in all."

"Well, how is he doing, Mary?"

"I really don't know."

"Oh, you haven't heard from him?"

"Well, yes, I have. In fact, that big stack of letters there on the coffee table are all from John, but I just haven't had the time to read them. You know, it's been such a busy year. There's the women's auxiliary, and then, of course, there's the tennis group, and time on the golf course. There's so much to do at the house too. I've been meaning to read those letters one of these days but I just haven't had the time yet. Someday I am sure that I will because I just love John with all my heart."

Is this scene difficult to imagine? Perhaps on your coffee table, or somewhere in your house, there sit sixty-six love letters from God. You profess in word and song to believe in Him and to love Him; but do you take the time to read His letters to you? The key to spiritual growth rests with our devouring the Scriptures.

Apart from the guidance and strength of the Word of God, your life here in this world will not be a success. You may say, "My life is already a success, and I don't read the Word of God. I've got a large house, two cars and a boat, a cabin in the mountains. My life is very successful." If that is your answer, you don't even know what success is because you haven't been reading the Word of God. God gave you your life and He will judge its success or failure by a higher standard: "One's life does not consist in the abundance of the things he possesses" (Luke 12:15).

We may succeed in the world's eyes, but our life will nevertheless be a failure in the end because we have aimed in the wrong direction. Jesus rhetorically asked, "For what will it profit a man if he gains the whole world, and loses his own soul?" (Mark 8:36).

The Word of God contains within it the secret of true success—both in this life, and in the life to come. The truths found in the Scripture are the source of successful living. When you find a successful person, you will find a person who practices those truths. To wit: Dr. Howard A. Kelly, the most famous medical practitioner in this country in the first half of this century. Dr. Kelly was professor of gynecology at Johns Hopkins University, and later the head surgeon and radiologist at the famous Howard A. Kelly Hospital in Baltimore. He wrote some twenty scientific books and five hundred medical and scientific articles. It took thirty lines in his biography just to indicate his honors in *Who's Who in America*.[2]

What was the secret of his greatness? He said the secret of whatever success he had was this:

> I rise regularly at six and, after dressing, give all of my time until our eight o'clock breakfast to the study of God's Word. I find time for brief studies during the day and again in the evening. I make it a general rule to touch nothing but the Bible after the evening meal.[3]

Grasp all that he said: He devoted about an hour and a half to Bible study in the morning before breakfast, had a number of brief times of study in little moments during the day, and then touched nothing but the Bible after the evening meal. That probably amounted to between three and four hours in God's Word *each day!* Here was a man who was the head of a hospital, author of twenty scientific texts, a busy surgeon—and yet he found time for studying the Word of God.

Is he a fluke, or does the reading of God's Word lead to greatness in life? George Washington, the great founder of this nation, arose regularly and spent the time from five until six in the morning on his knees before a chair on which lay an open Bible. He retired every evening at nine o'clock to the same study, to the same chair, to the same open Bible.[4]

Why was George Washington called "the wonder of the world"? Was it his political acumen, his great rhetorical abilities, his great military accomplishments? No, it was the character of George Washington that was said to be, in his day, the wonder of the world, so that even during the Revolutionary War there were no attacks on his personal character in the press—not even in England.

Consider the secret of success for other people of great accomplishment.

G. Campbell Morgan wrote magnificent commentaries on most of the Bible. Someone said it seemed as if he were inspired. He said that he never put pen to paper until he had read that particular book of the Bible through fifty times.

Arthur S. DeMoss was a friend of mine and a great businessman. He earned hundreds of millions of dollars, but his great desire was to share the gospel of Jesus Christ. That desire grew out of time he spent daily in the Word of God. He and his wife, Nancy, have seven children. They had a rule in their family. It was very simple: "No Bible, no breakfast." Their children learned early on what was the first priority of their day.

SUCCESS IN MARRIAGE

The Bible also provides the secret of success in marriage. Many people don't seem to know what causes trouble in marriages. It is one thing: sin! Whether it is pride, the unwillingness to forgive and be humble, selfishness, greed, lust, or whatever—all of these are sins. The Word of God is the great cleansing water that washes away our sin, wears down the rough edges in our personalities, and makes us people other people can live with.

I remember a couple in our church who were having great troubles in their marriage. They were about to split up; then they decided to spend an hour each day reading the Word of God and praying. It was not too long before they were back together again; their marriage was happier than it had ever been, and they were serving Christ together in the Church—as a family. The old saying is still true: the family that prays together stays together.

SUCCESS IN HEAVEN

Most of all, the Word of God is the guarantor of our success in heaven. The only way we can please God is by finding what it is He would have us to do and to be in this world, and that all comes through His Word. Lincoln said that all of the best gifts and greatest blessings of God had come to mankind through the Bible.[5] If you would have the rewards God promises to those who obediently serve Him, you must find them in His Word. The Bible teaches that heaven is free; we don't earn it by our obedience or by Bible reading. It is a free gift, paid for by Christ and offered to all who repent of their sins and trust Him as Savior. It is not earned or merited; it is free!

But there are degrees of reward, the Bible tells us, and they come from our faithful obedience.

It is not possible to eat one big meal and then go without food for the rest of the month; neither is it possible for a child of God to go without spiritual food. *Daily* reading of the Scriptures and prayer is the lifeline of the believer. Jesus said "I am the vine, you are the branches" (John 15:5). Without the Word, we are like a branch cut off from the tree.

MAKE A DECISION

A certain gentleman weighed 240 pounds, and he had a suitcase in each hand. He was running up the stairs of the train station to catch a train. By the time he reached the top, his heart almost completely failed him, and he had to sit down. He almost caught a train for which he had no ticket! But he made a decision right there. He decided he had to lose weight. He had to get rid of all that excess baggage. Result: he lost sixty-some pounds and was in better shape than he had been in for twenty-five years. He said that the most difficult thing of all was making the decision—determining that he was going to lose weight. After that, he said, it was all downhill.

That is the way it is with most things in the moral and spiritual realm, as well. The most important thing is making up our mind that we are going to do something. That is also very true about the study of God's Word. Have you made a decision to give yourself daily to systematic and in-depth Bible study? If not, I hope that you will. Most of all, we should study the person of Christ. As we saw in the last chapter, He is at the center of the revelation of God.

HOW DO WE READ THE BIBLE?

A recent survey by the George Gallup organization revealed that 11 percent of people in this country read the Bible every day. Assuming that the people who make up that 11 percent are part of the 40 percent of the people in America who attend church every week, you can conclude that about 26 or 27 percent of the people who attend church read the Bible daily. If yours is an average church, that would mean a little over a quarter of the congregation you belong to read the Bible every day. More Christians should read and study God's Word.

When Philip came to the Ethiopian eunuch in his chariot, the man was reading one of the passages from the prophet Isaiah. Philip said to him, "Do you understand what you are reading?" (Acts 8:30). The Ethiopian said, "How can I, unless someone guides me?" (v. 31). Today there are many study guides for Christians, and you can have your own private, portable Philip to go in your chariot to help you daily in the understanding of the Word.

How can you make Bible study more enjoyable and more profitable?

First, we need to understand how to use some of the study tools that are available, and second, we need to know some methods for profitable and enjoyable study of the Bible. There are many tools that can be used. Every Christian, especially every Christian in America, ought to have some of those tools readily available to him. First I recommend a complete concordance. A concordance is a book that lists words found in the Scripture and the verses where each word is found. You can use a concordance to find a verse when you know at least one word in the verse. Or you can use it to find verses on a particular subject.

A Bible dictionary will also help you understand many of the terms in the Bible. For example, there's *The Zondervan Pictorial Bible Dictionary* edited by Merrill Tenney.[6] Both *Eerdman's Dictionary of the Bible* (Grand Rapids, MI: Wm. B. Eerdman, 1998) and *Vine's Complete Expository Dictionary* (Nashville, TN: Thomas Nelson Publishers, 1985) are also excellent Bible dictionaries. The serious student of God's Word would do well to get a reliable dictionary of the Bible. It will illumine the Scripture.

Third, commentaries are great tools for exploring the depths of the Bible. There are hundreds of commentaries, but if I had to recommend one, it would be Matthew Henry's. For almost three hundred years it has stood the test of time. It has led thousands of people closer to God. Charles Spurgeon, the great preacher of England, said he read it continually. The great eighteenth-century evangelist George Whitefield said that he had read the entire six volumes of Matthew Henry's commentary four times.

These study aids will help you understand the Word of God. There are many others—such as *Halley's Bible Handbook*[7] (a one-volume resource that provides helpful background information) or *Search the Scriptures: A Three-Year Bible Study Course*[8]—but a concordance, a dictionary, and a commentary are the most basic.

We read the Bible in obedience to God; we must also read the Bible obediently:

> But be doers of the word, and not hearers only, deceiving yourselves. For if anyone is a hearer of the word and not a doer, he is like a man observing his natural face in a mirror; for he observes himself, goes away, and immediately forgets what kind of man he was. But he who looks into the perfect law of liberty and continues in it, and is not a forgetful hearer but a doer of the work, this one will be blessed in what he does. (James 1:22–25)

Dear friend, let me urge you to read the Word of God. It is the height of wisdom to read it, and to fail to read it is great folly. Note what several of our presidents have said on the subject:

- President John Adams, one of the founders of our nation and its second president, said, "I have made it a practice every year for several years to read through the Bible."[9]
- Ulysses S. Grant, eighteenth president of the United States, said, "Hold fast to the Bible as the anchor of your liberty; write its precepts in your hearts and practice them in your lives."[10]
- Theodore Roosevelt, twenty-sixth president of the United States, said, "If a man is not familiar with the Bible, he has suffered the loss which he had better make all possible haste to correct."[11]
- Ronald Reagan, fortieth president of the United States, said, "Inside the Bible's pages lie all of the answers to all of the problems man has ever known. I hope Americans will read and study the Bible. . . . It is my firm belief that the enduring values presented in its pages have a great meaning for each of us and for our nation. The Bible can touch our hearts, order our minds, and refresh our souls."[12]

> It has been said of the Bible:
> It is God's highway to Paradise.
> It crowns womanhood with beauty and manhood with strength.

> It furnishes adequate motives for self-sacrifice.
> Children grow in character under its influence.
> Youth is vitalized by its teachings.
> The most common work of life is glorified by it.[13]

Many years ago, as a young pastor, I found the work of the ministry could crowd the time for reading and studying the Word of God. I became very convicted about this. I committed myself before God that I would not allow a day to go by that I did not spend time in the Word. Would that everyone who reads this book make that same commitment—and do it today. You will be so grateful you have done so. Your life will be blessed; your home will be blessed; the success of your future years may indeed depend upon hiding the Bible's great truths in your heart and mind. I urge you to commit yourself to do that.

TECHNIQUES FOR STUDY

Read the Bible meditatively. The Bible has a great deal to say about meditating upon God's Word day and night—to think about it when we rise up, when we lie down, and when we walk in the way.

We should give our attention to what God has said in His Word. That means we must hide it in our hearts. We must write it upon the walls of our memory.

We should also read the Word of God "in Jesus' name." Christians all over the world begin reading with, "In Jesus' name." This signifies that all of the Bible centers around Christ, and it places us under Him when we read. We are in much less danger of sitting as judge and jury over the Bible if we read it in His holy name.

How should we study the Bible? Dr. Howard Kelly said:

> And now for my greatest secret for everyday common folks, known through the ages and yet ever needing to be restated and learned afresh as generation succeeds generation. It is this. The very best way to study the Bible is simply to read it daily with close attention and with prayer to see the light that shines from its pages, to meditate upon it, and to continue to read until somehow it works itself, its words, its expressions, its teachings, its habits of thought, and its presentation of God and His Christ into the very warp and woof of one's being.[14]

There is nothing remarkable about that; in fact, it is wonderfully simple. But it works.

What are the hindrances that keep people from diligent Bible study? First, I believe, is a feeling of repetitiveness. There are not many books that a person reads over three or four or five or even ten or twenty times—much less fifty or a hundred times. People sometimes have the been-there-done-that feeling when they read the Bible, especially when they are facing a story or a parable or a passage they've read many times. The problem is that these people are used to doing nothing more than "strip-mining." They just turn up the surface of the ground. They think that they have exhausted the treasures; they don't know that the Bible contains inexhaustible treasures. The problem is not with the Scripture; the problem is with the readers. They do not dig deeper to find the treasure that God has for them. They give little effort, and they find that they get little out of it. Little given gives little return. Conversely, much study yields much return. Dr. Kelly, whom we quoted above, said: "I have a feeling that the Bible is so profound a book that one ought to be able to give some fresh message to each and every audience year after year."[15]

Second, some people don't read the Bible often because they don't understand what they read. Sometimes people read repeatedly those passages that they feel they can understand, and ignore large sections of the Scripture that they find difficult. There are portions of the Bible that are very difficult to understand, but sometimes an in-depth study of those passages will yield great rewards. How many times have you struggled through the *begat*s and wondered why in the world God ever put these into the Bible? I remember three men who were Jews who were converted to Christ. Someone asked what passages of the Bible had the greatest impact upon them in their conversion. They replied, "The genealogies in Matthew and in Luke"—the *begat*s, where they saw the lineage of the Messiah, through Abraham and David.

The riches of the Scriptures are there for us to find, but sometimes it takes patience and time and effort. God has promised us:

> I will give you the treasures of darkness
> And hidden riches of secret places,
> That you may know that I, the LORD,
> Who call you by your name,
> Am the God of Israel. (Isa. 45:3)

J. Wilbur Chapman said, "The rule that governs my life is this: Anything that dims my vision of Christ, or takes away my taste for Bible study, or cramps my prayer life, or makes Christian work difficult, is wrong for me, and I must, as a Christian, turn away from it."[16]

The daily reading of the Scriptures is our greatest means of grace. It is the tool God uses in our sanctification process.

The Bible says that without holiness, no man shall see God (Heb. 12:14). How then do we obtain it? Sanctification is not merely an effort on the part of Christians to live a better Christian life. In fact, sanctification is not really the effort of man at all; sanctification is the work of God. I repeat, it is God who sanctifies. Salvation is of God, whether it be justification in the past tense, or sanctification in the present tense, or glorification in the future when the final vestiges of sin are removed. Salvation is wholly of God.

The agent of sanctification is not man but the Holy Spirit. It is the infusing of the holiness of Christ. There is no holiness in us.

This does not mean that we are passive in sanctification. We are passive in regeneration, but we are active in our sanctification, though it is still all of grace. We are to make use of the means of sanctification—the Word of God, prayer, sacraments, and worship. The Holy Spirit uses these things to sanctify us.

There are certain evidences of whether or not we are growing in grace. If we are growing, one of the fruits will be graciousness—becoming like Him who is the all-gracious God, having an unselfish love and concern for the needs of others. Another evidence of growth is joy. One of the meanings of *grace* is "that which brings gladness or joy or rejoicing" and if we are growing in grace we are rejoicing. Conversely, if we are grumbling and complaining, if we are sad and dejected and depressed, it is simply an indication that we are not growing in grace, that we are immature; that we are like babies. One of the characteristics of a baby is the tendency to fuss and complain whenever it does not get its own way. But the admonition of the Scriptures is "Rejoice. . . . Again I will say, rejoice!" (Phil. 4:4) and "Rejoice always" (1 Thess. 5:16), and it can only be fulfilled by those who have grown in grace and who know the working of God. Someone described a man in this way: "Every time I met him it was as if he had just come from a room that was filled with an atmosphere of grace and joy and wonder; it was as if this man were unable to escape the wonder and the marvel of God's grace, His ineffable grace to his soul." He was ever rejoicing in the goodness of God— a sure sign of the fact that we are growing in grace.

Another sign of growth is stability. When young people begin to learn to drive a car, they go all over the road. As they learn more and grow in their ability, this vacillation begins to smooth out until finally they are able to drive in a straight line. So it is with the Christian life. Many new Christians begin unsteadily, but they finally begin to smooth out those curves and their lives become more stable. Stability is one of the signs of spiritual maturity.

Another one is strength. Two people have been Christians for a number of years. One of them has spiritual limbs that are very short. He has spiritual rickets and frail arms, and if you place so much as a toothpick of burden or responsibility upon him, he falls into a heap on the ground and weeps and laments his inability to carry such overwhelming burdens. Pressures are more than he can handle. The other person, however, could have logs piled upon him and it would seem to not even slow him down because he has grown. When a young tree is first planted, a child can rip it up by the roots; but give that tree a number of years to grow until it becomes a great oak, and then many men cannot with all their strength move that tree. So it is with spiritual maturity. We grow in our ability to withstand temptation; we grow in our ability to serve. Some people demonstrate by their lack of ability or desire to serve the Lord that they are either spiritual babies or have no life in them at all.

God has also told us clearly in Galatians 5:22 what kind of fruit the Holy Spirit will bring forth in our lives: "love, joy, peace, patience, kindness, goodness, faithfulness, gentleness and self-control" (NIV). If we get discouraged and see no godly fruit in our lives, then let's remember the parable Jesus told about the tree that wasn't bearing fruit (Luke 13:6–8). For Jesus Himself is the master gardener. He will fertilize. He will dig around the tree, so that next year there will be fruit to the glory of God. He said, "Abide in Me, and I in you. As the branch cannot bear fruit of itself, unless it abides in the vine, neither can you, unless you abide in Me. I am the vine, you are the branches. He who abides in Me, and I in him, bears much fruit" (John 15:4–5).

Our love for the Lord grows when we draw near to Him, as we read His Word. If you have found your love for Him growing dim, I suggest you read afresh, in any of the four Gospels (perhaps starting with Luke[17]), of the passion of Jesus, the horrible suffering He underwent for us. You'd have to have a heart of stone to not be moved by what Christ underwent for our sake. Look to Christ and your love will grow. Jesus sticks closer than a brother. Look upon Him, and the love of Jesus Christ will reach out with its arresting power to give to your life a purpose and meaning that will compel you onward. As the sun shines in the heavens and melts the ice until there comes a great flow, you will be carried forward with that flow of love and with the apostle Paul you will be able to say, "The love of Christ compels [me]" (2 Cor. 5:14). And His love keeps us close to Him.

THE KEY

The Bible is the key to spiritual growth. We neglect it at our peril. One sage put it well: the Bible will keep us from sin, or sin will keep us from the Bible!

For centuries, children in America learned the alphabet through the *New England Primer.* Millions of young Americans were educationally weaned on this small book, which was full of biblical principles. Each letter of the alphabet pointed back to the Bible. "In Adam's fall, we sinned all" was how children learned the letter *A*. "Christ crucified, for sinners died" was how they learned *C*, and so on.[18] I close with the way they often learned the letter *B*. It summarizes in a sentence the entire point of this chapter—"Thy life to mend, the Bible attend."[19]

CHAPTER 15

FINAL THOUGHTS

*"Your word is a lamp to my feet
And a light to my path."*

—Psalm 119:105

One night in 1898 two traveling salesmen, John Nicholson and Samuel Hill, met each other in a hotel in Wisconsin. They rejoiced when they discovered they were both Christians. They shared their evening devotion and afterward they talked about how great it would be to have a Bible in the hotel room. That night a dream was born.

A year later at the YMCA in Janeville, Wisconsin, Nicholson and Hill met again, along with W. J. Knights. The three of them formed an organization in order to distribute Bibles in hotels and motels all over America. They prayed for a name and came up with "Gideon," based on Judges 6 and 7. Today, less than one hundred years later, the Gideons, International, works in 269 countries and provinces around the globe. The goal reaches far beyond motels and hotels. They distribute Bibles and New Testaments (with Psalms and Proverbs) at a rate of one million every eight days! The Gideons place Bibles in hospitals, prisons, and military bases. They distribute the Word of God to students and nurses. Today you can go to a hotel virtually anywhere in the world, and you will find that the Gideons have been there before you to place a Bible in your room![1]

In the last two centuries, Bible distribution has been going on in earnest. From 1815 to 1975, it's reported that 2.5 billion copies of the Bible were printed and distributed worldwide.[2] The United Bible Societies are distributing millions and millions of copies of the Scriptures worldwide *each year!* As we said in the first chapter, no book comes close in worldwide distribution to the Word of God. This reminds me of what the Scriptures say in Psalm 19 (about the witness of creation in the heavens, in the skies): "Day after day they pour forth speech; night after night they display knowledge. There is no speech or language where their voice is not heard. Their voice goes out into all the earth, their words to the ends of the world" (vv. 2–4 NIV).

CHALLENGES TO THE SPREAD OF THE BIBLE

But just as in the past in a multitude of different ways, so now there are a great number of challenges we face in spreading the Bible and its message. One of them is the decline of literacy.

Declining Literacy

As the Bible has been excluded from public education in recent decades, literacy has plummeted. Some high school graduates cannot even read their own diplomas, much less the Bible. This deplorable fact under-scores an important challenge facing the Church today. Literacy is not just a concern for the United States. Dr. Hilde Fjeldstad, the president of a Lutheran Bible College in Oslo, Norway, and member of the Lausanne Executive Committee on World Evangelization, gave a speech a few years ago that warns about what is happening in many parts of the world. She made three significant points worth pondering:

> 1. Common literacy is down in many parts of the world, including the industrialized nations. Many people do not read books at all. As the visual media [TV, film, video] takes over, many young people do not read.
> 2. The collective memory of Western culture, a common memory built upon the Bible, is being lost in our generation.
> 3. Among the intelligentsia, there is a relativistic movement claiming that the text has no specific message or truth contained in it, but only the meaning and message perceived by the individual reader. Applied to the Bible, this view is basically saying that the Bible says whatever you think it says, and what message or truth you get from it is entirely up to you.[3]

These trends make our efforts to distribute the message of the Bible more difficult. They show how important creative visual and audio means are for getting the message of the Bible out, along with the promotion of literacy so that people can read the Bible for themselves.[4]

Not Enough Bibles

Richard Worthing-Davies of the Evangelical Bible Society points out another challenge facing the Church. He estimates that only 25 percent of new converts in the world get their own Bible. To meet this enormous need for Bibles, a union was formed in Manila in 1992 at the International Lausanne Conference on World Evangelization. Several Bible societies joined together to work more effectively toward the goal of supplying Bibles to new converts, and in all the different languages of the world. The forum consists of the United Bible Societies, Wycliffe Bible Translators, International Bible Society, and Scripture Union.

It's exciting to see these ministries working together for this all-important goal. But of course, there are many in our society who would take issue with that goal. They view the Bible as a negative force, in part because of its occasional misuse.

Scripture-Twisting

What about instances of the Bible allegedly having a negative impact? What about people like David Koresh or other cult leaders? What about people who use the Bible to justify unjust practices? We must remember that even the devil can quote Scripture—as he did when he tempted our Lord (Matt. 4:6).

The Scriptures can be misconstrued, misinterpreted, and twisted to support all kinds of heretical views. I heard of one man who tried beating his wife into submission. He claimed he was justified because the Bible says, "Wives, submit to your own husbands" (Eph. 5:22). That man's behavior was evil, and deep down he knows it. The very same passage that he yanked out of context gives the husbands a more challenging assignment: "Husbands, love your wives, just as Christ also loved the church and gave Himself for her" (v. 25). You don't find Jesus abusing His Church! Any husband who loves his wife as Christ loved the Church will be of such good and noble character that the wife will gladly submit her will to him.

There have always been men who cloaked evil through the sanctions of the Scriptures, even if they didn't necessarily perceive this as wrong. Slavery was justified by Bible-quoting pastors in the antebellum South. But it's also true that the end of slavery came about by the efforts of those who were convinced it was evil—because of the *very same Bible!* Racism and apartheid have been justified by use of the Bible. Yet they conform more with an evolutionary view of man than a biblical one. Don't forget the full title of Darwin's book, *On the Origin of Species by Means of Natural Selection or The Preservation of Favoured Races in the Struggle for Life.*[5] In contrast, the Scriptures dispel all excuses for racism. Paul said in Acts 17:26: "From one man he made every nation of men, that they should inhabit the whole earth" (NIV). The Bible that white supremacist groups claim to read tells them they are physically related to blacks and people of all races! Such groups are twisting the Scriptures. They are badly mistaken.

Scripture-twisting is nothing new. The term itself comes from the Bible! Peter wrote about false teachers who were taking the writings of Paul and other Scriptures (already, the epistles of Paul were being recognized as holy Scripture) and distorting them. He wrote, "As also our beloved brother Paul, according to the wisdom given to him, has written to you, as also in all his epistles, speaking in them of these things, in which are some things hard to understand, which untaught and unstable people twist to their own destruction, as they do also the rest of the Scriptures" (2 Peter 3:15–16). Scripture-twisting will continue until the Lord's return. But it does not nullify the Word of God. We know the devil can quote Scripture, and that he often appears as an angel of light in order to deceive people (2 Cor. 11:14). We also know that the Bible says of man, "The heart is deceitful above all things, and desperately wicked" (Jer. 17:9). So we must guard ourselves as we handle the Word of God, lest we try to make the Scripture conform to our will.

TIME TO RECLAIM
OUR RICH HERITAGE

Christians should never apologize for who we are. Let us reclaim our rich Christian heritage. What has made Western civilization great? Samuel Huntington, a professor at Harvard and director of the John M. Olin Institute for Strategic Studies, wrote recently, "Western Christianity, first Catholicism and then Protestantism, is the single most important historical characteristic of Western civilization. Indeed, during most of its first millennium, what is now known as Western civilization was called Western Christendom."[6]

We are heirs to a great civilization, thanks in large part to the Bible. Yet, like Esau, who sold his birthright for a single meal, we seem bent on trading in our heritage for a mess of pottage. Consider the consequences of our society's rejection of the Bible. In the 1970s, restraints on the use of law that were in place since medieval times were removed, and the litigation nightmare followed. As one social critic puts it, "We're all one frivolous lawsuit away from bankruptcy." In colleges, Western civilization has been replaced by women's studies, by gay and lesbian pride curricula, by a host of multicultural, diversity programs. Even Shakespeare has fallen upon hard times in our major universities.

Meanwhile, our morality continues to plummet. We have rejected God's rules on sex and the family and substituted the Playboy philosophy. Consequently, marriage and the family have taken an incredible beating in our time. And the children pay the highest price. We've witnessed the rise of the militant homosexual movement; they are trying to force legal recognition of their perversion and to make it a crime to speak negatively of homosexual practices. The family, the very bedrock of society, has fallen on such hard times that many are trying to redefine the traditional family—right out of existence!

We are engaged in a cultural war, and at the heart of the matter is where we stand on the Bible. Is the Bible our final authority and do we allow it to rule for us, or are we the final arbiters of right and wrong, as we arrogantly sit in judgement on the very Word of God?

While our problems may seem modern, they really aren't. Virtually all of these matters are dealt with definitively in the Bible. Paul wrote in his letter to the Romans words that are relevant in today's cultural wars. Note how the floodlight of God's revelation exposes the depth of man's immorality and the fatal consequences:

> For the wrath of God is revealed from heaven against all ungodliness and unrighteousness of men, who suppress the truth in unrighteousness, because what may be known of God is manifest in them, for God has shown it to them. For since the creation of the world His invisible attributes are clearly seen, being understood by the things that are made, even His eternal power and Godhead, so that they are without excuse, because, although they knew God, they did not glorify Him as God, nor were thankful, but became futile in their thoughts, and their foolish hearts were darkened. Professing to be wise, they became fools, and changed the glory of the incorruptible God into an image made like corruptible man—and birds and four-footed animals and creeping things. Therefore God also gave them up to uncleanness, in the lusts of their hearts, to dishonor their bodies among themselves, who exchanged the truth of God for the lie, and worshiped and served the creature rather than the Creator, who is blessed forever. Amen. For this reason God gave them up to vile passions. For even their women exchanged the natural use for what is against nature. Likewise also the men, leaving the natural use of the woman, burned in their lust for one another, men with men committing what is shameful, and receiving in themselves the penalty of their error which was due. And even as they did not like to retain God in their knowledge, God gave them over to a debased mind, to do those things which are not fitting; being filled with all unrighteousness, sexual immorality, wickedness, covetousness, maliciousness; full of envy, murder, strife, deceit, evil-mindedness; they are whisperers, backbiters, haters of God, violent, proud, boasters, inventors of evil things, disobedient to parents, undiscerning,

untrustworthy, unloving, unforgiving, unmerciful; who, knowing the righteous judgment of God, that those who practice such things are deserving of death, not only do the same but also approve of those who practice them. (1:18–32)

This first-century passage describes America at the turn of the twenty-first century. It underscores our great need for repentance and returning to Christ. In short, it's time we get back to the Bible!

Every civilization must have a set of beliefs that act as a compass by which it is led through the morass of the fallen human condition to civility. These beliefs are to become manifest to all who are a part of a given society in the form of law. For this is the very thing by which civility is maintained. No other document was capable of such a task. Only God, through His written Word, could achieve such a universal feat. And this is the very foundation that God has granted us to build upon. He gave us liberty and justice, the very linchpins of freedom.

In this country we are blessed with "free speech." This liberty was the outgrowth of a tattered gathering of pilgrims, seeking refuge from persecution in their homeland. They laid the foundation for such a principle because they understood its importance. It is perhaps one of the greatest ironies of our time that the very thing that gave rise to free speech, the Holy Bible, is under siege daily by those who worship this First Amendment right. I'm thinking here about such groups as the ACLU (which some critics label as the Anti-Christian Liberties Union) and People for the American Way (or People for the Atheist Way). Some critics point out that organizations like this are in favor of free speech, as long as they approve of that speech—conservative Christians need not apply! They will no doubt find, much to their chagrin, that once they have removed the Bible from schools and public forums, tyranny will ultimately fill the void. There are signs of that coming tyranny virtually every day, but the intelligentsia never seem to make the connection!

As we detach ourselves and our nation from its biblical moorings, we can see the drift from civility and community that occurs. Our experience shows us that where the Bible is not present or does not hold sway, the void will be filled by police, metal detectors, and laws so stringent that the most basic human freedoms will be eradicated for the sake of social control. God fully understood the needed balance between the function of law and human freedom. It is this intricate balance that man has begun to tamper with. As we strip away the admonitions of the Word, we subsequently strip away our freedoms. Come now and let us reason together—remove any structure's foundation and it is sure to collapse.

And collapsing it is! But I believe an all-out collapse can be prevented. It can happen if true revival sweeps through the land.

THE BIBLE AND REVIVAL

Judge Robert Bork, a conservative critic and author of the best-selling *The Tempting of America* and *Slouching Toward Gomorrah*, says that the real hope for America rests with a revival of religion. He says that the evangelical movement and Promise Keepers could turn the tide. But he cautions that only time will tell if such changes will last and be far-sweeping enough.[7]

The greatest need in our time is revival. The Church, especially in the Western industrialized nations, is like a slumbering giant. There are many pockets of the Church that are wide awake and active, but the large part is no longer a force in our society. The Bible is the catalyst for waking the giant. The Bible is the spark that brings revival.

The word *revive* is often used in the Scripture. "O LORD, revive Your work in the midst of the years" (Hab. 3:2). The word refers to a quickening by the power of God. No one reading this book is likely to have seen a revival of Christianity unless that person was in the Hebrides, or perhaps in the South Seas during a revival that saw hundreds of thousands of Muslims swept into the faith. These are probably the only revivals that have taken place in the lifetime of most of us. However, in the spring of 1995 there were stirrings of revival on some Christian college campuses—beginning with Howard Payne University and going forth to Trinity in Deerfield, Illinois, Wheaton College, and others. Revival, some also say, has begun in a church in Pensacola, where they have been consistently holding packed-out services for more than two years now. Thankfully, there have been thousands who have been converted or who have recommitted their lives to Christ because of those meetings. Some would argue that Promise Keepers has the earmarks of an inkling of a revival, and I am very thankful for the thousands of men who have committed or recommitted their lives to Christ through that movement. Time alone will tell whether such movements are truly part of a *national* revival.

There are two aspects to revival. First there is the transformation of the people of God, which is the essential element. Revival primarily has to do with the people of God. It sparks a tremendous outbreak of evangelism, which works in ways people have not seen before.

Revivals in History

The Welsh revival of 1904 and 1905 is perhaps the most notable revival in this century. There people had been praying; churches that had been one-fourth filled with apathetic Christians began to come alive; the Spirit of God fell upon various towns; you could go through the streets and find men in great conviction and anguish because of their sins. Everywhere the Spirit of God was moving. People knew that God was there and that He was at work. The result was that in the small land of Wales, over a hundred thousand people were converted in five months! The outcome: the bars and taverns in many towns were shut down completely; the jails were emptied and closed! Wales was changed in a way that the people had never dreamed possible.

The Great Awakening in America in the mid-1700s was begun by a few people praying and seeking God's face, week after week, time after time, until finally God began to pour out His Spirit and people began to be converted. For years the revival went on. At its peak, tens of thousands of people a week were born into the kingdom of God. This statistic is all the more incredible when we consider that back then the country's population was roughly three million!

In England, a tremendous revival, also in the eighteenth century, that took place under George Whitefield and John and Charles Wesley may well have saved the country from a fate comparable to the French Revolution. It totally revolutionized the moral and spiritual life of the nation. Some historians make the point that France sowed the seeds for its own Revolution by killing or expelling the Huguenots—the French Calvinists, a sizable portion of the population who comprised the bulk of the middle class. By destroying the middle class in the sixteenth and seventeenth centuries, they paved the way for the bloodshed and chaos of the late eighteenth century. Unlike France, England did not butcher their dissenting Protestants—although some of their kings, notably James I, "harried them out of their land."[8] And a century and a half later, revival swept through Britain. That revival produced such Christians as William Wilberforce and Hannah More.

There can be a revival in America! The God who changed these men can change the hearts of anyone. The God who changed Saul of Tarsus, breathing out threats and slaughter, into Paul the apostle of the gospel of Christ, can change anyone. He can change America; He can restrain the evil that visits our mean city streets and spreads out from there. But there is a price to be paid! "If my people which are called by my name"—it begins with the people of God—"shall humble themselves and pray"—it begins in a prayer of brokenness, a prayer involving the humbling of ourselves, the acknowledgment of our own sins. For us to experience a revival in America, we need to repent and turn from our wicked ways. A Bible-centered revival in our nation and around the world is the great need of our time.

WHAT IF THE BIBLE HAD NEVER BEEN WRITTEN?

When a young lady who was not a Christian heard about this book, *What If The Bible Had Never Been Written?*, she immediately said, "Oh, the Bible has been nothing but oppressive toward women." This sentiment is often repeated in our biblically illiterate times. The truth is, the Bible has improved the treatment of women. Show me a country where women are treated well where the message of the Bible has not gone first. You can't because it doesn't exist. In fact, chivalry—where women became protected and cherished—was started by the Church in the Middle Ages. When hundreds of men on the *Titanic* voluntarily gave up their lives so that women and children could use the lifeboats, they were following a centuries-old, cultural norm that the Bible had established. However, since the Bible has lost sway among many people in our culture today, I daresay if the *Titanic* were to sink now, I doubt if most men would so readily give up on trying to get into a lifeboat.

The young lady's opposition to the Bible (which she has never bothered to read) is far too typical today. It comes from the school of ignorant thought that says Christianity is sexist, homophobic, racist, anti-science, anti-progress, and several other negative things.

What if the Bible had never been written? Consider the implications of such a scenario. There would be no salvation, no Salvation Army, no YMCA, virtually no charity, no modern science, no Red Cross. There would likely be no hospitals, for hospitals as we know them were born in the Christian era, and Christians have built hundreds of hospitals all over the globe. There would probably be no universities; they were created in the Middle Ages in order to reconcile Christian theology with the writings of Aristotle. There would probably be no capitalism, no accounting, no free enterprise. Millions of people would have been killed off by STDs (sexually transmitted diseases)—without any kind of inhibition against sexual promiscuity. Literacy and education might well be the exclusive domain of the elite. Many of the languages around the globe would never have been written down because there would have been no motive to do so. Many of the barbarians the world over would never have been civilized. Cannibalism and human sacrifice and the abandonment of children would still be widespread, even as abortion and infanticide plague us as we continue to move away from the Bible. Slavery might still be practiced, as it is in pockets of the world where the Bible is forbidden. And we might not even be in the New World—as Columbus clearly stated it was the Lord who inspired him to make his historic voyage. If the Bible had never been written, there would be no Mother Teresas, no David Livingstones, no Isaac Newtons, no William Wilberforces, no George Washingtons, no Lincolns, no Dantes, no Miltons, no Shakespeares, no Dickenses. Above all, if the Bible had never been written, we would be cut off from God, groping along in darkness without hope.[9]

But the Bible *has* been written, and we can embrace its wonderful message of the love of God, which was so great that He gave His only begotten Son that we might have eternal life. Because the Bible has been written, the wonderful story of how Jesus came to seek and to save the lost has gone out into all the world and has transformed millions of lives and scores of cultures and nations.

NO OTHER BOOK

No book can be rightfully compared to the Bible. No book has changed so many lives, so many cultures, so many nations. No book has inspired such great and noble deeds as those we have discussed in this book and in *What If Jesus Had Never Been Born?* And yet I imagine we've only managed to capture a fraction of the impact of the Scriptures on the world.

The Bible has no equal. Charles Dickens—a good judge of books—once wrote, "The New Testament is the best book the world has ever known or will know."[10] Ernest von Dobschutz sums it all up in his classic work, *The Influence of the Bible on Civilization:*

> There is a small book: one can put it in one's pocket, and yet all the libraries of America, numerous as they are, would hardly be large enough to hold all the books which have been inspired by this one little volume. The reader will know what I am speaking of; it is the Bible, as we are used to call it—the Book, the book of mankind, as has properly been called.[11]

The Bible is indeed the Book of books!
Soli Deo Gloria!

NOTES

Preface

1. "The Ultimate Hypothetical Question: What If Jesus Had Never Been Born?" *Christian Book Review*, March 1995, 16–17.
2. George Grant, "Outliving the conqueror," *World*, 11/18 May 1996, 22.
3. Ted Baehr, *Movieguide*, September A 1996, 15.
4. Abraham Lincoln, "Remarks upon the Holy Scriptures, in Receiving the Present of a Bible from a Negro Delegation," September 7, 1864, quoted in *Life and Works of Abraham Lincoln: Centenary Edition*, Marion Mills Miller, ed. (New York: The Current Literature Publishing Co., 1907), 5:209.

Chapter 1: The Book of Books

1. James C. Hefley, *What's So Great About the Bible?* (Elgin, IL: David C. Cook, 1969), 17–20.
2. Ibid., 18.
3. Quoted in Lee Williams, *No Room for Doubt* (Nashville: Broadman Press, 1977), 36.
4. Quoted in William J. Federer, *America's God and Country: Encyclopedia of Quotations* (Coppell, TX: FAME Publishing, Inc., 1994), 398.
5. Quoted in Federer, *America's God and Country*, 366.
6. Quoted in Hefley, *What's So Great About the Bible*, 71.
7. Ibid.
8. Quoted in Eleanor Doan, *Speakers Sourcebook II: 4,000 Illustrations and Quotations for Preachers and Other Public Speakers* (Grand Rapids: Zondervan, 1968), 47.
9. Quoted in Hefley, *What's So Great About the Bible*, 72.
10. Ibid.
11. Quoted in Doan, *Speakers Sourcebook II*, 48.
12. Reid Buckley, *Speaking in Public: Buckley's Techniques for Winning Arguments and Getting Your Point Across* (New York: Harper and Row, 1988), 46–47.
13. Allan Bloom, *The Closing of the American Mind* (New York: Simon and Schuster, 1987), 60.
14. Norman L. Geisler and William E. Nix, *A General Introduction to the Bible* (Chicago: Moody Press, 1968, 1988), 29.
15. Kenneth Scott Latourette, *A History of the Expansion of Christianity*, vol. 1, *First Five Centuries* (Grand Rapids: Zondervan, 1970), 214.
16. *World Annual Report 1995* (Reading, England), Bulletin Number 176/177, 271.
17. Reverend Jose Lopez, "Americas: Cuba: 'Something of an Explosion— Everyone Wants a Bible,'" *UBS [United Bible Societies] World Report* 316 (Reading, England), January 1997, 25.

18. "Bible Worth a 7-day Walk," *UBS World Report* 323, September 1997, 5.
19. *World Annual Report 1995*, 280.
20. Ibid., 3.
21. Ibid.
22. *UBS World Report* 316, 32.
23. Ibid.
24. "How often we read the Bible," *USA Today*, 1 February 1990. Source: *100 Questions and Answers: Religion in America*, Princeton Religious Research Center 1989.
25. Henry Van Dyke, "The Bible," quoted in Doan, *Speaker's Sourcebook II*, 45–46.

Chapter 2: The Bible and Morality

1. Miller, *Life and Works of Abraham Lincoln*, 5:209. Emphasis mine.
2. Immanuel E. Fichte, *The Way Toward the Blessed Life*, quoted in J. Gilchrist Lawson, *Greatest Thoughts About Jesus Christ* (New York: Richard R. Smith, Inc., 1930), 141.
3. Quoted in Lawson, *Greatest Thoughts About Jesus Christ*, 138.
4. Thomas Jefferson in a letter to John Adams in 1813, quoted in Douglas Lurton, foreword of *The Jefferson Bible* (Cleveland, OH: The World Publishing Company, 1942), ix.
5. J. T. Fisher and L. S. Hawley, *A Few Buttons Missing* (Philadelphia: J. B. Lippincott, 1951), 273.
6. Benjamin Disraeli, *Beaconsfield's Life of Lord Bentinck*, quoted in Lawson, *Greatest Thoughts About Jesus Christ*, 131.
7. *Liberty*, September/October 1984.
8. Miller, *Life and Works of Abraham Lincoln,* 5:146.
9. *Compton's Pictured Encyclopedia and Fact-Index* (Chicago: F. E. Compton Co., 1965), 13:483.
10. John R. Adams, *Harriet Beecher Stowe* (Boston: Twayne Publishers, 1963), 54.
11. Quoted in Adams, *Harriet Beecher Stowe*, 17–18.
12. Harriet Beecher Stowe, *Uncle Tom's Cabin* (New York: Washington Square Press, 1965), 458.
13. Nina Shea, *In the Lion's Den* (Nashville: Broadman and Holman, 1997), 33–34.
14. Erwin Lutzer, *Exploding the Myths That Could Destroy America* (Chicago: Moody Press, 1986), 57. Emphasis mine.
15. Paul Kurtz, ed., *Humanist Manifestos I and II* (Buffalo: Prometheus Books, 1981), 17.
16. Here are Ted Turner's "Ten Voluntary Initiatives":
    1. I promise to have love and respect for the planet earth and living things thereon, especially my fellow species—humankind.

2. I promise to treat all persons everywhere with dignity, respect, and friendliness.

3. I promise to have no more than two children, or no more than my nation suggests.

4. I promise to use my efforts to save what is left of our natural world in its untouched state and to restore undamaged or destroyed areas where practical.

5. I pledge to use as little nonrenewable resources as possible.

6. I pledge to use as little toxic chemical, pesticides, and other poisons as possible and to work for their reduction by others.

7. I promise to contribute to those less fortunate than myself, to help them become self-sufficient and enjoy the benefits of a decent life, including clean air and water, adequate food and health care, housing education, and individual rights.

8. I reject the use of force, in particular military force, and back United Nations arbitration of international disputes.

9. I support the total elimination of all nuclear, chemical, and biological weapons of mass destruction.

10. I support the United Nations and its efforts to collectively improve the conditions of the planet.

Source: "Turner's 'Voluntary Initiatives,'" *The Humanist*, November/December 1989, 6.

17. Quoted in Paul Lee Tan, *Encyclopedia of 7700 Illustrations: Signs of the Times* (Rockford, MD: Assurance Publishers, 1984), 176.

18. D. James Kennedy, "Absolutes in a Relativistic Age," speech delivered at Yale University, October 7, 1993.

19. Bloom, *The Closing of the American Mind*, 194.

20. Charles Darwin, *The Autobiography of Charles Darwin and Selected Letters* (New York: Dover, 1958), quoted in Lutzer, *Exploding the Myths*, 53–54.

21. Quoted in Lutzer, *Exploding the Myths*, 53.

22. Ibid., 27–28.

23. Ibid., 52.

24. Elizabeth Mehren, "Humans a mere afterthought, evolutionist says," *The Cleveland Plain Dealer*, 17 December 1989.

25. Lutzer, *Exploding the Myths*, 46–47, 54.

26. William H. McGuffey, *The Eclectic Fourth Reader: Containing Elegant Extracts in Prose and Poetry from the Best American and English Writers* (Cincinnati: Truman and Smith, 1838), 143–144, reproduced in John H. Westerhoff III, *McGuffey and His Readers: Pity, Morality and Education in Nineteenth-Century America* (Milford, MI: Mott Media, 1978, 1982), 151–152.

27. Bloom, *The Closing of the American Mind*, 25.

28. Paul Johnson, *Modern Times: The World from the Twenties to the Eighties* (New York: Harper and Row, 1983), 4–5.

29. John Warwick Montgomery, *The Law Above the Law* (Minneapolis: Bethany House, 1975), 25–26.
30. Ibid.
31. Michael Medved's comments were spoken on D. James Kennedy, *The Coral Ridge Hour* (Fort Lauderdale: Coral Ridge Ministries—TV), 3 March 1996.
32. See D. James Kennedy with Jerry Newcombe, *The Gates of Hell Shall Not Prevail: The Attack on Christianity and What You Need to Know to Combat It* (Nashville: Thomas Nelson, 1996). Movies depicting what I am describing here include *Johnny Mnemonic* (1994), *Seven* (1995), *Just Cause* (1995), *The Glimmer Man* (1996), ad infinitum, ad nauseum. As we pointed out in *The Gates of Hell Shall Not Prevail*, the vast majority of these bigoted, antireligious films bomb in the box office with, as Michael Medved puts it, "stunning predictability."
33. "Washington's Farewell Address," reproduced in *Compton's Pictured Encyclopedia,* 15:26.
34. Quoted in Federer, *America's God and Country*, 661, from Washington's farewell address.
35. Quoted in J. Gilchrist Lawson, *Greatest Thoughts About God* (New York: George H. Doran Company, 1920), 302.
36. William J. Bennett, *The Index of Leading Cultural Indicators: Facts and Figures on the State of American Society* (New York: Simon and Schuster, 1994), 8.
37. Ibid., 20, 23, 30, 35.
38. William Kilpatrick, *Why Johnny Can't Tell Right from Wrong* (New York: Simon and Schuster, 1992), 14.
39. Quoted in Gary DeMar, *America's Christian History: The Untold Story* (Atlanta: American Vision, Inc., 1995), 154.
40. Bertrand Russell, *Why I Am Not a Christian* (New York: Simon and Schuster, 1957).
41. Paul Johnson, *Intellectuals* (New York: Harper and Row, 1988), 212–218.
42. Quoted in Lawson, *Greatest Thoughts About God*, 120.
43. Judge Sharswood, quoted in Lawson, *Greatest Thoughts About God*, 122.
44. Quoted in "Britain's Margaret Thatcher speaks About Christian Responsibility," *Concerned Women for America*, February 1989, 20.

Chapter 3: The Bible and Society

1. W. H. McCutheon, *The Gospel Herald*, quoted Walter B. Knight, *Knight's Master Book of New Illustrations* (Grand Rapids: Eerdmans, 1956), 33.
2. Bill Wilson, featured in "Crisis in Character," *The Coral Ridge Hour* (Fort Lauderdale: Coral Ridge Ministries—TV), 16 October 1994.
3. Quoted in Lawson, *Greatest Thoughts About Jesus Christ,* 149.
4. For more details on the debauchery on Pitcairn Island, see Jerry Newcombe, "Tropical Paradise Lost and Found," *The Moral of the Story:*

Timeless Tales to Cherish and Share (Nashville: Broadman and Holman, 1996), 211–215.

5. Quoted in Newcombe, "Tropical Paradise," 214–215.
6. T. C. Roughley, "*Bounty* Descendants Live on Remote Norfolk Island," *National Geographic* 118, no. 4 (October 1960): 559–584.
7. Karl Marx, *Economic and Philosophical Manuscripts of 1844*, D. J. Struick, ed., M. Milligan, trans. (New York: International Publishing Co., 1971), quoted in David McLellan, *Karl Marx* (New York: Penguin Books, 1975), 32–33. Emphasis mine.
8. Of course, the Communists tried to completely squelch Christianity. Stalin is estimated to have killed about fifteen million Christians. (See Chapter 11 of *The Gates of Hell Shall Not Prevail* for details on the Communists' unsuccessful attempt to uproot Christianity.)
9. Karl Marx, *The Communist Manifesto*, Samuel Moore, trans. (Chicago: Henry Regnary Company, 1969) 56–57.
10. For example, Stalin killed between forty and sixty million people. Mao killed about 72 million people. See D. James Kennedy and Jerry Newcombe, *What If Jesus Had Never Been Born?* (Nashville: Thomas Nelson, 1994), 234–237.
11. Frederica Mathewes-Green, "The Genoveses Find God," *National Review*, 24 February 1997, 56.
12. Johnson, *Modern Times*, 729.
13. See Kennedy and Newcombe, *What If Jesus Had Never Been Born?*, 42–51.
14. John J. Dunphy, "Religion for a New Age," *The Humanist*, January/February 1983, 26.
15. The most direct way to read about these events is in *Pitcairn Island*, Part 3 of Charles Nordhoff and James Norman Hall, *The Bounty Trilogy* (Boston: Little, Brown and Company, 1962).
16. See Ernest Gordon, *Through the Valley of the Kwai* (New York: Harper and Row, 1962).
17. St. Augustine, *The Confessions of St. Augustine*, trans. by John K. Ryan (Garden City, NY: Doubleday, 1960), 43.
18. If you would like information on this ministry and how to implement it in your church, please write to Evangelism Explosions III, International, 5554 N. Federal Highway, Fort Lauderdale, FL 33308; or call 954-491-6100.
19. Louisa Fletcher, "The Land of Beginning Again," *Best Loved Poems*, Hazel Felleman, ed. (Garden City, NY: Garden City Books, 1936), 101–102.
20. Earle Albert Rowell, *Prophecy Speaks: Dissolving Doubts* (Washington, DC: Review and Herald Publishing Association, 1933), 123, 125–126.
21. C. E. M. Joad, *The Recovery of Belief* (London: Faber, 1952).
22. Jane Chastain, *Dispatches*, 22 May 1996, reported in *The Washington Times*, 2 July 1996.

23. "Eat Right, Exercise Regularly, and Go to Church on Sunday," *Christian News*, 30 December 1996, 3.

24. See Dr. Kenneth H. Cooper, *Faith-Based Fitness* (Nashville: Thomas Nelson, 1995).

25. "Survey finds churchgoers more stable, productive, charitable," *The Washington Times*, 30 March 1990.

26. "Go to church, live longer," in the "Briefing" subsection under "Heath-Fitness-Families," Fort Lauderdale *Sun-Sentinel*, 10 August 1997, 3E. The findings were reported in the *American Journal of Public Health*.

27. Ibid.

28. "Religion's role in health studied," *The Washington Times*, 30 July 1996, A2.

29. Joseph P. Shapiro with Andrea R. Wright, "Can Churches Save America?" *U.S. News and World Report*, 9 September 1996, 50.

30. Ibid., 52.

31. "Unlocking Hearts with the 'Key to Life,'" *UBS World Report*, September 1996, 22.

32. Lawson, *Greatest Thoughts*, 122.

33. Quoted in Lawson, *Greatest Thoughts*, 27.

Chapter 4: The Bible and Law

1. A cartoon by Baloo from *The Saturday Evening Post*, reproduced on the back side of an undated press release from Zondervan Publishing House for Steve Pettinga, ed., *The Best Cartoons from* The Saturday Evening Post.

2. Al Ries and Jack Trout, *Positioning: The Battle for Your Mind* (New York: Warner Books, 1981, 1986), 13.

3. René A. Wormser, *The Story of Law and the Men Who Made It—From the Earliest Times to the Present* (New York: Simon and Schuster, 1962), 7.

4. Ibid., 3.

5. Ibid.

6. Will and Ariel Durant, *The Lessons of History* (New York: Simon and Schuster, 1968), 58.

7. Sara Robbins, ed., *Law: A Treasury of Art and Literature* (New York: Hugh Levin Associates, Inc., distributed by Macmillan Publishing Company, 1990), 20–21.

8. Will Durant, *Our Oriental Heritage*, vol. 1 of *The Story of Civilization* (New York: Simon and Schuster, 1954), 232.

9. Max Dimont, "Jews, God and History," quoted in Robbins, *Law*, 27.

10. Wormser, *The Story of Law*, 28.

11. Dimont, "Jews, God, and History," 27.

12. Durant, *Our Oriental Heritage*, 333.

13. Ibid., 335.

14. Ibid., 337.

15. Wormser, *The Story of Law*, 13.
16. Ibid.
17. Israel Drapkin, M. D., *Crime and Punishment in the Ancient World* (Lexington, MA: Lexington Books, 1989), 50.
18. Wormser, *The Story of Law*, 27.
19. Ibid., 27–28.
20. J. M. Roberts, *History of the World* (New York: Oxford University Press, 1993), 243–244.
21. Will Durant, *The Age of Faith*, vol. 4 of *The Story of Civilization* (New York: Simon and Schuster, 1960), 111.
22. Charles Diehl, *History of the Byzantine Empire*, George B. Ives, trans. (New York: AMS Press 1969), 19.
23. P. N. Ure, *Justinian and His Age* (Westport, CT: Greenwood Press, 1979), 139.
24. Durant, *The Age of Faith*, 111.
25. George Ostrogorsky, *History of the Byzantine State* (New Brunswick, NJ: Rutgers University Press, 1969), 75.
26. Quoted in John Julius Norwick, *Byzantium: The Early Centuries* (New York: Alfred A. Knopf, Inc., 1988), 181.
27. Quoted in Ure, *Justinian and His Age*, 142.
28. Durant, *The Age of Faith*, 112–114.
29. Ibid., 112.
30. Ostrogorsky, *History of the Byzantine State*, 76.
31. Ibid., 77.
32. Norman A. Cantor, *Western Civilization: Its Genesis and Destiny*, vol. 1, *From the Prehistoric Era to 1715* (Glenview, IL: Scott, Foresman, Company, 1969), 276.
33. Diehl, *History of the Byzantine Empire*, 31.
34. Ibid.
35. Durant, *The Age of Faith*, 114.
36. Percy H. Winfield, *The Chief Sources of English Legal History* (New York: Burt Franklin, 1925), 58–59.
37. Wormser, *The Story of Law*, 147.
38. Drapkin, *Crime and Punishment*, 243.
39. Allen J. Frantzen, *King Alfred* (Boston: Twayne Publishers, 1986), 11.
40. J. M. Roberts, *History of the World*, 326.
41. Winston Churchill, *A History of the English-Speaking Peoples: The British* (New York: Dodd, Mead and Company, 1956), 122.
42. Quoted in Durant, *The Age of Faith*.
43. Pauline Stafford, *Unification and Conquest: A Political and Social History of England in the Tenth and Eleventh Centuries* (London: Edward Arnold, 1989), 134.
44. Frantzen, *King Alfred,* 13.
45. Churchill, *A History of the English-Speaking Peoples*, 120.

46. Philip Schaff, *History of the Christian Church*, vol. 4, *Medieval Christianity A.D. 590–1073* (Grand Rapids: Eerdmans, 1910), 393–395.
47. Frantzen, *King Alfred*, 13–14.
48. Stafford, *Unification and Conquest*, 5.
49. John Richard Green, *History of the English People*, quoted in Verna Hall, *The Christian History of the Constitution of the United States of America* (San Francisco: Foundation for American Christian Education, 1966, 1993), 38.
50. Archbishop Steven Langdon, The Magna Charta, quoted in Hall, *The Christian History of the Constitution*, 38.
51. Joseph A. Wapner, "From a Judge's Study," *Guideposts*, November 1988, 3–4.
52. Joseph Reither, *World History at a Glance* (New York: The New Home Library, 1942), 184.
53. Wormser, *The Story of Law*, 507.
54. Charles Edwards, *Hugo Grotius, the Miracle of Holland: A Study in Political and Legal Thought* (Chicago: Nelson-Hall, 1981), 1.
55. Will and Ariel Durant, *The Age of Reason Begins*, vol. 7 of *The Story of Civilization* (New York: Simon and Schuster, 1963), 632.
56. W. E. Butler, "Grotius and the Law of the Sea," *Hugo Grotius and International Relations*, Hedley Bull, Benedict Kingsbury, and Adam Roberts, eds. (Oxford: Claredon Press, 1990), 213.
57. Wormser, *The Story of Law*, 508.
58. Quoted in Durant, *The Age of Reason Begins*, 633.
59. Hedley Bull, "The Importance of Grotius in the Study of International Relations," *Hugo Grotius and International Relations*, 65.
60. Quoted in Edwards, *Hugo Grotius*, 60.
61. Edwards, *Hugo Grotius*, 60.
62. Quoted in Edwards, *Hugo Grotius*, 129.
63. Quoted in Edwards, *Hugo Grotius*, 61.
64. Bull, "The Importance of Grotius," 75.
65. Wormser, *The Story of Law*, 507.
66. W. N. Welsby, "Lives of Eminent English Judges," 1846, quoted in Hall, *The Christian History of the Constitution*, 139.
67. Judge Moore was given this award by the D. James Kennedy Center for Christian Statesmanship in Washington, D.C., by Dr. Frank Wright, the center's director.
68. I have benefited tremendously from Roy Moore's affidavit for this section on Blackstone. See Roy S. Moore, *Affidavit and Statement of Facts* (Etowah County, AL: unpublished, July 1996). For information on how to obtain a copy, write to Judge Moore Legal Defense Fund, 800 Forrest Ave., Gadsden, AL 35901.
69. Moore, *Affidavit*, 7.
70. Ibid., 129, 125.
71. Ibid., 41.

72. William Blackstone, *Commentaries on the Laws of England* (Philadelphia: Robert Bell, 1771), 2:2–3.
73. Moore, 39.
74. Blackstone, *Commentaries*, 1:38.
75. Ibid., 1:41.
76. Blackstone, quoted in Hall, *The Christian History of the Constitution*, 141.
77. Blackstone, *Commentaries*, 1:42.
78. Ibid.
79. Quoted in Moore, *Affidavit*, 86–87. From Washington's "Farewell Address," 17 September 1796.
80. Blackstone, *Commentaries*, 3:31.
81. Ibid., 4:43–44.

Chapter 5: The Bible and Politics

1. Abraham Kuyper, *You Can Do Greater Things Than Christ*, Jan H. Boer, trans. (Jos, Nigeria: Institute of Church and Society, 1991), 74. This quote comes from the first volume of Kuyper's book, which was first published as *Pro Rege, of Het Koningschap van Christus* in 1911.
2. John Eidsmoe, *God and Caesar: Christian Faith and Political Action* (Westchester, IL: Crossway Books, 1985), 14.
3. Quoted in James Madison, *The Papers of James Madison*, Henry D. Gilpin, ed. (Washington, DC: Langtree and O'Sullivan, 1840), 2:984–986.
4. Quoted in Eidsmoe, *God and Caesar*, 102.
5. Ibid.
6. Ibid.
7. Quoted in David Barton, *Original Intent: The Courts, the Constitution, and Religion* (Aledo, TX: WallBuilders, Inc., 1996), 425.
8. These prayers were found in the 1890s along with a cache of other writings and effects of George Washington. Experts have judged them to be authentic. John Eidsmoe points out that it's not known whether these prayers were original or not. Even if they weren't original, for Washington to transcribe them shows a great deal about his earnestness to know God and to do His will. John Eidsmoe, *Christianity and the Constitution* (Grand Rapids: Baker Book House, 1987), 130.
9. George Washington's personal prayer book in his own handwriting. Quoted in Federer, *America's God and Country*, 657–658.
10. George Washington, *Writings* (1932), 15:55; from his speech to the Delaware Indian Chiefs on May 12, 1779. Quoted in Barton, *Original Intent*, 168.
11. Quoted in Lawson, *Greatest Thoughts About Jesus Christ*, 130.
12. Henry Cabot Lodge, letter to *New York Daily Tribune*, 26 May 1902, quoted in John Eidsmoe, *Christianity and the Constitution*, 138.
13. Nelly Custis, letter to Jared Sparks, 23 February 1833, quoted in Eidsmoe, *Christianity and the Constitution*, 141.

14. Quoted in Eidsmoe, *Christianity and the Constitution*, 139.
15. William J. Johnson, *Abraham Lincoln: The Christian* (New York: The Abingdon Press, 1913), 149.
16. Henry C. Whitney, *Lincoln the Citizen* (New York: The Current Literature Publishing Co., 1907), 201.
17. Quoted in Whitney, *Lincoln the Citizen*, 201–202.
18. Comment from George Grant on D. James Kennedy, "The ACLU: Children in the Balance," *The Coral Ridge Hour* (Fort Lauderdale: Coral Ridge Ministries—TV), 30 June 1996.
19. Miller, ed., *Life and Works of Abraham Lincoln*, 6:153.
20. Ibid., 6:156–157.
21. Ibid., 6: 204–205.
22. Ibid., 6: 205.
23. Quoted in *Speeches and Presidential Addresses, 1859–1865* (New York: The Current Literature Publishing Co., 1907), 5:224–225.
24. Johnson, *Abraham Lincoln: The Christian*, 182.
25. Quoted in Dale Carnegie, *How to Win Friends and Influence People* (New York: Simon and Schuster, 1936, 1964), 23.
26. Charles Ludwig, *He Freed Britain's Slaves* (Scottdale, PA: Herald Press, 1977), 78–79.
27. Quoted in Charles W. Colson, "Standing tough against all odds," *Christianity Today*, 6 September 1985, 27.
28. Quoted in Basil Miller, *Ten Handicapped Boys and Girls Who Became Famous*, 29.
29. Quoted in "Standing tough against all odds," 27.
30. Quoted in Travers Buxton, *William Wilberforce: The Story of a Great Crusade* (London: The Religious Tract Society, undated), 80.
31. Quoted on the back cover of Ludwig, *He Freed Britain's Slaves*.

Chapter 6: The Bible and the Founding of America

1. Kenneth L. Woodward with David Gates, "How the Bible Made America," *Newsweek*, 27 December 1982, 44.
2. "Looking to Its Roots," *TIME*, 25 May 1987.
3. Clarence B. Carson, *A Basic History of the United States*, vol. 1, *The Colonial Experience 1607–1774* (Wadley, AL: American Textbook Committee, 1983, 1987), 17.
4. Albert Matthews, *The Term Pilgrim Fathers*. Reprinted from the publications of the Colonial Society of Massachusetts, vol. 17 (Cambridge: John Wilson and Son University Press, 1915), 293–294, quoted in Catherine Millard, *The Rewriting of America's History* (Camp Hill, PA: Horizon House Publishers, 1991), 35.
5. Henry Cabot Lodge, "English Colonies in America," (1881), quoted in Hall, *The Christian History of the Constitution*, 150B.
6. *NEA Handbook 1995–1996* (Washington, DC: National Education Association, 1995), 266.

7. William Bradford, *Of Plymouth Plantation* (1650), rendered into modern English in 1909 by Harold Paget and retitled *Bradford's History of the Plymouth Settlement 1608–1650* (San Antonio, TX: Mantle Ministries, 1988), 21.

8. Leonard Bacon, "Genesis of the New England Churches," (1874), quoted in Hall, *The Christian History of the Constitution*, 23.

9. The word *pilgrims* as applied to the Separatists who founded Plymouth was first used in writings of William Bradford, who wrote the historic book *Of Plymouth Plantation*.

10. Quoted in William B. Sprague, "Annals of the American Pulpit," (1857), cited in Hall, *The Christian History of the United States*, 184.

11. Millard, *The Rewriting of American History*, 19.

12. Daniel Webster, *The Works of Daniel Webster* (Boston: Little, Brown and Company, 1853), 1:48.

13. C. S. Lewis, *English in the Sixteenth Century, Excluding Drama* (London: Oxford University Press, 1973), 34.

14. Eidsmoe, *Christianity and the Constitution*, 24.

15. Clarence Carson, *A Basic History*, 72.

16. John Winthrop, *A Model of Christian Charity*, written 11 June 1630, aboard the ship *Arbella*, quoted in Federer, *America's God and Country*, 700.

17. Quoted in Federer, *America's God and Country*, 700.

18. Clarence Carson, *A Basic History*, 72–73.

19. John Fiske, *Civil Government in the United States* (1890), cited in Hall, *The Christian History of the Constitution*, 271–272.

20. Ibid., 272.

21. Quoted in Hall, *The Christian History of the Constitution*, 279.

22. Quoted in Millard, *The Rewriting of America's History*, 38.

23. Quoted in Millard, *The Rewriting of America's History*, 43.

24. B. F. Morris, *The Christian Life and Character of the Civil Institutions of the United States* (Philadelphia: George W. Childs, 1864), 83.

25. Although John Robinson was the pastor of the Pilgrims, it was mutually decided that he would not join the first voyage over to the New World. Instead, he was to continue to minister to the flock that remained in Holland, which would later come to America. He died in 1625 before he got the chance to come.

26. Loraine Boettner, *The Reformed Doctrine of Predestination* (Philadelphia: The Presbyterian and Reformed Publishing Company, 1975), 382.

27. Eidsmoe, *Christianity and the Constitution*, 18.

28. Ibid., 17–26.

29. Quoted in Boettner, *The Reformed Doctrine*, 389.

30. Quoted in Hall, *The Christian History of the Constitution*, 28.

31. See DeMar, *America's Christian History* (1993 edition), 40–44, and Kennedy and Newcombe, *What If Jesus Had Never Been Born?*, 52–53.

32. Quoted in DeMar, *America's Christian History* (1995 edition) 103. Emphasis author's.
33. Quoted in Tan, *Encyclopedia of 7700 Illustrations*, 157.
34. DeMar, *America's Christian History* (1995 edition), 5.
35. M. E. Bradford, *A Worthy Company* (Marlborough, NH: Plymouth Rock Foundation, 1982) or see Kennedy and Newcombe, *What If Jesus Had Never Been Born?*, 70.
36. Again, I would point out that Calvinism transcended denominational boundaries. For example, many Anglicans at the time were Calvinists and virtually all the Congregationalists were Calvinists.
37. Federer, *America's God and Country*, 180.
38. We recommend for starters Gary DeMar's excellent book *America's Christian History: The Untold Story*. Other recommended books are David Barton's *Original Intent: The Courts, the Constitution, and Religion*; John Eidsmoe's *Christianity and the Constitution: The Faith of Our Founding Fathers*; *The Rewriting of America's History* by Catherine Millard; *The Christian History of the Constitution of the United States of America* edited by Verna Hall; and William J. Federer's *America's God and Country: Encyclopedia of Quotations*. All of these books are well documented.
39. See Hall, *The Christian History of the Constitution*, 261.
40. Rev. Nathaniel Ward of Ipswich, MA, "Body of Liberties," quoted in Hall, *The Christian History of the Constitution*, 257.
41. Palfrey, *History of New England*, quoted in Hall, *The Christian History of the Constitution*, 257.
42. Rush H. Limbaugh III, *See, I Told You So* (New York: Simon and Schuster, 1993), 69–73, quoted in Federer, *America's God and Country*, 373.
43. John Winthrop, "Little Speech on Liberty: (1645), quoted in Federer, *America's God and Country*, 262.
44. Quoted in Federer, *America's God and Country*, 262A.
45. Alexis de Tocqueville, *Democracy in America*, Henry Reeve, trans., revised by Francis Bowen, further corrected and edited by Phillips Bradley (New York: Vintage Books, 1990), 307.
46. John Locke, *An Essay Concerning Human Understanding* (Brattleboro, VT: 1806), quoted in Hall, *The Christian History of the Constitution*, 56.
47. Quoted in Hall, *The Christian History of the Constitution*, 130.
48. John Locke, *The Reasonableness of Christianity* (1695), quoted in Hall, *The Christian History of the Constitution*, xiii.
49. Gary DeMar, *America's Christian History* (1995 edition), 114.
50. *The World Almanac and Book of Facts 1991*, 472.
51. Quoted in Kennedy and Newcombe, *What If Jesus Had Never Been Born?*, 64.
52. Quoted in David Barton, *The Myth of Separation: What Is the Correct Relationship Between Church and State?* (Aledo, TX: WallBuilder Press, 1992), 88. Used by permission.

53. "Fundamental Orders of Connecticut," 14 January 1639. *Documents of American History*, sixth edition, Henry Steel Commager, ed. (New York: Appleton-Century-Crofts, 1958), 26, quoted in DeMar, *America's Christian History* (1993 edition), 37.

54. George Leon Walker, *History of the First Church in Hartford* (Brown and Gross, 1884), quoted in Hall, *The Christian History of the Constitution*, 249.

55. Quoted in David Barton, *Original Intent*, 173.

56. *The Washington Times*, 23 November 1992.

57. *Church of the Holy Trinity* v. *The United States;* 143 U.S. 457, 471 (1892).

58. *The Washington Post*, 15 November 1986.

59. Quoted in Robert Faulkner, *The Jurisprudence of John Marshall* (Westprot, CT: Greenwood Press, 1968), 139.

60. Public Law 97-280, 96 Stat. 1211, approved 4 October 1982, quoted in DeMar, *America's Christian History*, 121.

Chapter 7: The Bible and Science

1. Isaac Watts, "Joy to the World!" *Choice Hymns of the Faith* (Fort Dodge, IA: Gospel Perpetuating Fund, 1945), hymn number 522.

2. Donald E. Chittick, *The Controversy: Roots of the Creation-Evolution Conflict* (Compass Press, 1984), 16.

3. Francis A. Schaeffer, *Escape from Reason* (Downers Grove, IL: InterVarsity Press, 1968), 31.

4. J. Robert Oppenheimer, "On Science and Culture," *Encounter*, October 1962, 5.

5. Quoted in Henry Morris, *Men of Science — Men of God* (San Diego: Master Books, 1984), 35.

6. Robert G. Frank Jr., review of *The Great Instauration* by Charles Webster, *Science*, 28 January 1977, 386.

7. Morris, *Men of Science — Men of God*, 39.

8. Ibid., 56.

9. Ibid.

10. Ibid., 89.

11. Johannes Kepler, quoted in Durant, *The Age of Reason Begins*, 600.

12. Charles E. Hummel, *The Galileo Connection: Resolving Conflicts Between Science and the Bible* (Downers Grove, IL: InterVarsity Press, 1986), 57–58.

13. Job Kozhamthadam, S. J., *The Discovery of Kepler's Laws: The Interaction of Science, Philosophy, and Religion* (South Bend, IN: University of Notre Dame Press, 1994), 181.

14. Durant, *The Age of Reason Begins*, 598.

15. Kozhamthadam, *The Discovery of Kepler's Laws*, 44.

16. Ibid., 21.

17. Richard J. Blackwell, *Galileo, Bellarmine, and the Bible* (South Bend, IN: University of Notre Dame Press, 1991), 56.

18. Hummel, *The Galileo Connection*, 102.
19. Durant, *The Age of Reason Begins*, 602.
20. Ibid., 603.
21. This quote is taken from a summary of *Blackwell, Galileo, Bellarmine, and the Bible*, located on the inside flap of the dust jacket.
22. Quoted in Stillman Drake, *Galileo at Word: His Scientific Biography* (Chicago: University of Chicago Press, 1978), 224.
23. Derek Gjertsen, *The Newton Handbook* (New York: Routledge and Kegan Paul, Inc., 1986), 69–70.
24. Some critics charge that Newton was not orthodox in his theology all of his life. But the Durants point out: "Newton was, or became, quite orthodox. He seems to have taken every word of the Bible as the word of God, and to have accepted the books of Daniel and Revelation as literal truth." Ibid.
25. This idea is similar to what we find in Psalm 19, where David talks about the acts of the Lord as seen in creation and the Law of the Lord as seen in His revealed Word.
26. Gale E. Christianson, *In the Presence of the Creator: Isaac and His Times* (New York: Free Press, 1984), 41.
27. Ibid., 248.
28. Will and Ariel Durant, *The Age of Voltaire*, vol. 9 of *The Story of Civilization* (New York: Simon and Schuster, 1965), 561.
29. Ian T. Taylor, *In the Minds of Men: Darwin and the New World Order* (Toronto: TFE Publishing, 1987), 38.
30. Stephen Jay Gould, *Dinosaur in a Haystack: Reflections in Natural History* (New York: Harmony Books, 1995), 421.
31. Alice Dickinson, *Carl Linnaeus: Pioneer of Modern Botany* (New York: Franklin Watts, Inc., 1967), 34.
32. Taylor, *In the Minds of Men*, 39.
33. Gould, *Dinosaur in a Haystack*, 422.
34. Ibid.
35. Durant and Durant, *The Age of Voltaire*, 564.
36. Dickinson, *Carl Linnaeus*, 486.
37. Ibid., 121.
38. Ibid., 197.
39. *Encyclopedia Americana* (New York: Americana Corporation, 1966).
40. David Knight, *The Age of Science: The Scientific World-View in the Nineteenth Century* (Oxford: Basil Blackwell, 1986), 46.
41. Quoted in H. W. Buxton, *Memoirs of the Life and Labours of Charles Babbage ESQ. F. R. S.* (Cambridge, MA: The MIT Press, 1988), 316.
42. Anthony Hyman, *Science and Reform: Selected Works of Charles Babbage* (Cambridge, England: Cambridge University Press, 1989), 208.
43. Buxton, *Memoirs*, 324.
44. Ibid., 330.
45. Ibid., 351.

46. See James M. Houston, ed., *The Mind on Fire: An Anthology of the Writings of Blaise Pascal* (Portland, OR: Multnomah Press, 1989).
47. Paul J. Staiti, *Samuel F. B. Morse* (Cambridge, England: Cambridge University Press, 1989), 1.
48. *Compton's Pictured Encyclopedia*, 9:492.
49. Ibid.
50. William Kloss, *Samuel F. Morse* (New York: Harry A. Abrams, Inc., Publishers, 1988), 148.
51. Ibid.
52. Quoted in Kloss, *Samuel F. Morse*, 148.
53. Quoted in Staiti, *Samuel F. B. Morse*, 135.
54. Quoted in Staiti, *Samuel F. B. Morse*, 136.
55. Staiti, *Samuel F. B. Morse*, 223.
56. John A. Garraty and Jerome L. Sternstein, eds., *Encyclopedia of American Biography* (New York: Harper and Row, 1974), 788.
57. Don Groves, *The Oceans: A Book of Questions and Answers* (New York: John Wiley and Sons, Inc., 1989), 9.
58. Donald G. Groves and Lee M. Hunt, *The Ocean World Encyclopedia* (New York: McGraw-Hill Book Co., 1980), 222.
59. Ibid.
60. Barbara Charton, ed., *Facts on File: Dictionary of Marine Science* (New York: Facts on File Publications, 1988).
61. Gardner Soule, *Men Who Dared the Sea: The Ocean Adventures of the Ancient Mariners* (New York: Thomas Y. Crowell Co., 1976), 228.
62. Frances Leigh Williams, *Matthew Fontaine Maury, Scientist of the Sea* (New Brunswick: Rutgers University Press, 1963), 339. Emphasis mine.
63. Quoted in Williams, *Matthew Fontaine Maury*, 340.
64. Roberto Margotta, *The Story of Medicine: Man's Struggle Against Disease—from Ancient Sorcery to Modern Miracles of Vaccines, Drugs, and Surgery* (New York: Golden Press, 1968), 254.
65. Roderick E. McGrew, *Encyclopedia of Medical History* (New York: McGraw-Hill Book Company, 1985), 17.
66. Margotta, *The Story of Medicine*, 256.
67. Garraty and Sternstein, *Encyclopedia of American Biography*, 179.
68. *Encyclopedia Americana*, 5:689.
69. Ibid.
70. Gary R. Kremer, *George Washington Carver: In His Own Words* (Columbia, MO: University of Missouri Press, 1987), 133.
71. Ibid., 142.
72. Rackham Holt, *George Washington Carver: An American Biography* (Garden City, NY: Doubleday and Company, Inc., 1963), 232–233.
73. Linda O. McMurry, *George Washington Carver, Scientist and Symbol* (New York: Oxford University Press, 1981), 96–97.
74. Ibid., 180.
75. Ibid., 105.

76. Ibid., 105–106.

77. *Compton's Pictured Encyclopedia*, 3:147.

78. Quoted in Wilbur M. Smith, *Profitable Bible Study: Seven Simple Methods* (Natick, MA: W. A. Wilde Company, 1963), 82–83. Emphasis mine.

Chapter 8: The Bible and Literature

1. Charlotte Brontë, *Jane Eyre* (New York: The New American Library, Inc., 1960), 456.

2. Terry W. Glaspey, *Great Books of the Christian Tradition, and Other Books Which Have Shaped Our World* (Eugene, OR: Harvest House Publishers, 1996), 39.

3. See Kennedy and Newcombe, *The Gates of Hell Shall Not Prevail*.

4. Glaspey, *Great Books of the Christian Tradition*, 28.

5. T. S. Eliot, "Religion and Literature," *Religion and Modern Literature: Essays in Theory and Criticism*, G. B. Tennyson and Edward E. Ericson Jr., eds. (Grand Rapids: Eerdman, 1975), 22.

6. David H. Higgins, introduction *The Divine Comedy*, by Dante, trans. C. H. Sisson (Chicago: Regnery Gateway, 1980).

7. Harold Bloom, introduction to *Modern Critical Interpretations: The Divine Comedy*, edited by Harold Bloom (New York: Chelsea House Publishers, 1987), 1.

8. J. H. Whitfield, *A Short History of Italian Literature* (Westport, CT: Greenwood Press, Publishers, 1960), 49.

9. Colin Manlove, *Christian Fantasy: From 1200 to the Present* (South Bend, IN: Notre Dame University Press, 1992), 22.

10. Ibid.

11. Ernest Hatch Wilkins, *A History of Italian Literature* (Cambridge, MA: Harvard University Press, 1978), 61. This edition was revised by Thomas G. Bergin.

12. Edward Moore, *Studies in Dante: The First Series* (New York: Haskell House Publishers, 1968), 4.

13. Ibid.

14. Dante, *Purgatory*, in *The Divine Comedy*, canto XI, line 97, quoted in John Bartlett, *Familiar Quotations* (Boston: Little, Brown and Company, 1937), 1021.

15. Manlove, *Christian Fantasy*, 21.

16. Dante, *The Divine Comedy*, 47.

17. Ibid.

18. Francis X. Newman, "St. Augustine's Three Visions and the Structure of the 'Commedia,'" *Modern Critical Views: Dante*, ed. Harold Bloom (New York: Chelsea House Publishers, 1986), 65.

19. Dante, *Inferno*, in *The Divine Comedy*, canto III, line 9, quoted in Bartlett, *Familiar Quotations*, 1020. Technically the line reads: "All hope abandon, ye who enter here." In another translation it reads: "No room for hope when you enter this place."

20. Ibid.
21. Dante, *The Divine Comedy*, 351.
22. Ibid., 365.
23. Ibid., 498–499.
24. Susan Gallagher and Roger Lundin, *Literature Through the Eyes of Faith* (San Francisco: Harper and Row, 1989), XVI.
25. Ibid.
26. Colin Manlove, *Christian Fantasy*, 25.
27. Wayne Martindale and Jerry Root, eds. *The Quotable Lewis* (Wheaton, IL: Tyndale House Publishers, 1989), 141.
28. Ibid., 142.
29. Wilbur L. Cross and Tucker Brooke, introduction to *The Yale Shakespeare: The Complete Works* (New York: Barnes and Noble Books, 1993), vii.
30. Among Elizabethan scholars, a debate rages as to whether William Shakespeare of Stratford-upon-Avon is the author of the body of works historically ascribed to him. There are at least two schools of thought here, and for now the jury is out. Whatever the outcome of that dispute, there is no doubt that the author of those plays, perhaps the greatest literature in the English language, *knew the Bible backward and forward!*
31. Allan Bloom, "Political Philosophy and Poetry," *Giants and Dwarfs: Essays 1960–1990* (New York: Simon and Schuster, 1990), 61.
32. Peter Milward, *Shakespeare's Religious Background* (Chicago: Loyola University Press, 1985), 87.
33. Peter Alexander, *Shakespeare's Life and Art* (Westport, CT: Greenwood Press, 1979), 228.
34. Naseeb Shaheen, *Biblical References in Shakespeare's Comedies* (Newark, DE: University of Delaware Press, 1993), 22.
35. Ibid.
36. Milward, *Shakespeare's Religious Background*, 86.
37. Shaheen, *Biblical References in Shakespeare's Comedies*, 26.
38. Philip Edwards, *Shakespeare: A Writer's Progress* (Oxford: Oxford University Press, 1986), 2. Emphasis mine.
39. Peter Milward, *Biblical References in Shakespeare's Great Tragedies* (Bloomington, IN: Indiana University Press, 1987), 2.
40. Milward, *Shakespeare's Religious Background*, 97.
41. S. Schoenbaum, *William Shakespeare: A Compact Documentary Life* (New York: Oxford University Press, 1977), 58.
42. Shakespeare, *Hamlet*, in *The Yale Shakespeare*, 984.
43. Milward, *Biblical Influences in Shakespeare's Great Tragedies*, 14–15.
44. Shakespeare, *Hamlet*, in *The Yale Shakespeare*, 995.
45. Milward, *Biblical Influences in Shakespeare's Great Tragedies*, 28.
46. Alexander, *Shakespeare's Life and Art*, 117.
47. Shakespeare, *Henry the Sixth*, in *The Yale Shakespeare*, 543.
48. Shaheen, *Biblical References in Shakespeare's Comedies*, 186.

49. Russell Fraser, *Shakespeare: The Later Years* (New York: Columbia University Press, 1992), 85.

50. Milward, *Shakespeare's Religious Background*, 103.

51. "NAF Study Reveals Shakespeare in Decline," *Inside Academia*, Fall 1996, vol. II, no. 1, 1.

52. Jonathan Yardley, "For English Departments, a Major Change," *The Washington Post*, 30 December 1996, D2.

53. F. W. Boreham, *A Temple of Topaz* (Philadelphia: The Judson Press, 1951), 219.

54. Ibid., 128.

55. Glaspey, *Great Books of the Christian Tradition*, 63.

56. Quoted in Douglas Bush, introduction to *The Complete Poetical Works of John Milton* (Boston: Houghton Mifflin company, 1965), xx.

57. Milton, *Paradise Lost*, in *The Complete Poetical Works*, 213–215.

58. Ibid., 218.

59. Coauthor Jerry Newcombe summarized a few choice portions of *Paradise Lost* in his book of Christian-oriented short stories entitled *The Moral of the Story*. The Milton selection is found in the category of "Pride" in Part II, stories centered on the Seven Deadly Sins.

60. Kerry M. Wood, Helen McDonnell, John Pfordresher, Mary Alice Fite, and Paul Lankford, *Classics in World Literature* (Glenview, IL: Scott, Foresman and Company, 1989), 500.

61. John Bunyan, *The Pilgrim's Progress* (Springdale, PA: Whitaker House, 1678, 1973), 5–6.

62. Herbert Lockyer, *The Man Who Changed the World* (Grand Rapids: Zondervan, 1966), 2:63.

63. J. D. Douglas, gen. ed., *The New International Dictionary of the Christian Church* (Grand Rapids: Zondervan, 1974, 1978), 167.

64. Roger L. Cox, *Between Earth and Heaven: Shakespeare, Dostoevsky, and the Meaning of Christian Tragedy* (New York: Holt, Rinehart and Winston, 1969), 123.

65. Geir Kjetsaa, *Fyodor Dostoevsky: A Writer's Life*, trans. Siri Hustvedt and David McDuff (New York: Viking Penguin, Inc., 1987), 8.

66. Joseph Frank and David Goldstein, eds. *Selected Letters of Fyodor Dostoevsky* (New Brunswick, NJ: Rutgers University Press, 1987), 47. It is interesting to note that when first imprisoned, Dostoevsky received three different books. Two of them were the Bible and Shakespeare, and in his letter to his brother he expresses tremendous gratitude for the Shakespeare, which he did not originally request.

67. Quoted in Kjetsaa, *Fyodor Dostoevsky*, 88.

68. Kjetsaa, *Fyodor Dostoevsky,* 99.

69. Frank and Goldstein, *Selected Letters of Fyodor Dostoevsky,* 450.

70. Alba Amoia, *Feodor Dostoevsky* (New York: The Continuum Publishing Company, 1993), 65.

71. Ibid.

72. Fyodor Dostoevsky, *Crime and Punishment*, trans. Constance Garnett (New York: Barnes and Noble Books, 1866, 1994), 449.
73. Kjetsaa, *Fyodor Dostoevsky*, 221.
74. Ibid. This quote was in its original form a complete sentence.
75. Quoted in Kjetsaa, *Fyodor Dostoevsky*, 221–222.
76. Kjetsaa, *Fyodor Dostoevsky*, 224.
77. Amoia, *Feodor Dostoevsky*, 125.
78. Cox, *Between Earth and Heaven*, 129–130.
79. Konstantin Mochulsky, *Dostoevsky: His Life and Work,* trans. Michael A. Minihan (Princeton: Princeton University Press, 1967), 4.
80. Ibid., 597.
81. Ibid., 599.
82. Cox, *Between Earth and Heaven*, 228.
83. Fyodor Dostoevsky, *The Brothers Karamazov*, trans. Constance Garnett (New York: Barnes and Noble Books, 1880, 1995), 3.
84. Robert L. Belknap, *The Genesis of The Brothers Karamazov: The Aesthetics, Ideology, and Psychology of Text Making* (Evanston, IL: Northwestern University Press, 1990), 19.
85. Ibid., 269.
86. Frank and Goldstein, *Selected Letters of Fyodor Dostoevsky,* 469–470.
87. Harold Bloom, introduction to *Modern Critical View: Miguel de Cervantes*, ed. Harold Bloom (New York: Chelsea House Publishers, 1987), 1.
88. Leo Spitzer, "Linguistic Perspectivism in the Don Quijote," *Modern Critical Views: Miguel de Cervantes*, 29.
89. Juan Bautista Avalle-Arce, "Reality, Realism, Literary Tradition," *Modern Critical Views: Miguel de Cervantes,* 148.
90. Durant, *The Age of Reason Begins,* 304.
91. Ibid.
92. Miguel de Cervantes, *Don Quixote* (New York: Mentor Books, 1957), 15.
93. Ibid., 16.
94. Durant, *The Age of Reason Begins,* 302.
95. Cervantes, *Don Quixote*, 241.
96. Ibid., 250.
97. Ibid., 432.
98. Durant, *The Age of Reason Begins,* 154.
99. Ibid., 154–156.
100. John Donne, "Death Be Not Proud," in *The Book of Virtues: A Treasure of Great Moral Stories* (New York: Simon and Schuster, 1993), 809.
101. Quoted in Durant, *The Age of Reason Begins*, 156.
102. See Evelyn Simpson, ed., *John Donne's Sermons on the Psalms and Gospels* (Berkeley, CA: University of California Press, 1963).
103 Glaspey, *Great Books of the Christian Tradition,* 68.
104. Quoted in Peter Ackroyd, *Dickens* (New York: HarperCollins, 1990), 504.

105. Ibid.
106. Quoted in Bennett, *The Book of Virtues*, 155.
107. Quoted in Bennett, *The Book of Virtues*, 156.
108. Charles Dickens, *A Tale of Two Cities* (New York: Collier Books, 1962), 19.
109. Ibid., 110.
110. Ibid., 138.
111. This quote comes from the transcript of an interview of Chris Mitchell by Jerry Newcombe for Coral Ridge Ministries TV, on the subject of C. S. Lewis, on location at the Marion E. Wade Center, Wheaton College, Wheaton, Illinois, 21 September 1995.
112. C. S. Lewis, *The Last Battle* (New York: Collier/Macmillan, 1970), 140–41.
113. C. S. Lewis, *Till We Have Faces* (Grand Rapids, MI: Wm. B. Eerdman, 1966), 279.
114. C. S. Lewis, *Mere Christianity* (New York: Macmillan Publishing Company, 1952), 124.
115. *Funk and Wagnalls New Encyclopedia* (New York: Funk and Wagnalls, Inc., 1979), 18:92.
116. Ibid.
117. Flannery O'Connor, "Novelist and Believer," *Religion and Modern Literature*, 71.
118. Ibid., 74.
119. Flannery O'Connor, "The River," *The Complete Stories* (New York: Farrar, Strauss and Giroux, 1982), 165.
120. Ibid.
121. See Glaspey, *Great Books of the Christian Tradition* or Beatrice Batson, *A Reader's Guide to Religious Literature* (Chicago: Moody Press, 1968).
122. See Newcombe, *The Moral of the Story*, 331–348.
123. Douglas, *The New International Dictionary of the Christian Church*, 979.
124. David Lyle Jeffrey, gen. ed., *A Dictionary of Biblical Tradition in English Literature* (Grand Rapids, MI: Wm. B Eerdman, 1992), 937–949, 953–957.
125. Ibid., xi.

Chapter 9: The Bible and Missions

1. Stephen Neill, *A History of Christian Missions* (New York: Penguin Books, 1964, 1977), 559.
2. Ibid., 207.
3. John Foxe, *Foxe's Book of Martyrs* (1563).
4. John Foxe, *Foxe's Book of Martyrs*, quoted in Newcombe, *The Moral of the Story*, 59.
5. Will Durant, *Caesar and Christ: A History of Roman Civilization and of Christianity from Their Beginnings to A.D. 325* (New York: Simon and Schuster, 1944), 652.

6. Tom Cahill, *How the Irish Saved Civilization: The Untold Story of Ireland's Heroic Role from the Fall of Rome to the Rise of Medieval Europe* (New York: Doubleday, 1995), 17.

7. Ibid., 11–31.

8. Ibid., 5.

9. Ibid., 3–4.

10. Ibid., 101–102.

11. A. Guggenberger, *A General History of the Christian Church*, vol. 1, *The Papacy and the Empire* (St. Louis: B. Herder, 1907), 98–99.

12. Quoted in Cahill, *How the Irish Saved Civilization,* 108.

13. Ibid.

14. Guggenberger, *A History of the Christian Church,* 99.

15. Cahill, *How the Irish Saved Civilization,* 116.

16. Quoted in Cahill, *How the Irish Saved Civilization,* 117–119.

17. Adam Loughridge, "Ireland," *The New International Dictionary of the Christian Church,* 515.

18. Adam Loughridge, "Columba," *The New International Dictionary of the Christian Church,* 241.

19. Ibid.

20. Neill, *A History of Christian Missions,* 112.

21. Quoted in William L. Shirer, *The Rise and Fall of the Third Reich: A History of Nazi Germany* (New York: Simon and Schuster, 1960), 101.

22. Neill, *A History of Christian Missions,* 75.

23. David Barrett, *Cosmos, Chaos, and Gospel: A Chronology of World Evangelization from Creation to New Creation* (Birmingham, AL: New Hope, 1990), 27.

24. Ibid.

25. Ibid., 28.

26. Barbara L. Faulkner, "Eastern Orthodox Church," Douglas, *The New International Dictionary of the Christian Church,* 323–324.

27. Neill, *A History of Christian Missions,* 177.

28. Ibid., 117.

29. Quoted in Neill, *A History of Christian Missions,* 117.

30. Neill, *A History of Christian Missions,* 153–166.

31. John D. Woodridge, gen. ed., *Great Leaders of the Christian Church* (Chicago: Moody Press, 1988), 329.

32. Neill, *A History of Christian Missions,* 156.

33. Ibid., 221.

34. See Allen W. Schattschneider, *Through Five Hundred Years: A Popular History of the Moravian Church* (Bethlehem, PA: Comenius Press, 1956).

35. Ibid., 262.

36. Robert Linder, "God's Extraordinary Plodder: William Carey," *Ambassadors for Christ: Distinguished Representatives of the Message Throughtout the World,* John D. Woodbridge, gen. ed. (Chicago: Moody Press, 1994), 23.

37. Neill, *A History of Christian Missions,* 265.

38. Quoted in *Ambassadors for Christ,* 20.
39. Quoted in W. G. Blaikie, *The Personal Life of David Livingstone* (London, 1880), 28.
40. Horace Walker, ed., *The Last Journals of David Livingstone in Central Africa* (London, 1874), 2:2.
41. Ibid., 2:182.
42. Tim Jeal, *Livingstone* (New York: G. P. Putnam's Sons, 1973), 336. From a letter from David Livingstone to R. Murchison, 1867, *National Archives in Rhodesia.*
43. Jeal, *Livingstone,* 337. This is a paraphrase of what Bennett said to Stanley.
44. *The Last Journals of David Livingstone,* 2:182.
45. Jeal, *Livingstone,* 366.
46. Quoted in Neill, *A History of Christian Missions,* 315.
47. David Barrett and Todd Johnson, *Our Globe and How to Reach It* (Birmingham, AL: New Hope, 1990), 54.
48. J. C. Pollock, *Hudson Taylor and Maria: Pioneers in China* (New York: McGraw-Hill Book Company, Inc., 1962), 170.
49. Quoted in *Ambassadors for Christ,* 160.
50. Harald Stene Dehlin, *Pionerer I Skjort [Pioneers in Skirts]* (Oslo, Norway: Norsk Luthersk Forlag A/S, 1985), 146. This passage was translated by Kirsti Sæbø Newcombe.
51. Dr. and Mrs. Howard Taylor, *Hudson Taylor's Spiritual Secret* (Chicago: Moody Press, 1989), 115.
52. Quoted in Pollock, *Hudson Taylor and Maria,* 140.
53. Alvyn Austin, "Missions Dream Team," *Christian History,* issue 52 (vol. XV, no. 4) 1996, 19.
54. Quoted in Taylor and Taylor, *Hudson Taylor's Spiritual Secret,* 201–202.
55. Transcript of an interview of Dr. David Barrett, conducted by Jerry Newcombe on location in Richmond, Virginia, for Coral Ridge Ministries—TV, 19 January 1996.
56. "The Miracles after Missions," an interview with Kim-Kwong Chan, *Christian History,* 43. Note that Chan's estimate of Christians in China is less than Barrett's. But Barrett has access to all sorts of databases from which he draws.
57. Quoted in Walter B. Knight, *Knight's Treasury of Illustrations* (Grand Rapids: Eerdmans, 1963), 203.
58. Transcript of Barrett interview.
59. *TIME,* 16 December 1996.
60. Arne Fjeldstad, "Christians on the Internet," an unpublished essay for a doctorate at Fuller Seminary, Pasadena, California, December 1996.
61. Charles R. Woodson, quoted in Doàn, *Speakers Sourcebook II,* 260.

Chapter 10: The Bible and Exploration

1. Carl Waldman and Alan Wexler, *Who Was Who in World Exploration* (New York: Facts on File, 1992), 231.

2. *Funk and Wagnalls New Encyclopedia* (Rand McNally and Company, 1983), 9:336.

3. Robin Hanbury-Tenison, *The Oxford Book of Exploration* (Oxford: Oxford University Press, 1993), 221.

4. John Eidsmoe, *Columbus and Cortez, Conquerors for Christ: The Controversy, the Conquest, the Mission, the Vision* (Green Forest, AR: New Leaf Press, 1992), 204.

5. *Ripley's Believe It or Not: Wonder Book of Strange Facts* (New York: The Universal Guild, Inc., 1957), 268.

6. Samuel P. Huntington, "The West Unique, Not Universal," *Foreign Affairs,* November/December 1996, 30.

7. Quoted in Ian Cameron, *Magellan and the First Circumnavigation of the World* (New York: Saturday Review Press, 1973), 215.

8. Quoted in Tim Joyner, *Magellan* (Camden, ME: International Marne, 1992), 299.

9. Cameron, *Magellan and the First Circumnavigation,* 96.

10. *Funk and Wagnalls New Encyclopedia* (1983), 16:321.

11. Joyner, *Magellan,* 185.

12. Quoted in Cameron, *Magellan and the First Circumnavigation,* 184.

13. Desmond Wilcox, *Ten Who Dared* (Boston: Little, Brown and Company, 1977), 14.

14. Quoted in *The World Almanac and Book of Facts 1997* (Mahwah, NJ: World Almanac Books, 1996), 511. This famous phrase comes from the Mayflower Compact.

15. *Encyclopedia Americana,* 73.

16. Waldman and Wexler, *Who Was Who in World Exploration,* 35.

17. Hanbury-Tenison, *The Oxford Book of Exploration,* 329.

18. *Great Adventures That Changed Our World: The World's Great Explorers—Their Triumphs and Tragedies* (Pleasantville, NY: The Reader's Digest Association, Inc., 1978), 95.

19. Wilcox, *Ten Who Dared,* 13.

20. Quoted in George Grant, *The Last Crusader: The Untold Story of Christopher Columbus* (Wheaton, IL: Crossway Books, 1992), 117.

21. Ibid.

22. Eidsmoe, *Columbus and Cortez,* 15.

23. Ibid., 16.

24. Quoted in Eidsmoe, *Columbus and Cortez,* 107.

25. Eidsmoe, *Columbus and Cortez,* 107.

26. Christopher Columbus, *Book of Prophecies,* trans. Kay Brigham (Fort Lauderdale: TSELF, Inc., 1992), 23. The quote is from Folios 5 and 6.

27. Ibid., 23–24.

28. The Roman Catholic Bible has a few extra books in the Old Testament known as the Apocrypha, which Protestants do not consider to be divinely inspired.

29. Columbus, *Book of Prophecies,* 178–179.

30. Ibid., 179.
31. Quoted in Eidsmoe, *Columbus and Cortez*, 90–91.
32. Quoted in Grant, *The Last Crusader*, 68.
33. Quoted in Eidsmoe, *Columbus and Cortez*, 85.
34. Ibid.
35. Ibid., 139.
36. *Great Adventures,* 164.
37. Waldman and Wexler, *Who Was Who in World Exploration,* 351.
38. Ibid.
39. Wilcox, *Ten Who Dared*, 87.
40. Ibid., 103.
41. *Great Adventures,* 247.
42. Ibid.
43. *Into the Unknown: The Story of Exploration* (Washington, DC: The National Geographic Society, 1987), 207.
44. Ibid., 209.
45. Ibid.
46. Ibid.
47. *Great Adventures,* 244.
48. Quoted in Hanbury-Tenison, *The Oxford Book of Exploration*, 180.
49. *Great Adventures,* 255.
50. Wilcox, *Ten Who Dared*, 215.
51. Ibid., 209.
52. David Nevin, introduction to *Ten Who Dared*, by Desmond Wilcox, 8.
53. Quoted in Neill, *A History of Christian Missions,* 126.
54. Wilcox, *Ten Who Dared*, 149, 154.
55. Bradford, *Of Plymouth Plantation: 1620–1647*, ed. Samuel Eliot Morison (New York: Alfred A. Knopf, Inc. 1952), 77.

Chapter 11: The Bible and Everyday Things

1. "Business leaders credit Bible," *International Religion Report*, 18 July 1990. This survey was conducted under the auspices of National College of Education, Evanston, Illinois. "Heads of 1,000 major American companies and presidents of 1,200 U.S. universities participated in the survey."
2. John Ayto, *Dictionary of Word Origins* (New York: Little, Brown and Company, 1990), 77.
3. Peter Gardella, *Innocent Ecstasy: How Christianity Gave America an Ethic of Sexual Pleasure* (New York: Oxford University Press, 1985), 44.
4. *Ripley's Believe It or Not!* 27th series (New York: Simon and Schuster, 1977), 159.
5. Tan, *Encyclopedia of 7700 Illustrations,* 478–479.
6. *Ripley's Believe It or Not!*, 159.
7. *Auntie Anne's Location Guide* (Gap, PA: Auntie Anne's Inc., 1995).
8. *Wonder Book of Strange Facts,* 444.

9. Ibid.

10. Walter Grab, *The French Revolution: The Beginning of Modern Democracy* (London: Bracken Books, 1989), 165, quoted in DeMar, *America's Christian History,* 89, 91.

11. Jess Stein, ed., *The Basic Everyday Encyclopedia* (New York: Random House, 1954), 87.

12. In *The Gates of Hell Shall Not Prevail* we explore seven pieces of evidence more striking and significant than the Sabbath shift for the bodily resurrection of Jesus Christ from the dead. See Chapter 2 of that book.

13. *The Basic Everyday Encyclopedia,* 87.

14. Ibid.

15. Ibid.

16. That Bible translation has caused many languages to be written down for the first time and that missionaries have sometimes created alphabets for the same reason is documented in *What If Jesus Had Never Been Born?,* 41–42.

17. James Harvey Robinson, *An Introduction to the History of Western Europe* (Boston: Ginn and Company, New Edition, 1934), 372.

18. Ibid., 373.

19. Will Durant, *The Reformation: A History of European Civilization from Wycliff to Calvin: 1300–1654, vol. 4 of The Story of Civilization* (New York: Simon and Schuster, 1957), 368–369.

20. *Carolingian* refers to the reign in eighth-, ninth-, and tenth-century France that was begun by Pepin the Short and that peaked under Charlemagne.

21. H. W. Janson and Joseph Kerman, *A History of Art and Music* (Englewood Cliffs, NJ: Prentice-Hall, Inc.), 51.

22. Ancient peoples of Northern Europe carved marks in stone using an alphabet called "runes." This was especially true in Scandinavia. These marks were used "mainly for inscriptions of a religious or magical nature." Stein, *The Basic Everyday Encyclopedia,* 455.

23. This quote can be found at the United Nations.

24. When Abraham Lincoln used this famous sentence, he knew that his hearers were biblically literate. Most of them knew that Jesus first spoke this memorable phrase. Today many Americans think the phrase originated with Lincoln.

25. Many people misquote this verse and say, "Money is the root of all evil." But that's not what the Bible teaches. It condemns the love and worship of money, not money per se.

26. Ayto, *Dictionary of Word Origins,* 58–59.

27. *Wonder Book of Strange Facts,* 464.

28. Ayto, *Dictionary of Word Origins,* 259.

29. R. F. Patterson, ed., *New Webster's Dictionary* (Miami: P. S. I. and Associates, 1993), 167.

30. Sometimes the names Ahab, Jezebel, or other wicked people of the Bible pop up, such as the rock group calling itself Judas Priest. But just the use

of the name in this context shows the anti-Christian nature of the band at
its outset.

31. Carnegie, *How to Win Friends and Influence People,* 79.
32. For example, the 1941 *Webster's Collegiate Dictionary* (Springfield, MA: G & C Merriam Co., Publishers) contains an appendix called "Pronouncing Vocabulary of Common English Christian Names."
33. *Encyclopedia of American Biography,* 1168.
34. Richard Moss, *Noah Webster* (Boston: Twayne Publishers, 1984), 104.
35. Oscar Handlin, *The History of the United States* (New York: Holt, Rinehart and Winston, 1967), 1:257.
36. Ibid., 1:393.
37. Moss, *Noah Webster,* 17.
38. Quoted in Moss, *Noah Webster,* 17.
39. *American Dictionary of the English Language* (San Francisco: Foundation for American Christian Education, 1995), 20. This edition is a facsimile of the first edition originally published in 1828. This quote is taken from a series of Webster's writings found at the front of this edition.
40. Moss, *Noah Webster,* 104.
41. Ibid.
42. Ibid.
43. *American Dictionary of the English Language.* Note: Webster's 1828 dictionary is without page numbers; the reference is to be found by the word itself.
44. Ibid.
45. Ibid.
46. Ibid.
47. Moss, *Noah Webster,* 115.
48. Ibid.
49. Millar, *The Rewriting of America's History,* 215.
50. *The New International Dictionary of the Christian Church,* 1067.
51. Ibid., 49.
52. Vergilius Ferm, *Pictorial History of Protestantism: A Panoramic View of Western Europe and the United States* (New York: Philosophical Library, 1957), 284.
53. Ayto, *Dictionary of Word Origins,* 98.
54. We covered this influence quite extensively in *What If Jesus Had Never Been Born?*
55. Charlie Chaplin, *My Autobiography* (New York: Simon and Schuster, 1964, 1996), 13.
56. Ibid.
57. See Kennedy and Newcombe, *The Gates of Hell Shall Not Prevail.*
58. Zig Ziglar, *See You at the Top* (Gretna, LA: Pelican Publishing Company, 1977), 18.
59. Jeffrey Satinover, *Homosexuality and the Politics of Truth* (Grand Rapids: Baker Books, 1996), 171.

60. Ann Rodgers-Melnick, "Secular trend sees AA's success falter," *The Washington Times*, 25 May 1996, reproduced from the *Pittsburgh Post-Gazette*.
61. Thomas Montalbo, "1924–1994: After 70 Years, Ralph Smedley's investment continues to provide dividends," *The Toastmaster*, 16.
62. Ibid., 17.
63. Ted Engstrom and R. Alec MacKenzie, *Managing Your Time: Practical Guidelines on the Effective Use of Time* (Grand Rapids: Zondervan, 1967, 1980), 89.
64. "Instruction Manual for Floor Clocks" (Zeeland, MI: Howard Miller Clock Company, undated, c. 1980s), 26.

Chapter 12: The Reliability of the Bible

1. John Shelby Spong, *Rescuing the Bible from Fundamentalism: A Bishop Rethinks the Meaning of Scripture* (New York: HarperCollins, 1991), 20–21.
2. Amazingly, Spong is discontent to become a new type of savior—one who will save the Bible from those naughty fundamentalists. No, he wants to do more than be a savior; he goes on to denigrate the Savior Himself! Spong writes:
   "There are passages in the Gospels that portray Jesus of Nazareth as narrow-minded, vindictive, and even hypocritical. Jesus exhorted people to love their enemies and to pray for their persecutors (Matt. 5:44) and never to call others by demeaning or hurtful names (5:22), yet he called his enemies a 'brood of snakes' (Matt. 12:34), 'sons of vipers' (Matt. 23:33), 'blind fools' (Matt. 23:17). . . . How divine is the message that says for your finite failings you will be cast into the outer darkness, where there will be weeping and gnashing of teeth (Matt. 25:30)?" Spong, 21.
   By the same token, Jesus said that we are not to judge, yet in the very same chapter (Matt. 7), He warns us to watch out for wolves in sheep's clothing. But how are we to know these wolves? Isn't that judging? Or maybe what people often commonly mistake for "judging" is different from what our Lord meant. We have to recognize that the best interpreter of Scripture is Scripture. We can best understand what the Bible means by understanding the total message of the Bible. When we do that, we won't be fooled by the wolves in sheep's clothing!
3. See Thomas J. Billitteri, "The Gospels: Was Jesus Misquoted?" *St. Petersburg Times*, 29 January 1994, A-1.
4. Ibid.
5. Robert Funk, Roy Hoover, and the Jesus Seminar, *The Five Gospels: What Did Jesus Really Say?* (New York: Macmillan, 1993).
6. If there are things in question in the Gospels, then they are all listed in the critical apparatus. But the people of the Jesus Seminar weren't dealing with the *manuscript* evidence, they were dealing with, frankly, their own feelings, and with extrabiblical writings (primarily, the Gospel of

Thomas—which the early Church decidedly rejected as Gnostic heresy). Material in the Gospels where manuscripts differ in spelling or in words deals with maybe 1 or 2 percent of the text; the New Testament documents are very reliable. Instead, what the Jesus Seminar has done is to get rid of 82 percent of the text! Textually, they stand on quicksand. An important book deals with the Jesus Seminar from an evangelical perspective. See *Jesus Under Fire: Modern Scholarship Reinvents the Historical Jesus*, ed. Michael J. Wilkins and J. P. Moreland (Grand Rapids: Zondervan, 1995).

7. Kennedy and Newcombe, *The Gates of Hell Shall Not Prevail.*
8. John R. W. Stott, *The Authority of the Bible* (Downers Grove, IL: Inter-Varsity Press, 1974), 7, 17.
9. Ibid., 29.
10. Quoted in Stott, *The Authority of the Bible*, 27.
11. Lee Strobel, quoted in D. James Kennedy, *The Bible: Fable, Fraud, or Fact?* (Fort Lauderdale: Coral Ridge Ministries—TV), 8 December 1996.
12. Lee Strobel, *Inside the Mind of Unchurched Harry and Mary: How to Reach Friends and Family Who Avoid God and the Church* (Grand Rapids: Zondervan, 1993), 36.
13. Mathematician Peter Stoner had his graduate students calculate what the odds would be of any one person fulfilling just eight of these prophecies. He found the chance was one in 10^{17}!—One in 100,000,000,000,000,000! Stoner gives an analogy:

      Take 10^{17} silver dollars and lay them on the face of Texas. They will cover all of the state two feet deep. Now mark one of these silver dollars and stir the whole mass thoroughly, all over the state. Blindfold a man and tell him that he can travel as far as he wishes, but he must pick up one silver dollar and say that this is the right one. What chance would he have of getting the right one? Just the same chance that the prophets would have had of writing these eight prophecies and having them all come true in any one man, from their day to the present time. Peter Stoner, *Science Speaks* (Chicago: Moody Press, 1963), 109.
14. Strobel, *Inside the Mind of Unchurched Harry and Mary,* 37.
15. Ibid.
16. Ibid. Author's emphasis.
17. Hefley, *What's So Great About the Bible,* 46.
18. Ibid., 45–47.
19. Werner Keller, *The Bible as History: A Confirmation of the Book of Books*, trans. William Neil (New York: Bantam Books, 1956, 1976), xxiii.
20. Josh McDowell, *Evidence That Demands a Verdict* (San Bernadino, CA: Campus Crusade for Christ, 1972), 68.
21. Ravi Zacharias, quoted in Kennedy, *The Bible: Fable, Fraud, or Fact?*
22. See Geisler and Nix, *A General Introduction to the Bible,* 385–408, and McDowell, *Evidence That Demands a Verdict,* 43–56.

23. Sir Federic G. Kenyon, *The Bible and Archaeology*, 288 f., quoted in Geisler and Nix, *A General Introduction to the Bible*, 405.
24. Dr. Randall Price, *Secrets of the Dead Sea Scrolls* (Eugene, OR: Harvest House, 1996), 126–127.
25. Ravi Zacharias, quoted in Kennedy, *The Bible: Fable, Fraud, or Fact?*

Chapter 13: The Central Message of the Bible

1. Quoted in Lawson, *Greatest Thoughts*, 81–82.
2. C. S. Lewis, *The Letters of C. S. Lewis,* 247, quoted *in The Quotable Lewis,* 72.
3. John Wenham, *The Goodness of God* (Downers Grove, IL: InterVarsity Press, 1974), 55.
4. Johnny Hart, "The Suffering Prince," *B.C.* comic strip. Copyright © 1997, Creators Syndicate. Used by permission.
5. Write to me at Coral Ridge Ministries, P.O. Box 40, Fort Lauderdale, FL 33308. Ask for *Beginning Again*.
6. Coauthor Jerry Newcombe highly recommends a book that has helped him. It is a three-year-through-the-Bible study guide, *Search the Scriptures*, ed. Alan Stibbs (Downers Grove, IL: InterVarsity Press, 1949, 1974).
7. If you are in the continental United States, my staff at Coral Ridge Ministries can assist you in finding a church in your area. Just write to me with the appropriate details at Coral Ridge Ministries, P.O. Box 40, Fort Lauderdale, FL 33308.
8. If you would like more information on how to share your faith, I suggest you get my book *Evangelism Explosion* (Wheaton, IL: Tyndale House Publishers, 1972). Or call the office of Evangelism Explosion III, International, at 954-491-610.

Chapter 14: The Vital Importance of the Bible

1. Bå Giertz, *Å Tro På Kristus [To Believe in Christ]* (Askim, Norway: Luther Forlag, 1973, 1976), 22–23. This passage was translated by Kirsti Sæbø Newcombe.
2. Smith, *Profitable Bible Study,* 81–82.
3. Ibid., 84.
4. This is the testimony of Robert Lewis of Fredericksburg, Virginia. Lewis was Washington's nephew. Lewis served as his uncle's "private secretary during the first part of his presidency." Furthermore, "Mr. Lewis lived with him on terms of intimacy, and had the best opportunity for observing his habits. Mr. Lewis said he had accidentally witnessed his private devotions in his library both morning and evening." William J. Johnson, *George Washington the Christian* (New York: Abingdon Press, 1919), 245–246.
5. *Life and Works of Abraham Lincoln,* 209.

6. Merrill C. Tenney, gen. ed., *The Zondervan Pictorial Bible Dictionary* (Grand Rapids: Zondervan, 1963).

7. Henry Halley, *Halley's Bible Handbook* (Grand Rapids: Zondervan, 1926, 1965).

8. Alan Stibbs, gen. ed., *Search the Scriptures*.

9. Quoted in John A. Hash, ed., *The Winning Way* (Murfreesboro, TN: Bible Pathway Ministries, undated), 2.

10. Frank Mead, *The Encyclopedia of Religious Quotations* (Old Tappan, NJ: Fleming H. Revell, 1965), 28.

11. Hash, *The Winning Way*, 2.

12. Ibid.

13. Vernon C. Grounds, *The Reason for Our Hope* (Chicago: Moody Press, 1945), 46.

14. Smith, *Profitable Bible Study*, 85.

15. Ibid., 84.

16. Mead, *The Encyclopedia of Religious Quotations*, 269.

17. The Luke account begins in 22:19.

18. *The New England Primer* (Boston: Edward Draper, 1777), reproduced by WallBuilder Press, 1991.

19. Sometimes, these sentences would be changed in different updated versions of the *Primer*, but they were always based on the Bible. For example, *B* is often found: "Heaven to find, the Bible mind." Sometimes it's, "Thy life to mend, this book attend," and it has a picture of an open Bible next to it.

Chapter 15: Final Thoughts

1. For more information about the Gideons, write to Gideons, International, 2900 Lebanon Road, Nashville, TN 37214.

2. Tan, *Encyclopedia of 7700 Illustrations*, 195.

3. Hilde M. Fjeldstad, speech given at the Lutheran Evangelical Free Church, Kristiansand, Norway, 13 February 1993. This passage was translated by Kirsti Sæbø Newcombe.

4. Quite frankly, the rise and fall of literacy are often directly related to the importance of the Bible. As we show in *What If Jesus Had Never Been Born?*, historically the whole idea of education for the masses came about so that people could read the Bible for themselves! See *What If Jesus Had Never Been Born?*, 41–49.

5. Charles Darwin, *On the Origin of Species by Means of Natural Selection or The Preservation of Favoured Races in the Struggle for Life* (London: John Murray, 1859).

6. Huntington, "The West Unique, Not Universal," 30.

7. Remarks made by Robert Bork at a public appearance and book signing for *Slouching Toward Gomorrah*, Liberties Bookstore, Boca Raton, Florida, October 1996.

8. A paraphrase of King James I, who said of the dissenting Protestants, "I will make them conform themselves, or else I will harry them out of the land, or else do worse!" Quoted in Robert Merrill Bartlett, *The Pilgrim Way* (Philadelphia: Pilgrim Press, 1971), 235.

9. Material included in this paragraph comes from *What If Jesus Had Never Been Born?*

10. Mead, *The Encyclopedia of Religious Quotations,* 26.

11. Ibid.

INDEX

ABOUT THE AUTHORS

D. James Kennedy, Ph.D., is the senior minister of Coral Ridge Presbyterian Church in Fort Lauderdale, Florida, and speaker for the international "Coral Ridge Hour" telecasts. He also serves as president of Evangelism Explosion International and chancellor of Knox Theological Seminary. The Kennedys have one daughter.

Jerry Newcombe is an award-winning producer for Coral Ridge Ministries, the television outreach of Coral Ridge Presbyterian Church. The Newcombes have two children, a daughter and a son.

LOOK FOR THESE OTHER BESTSELLING BOOKS BY D. JAMES KENNEDY AND JERRY NEWCOMBE

What if Jesus Had Never Been Born?

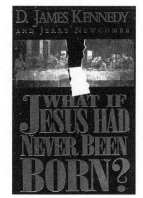

This book provides an extensive overview of the enormous impact Jesus Christ had on every aspect of human culture. Arranged topically, this book presents compelling, little-known historical facts and demonstrates the many benefits that would not exist if Christ had not lived.

0-7852-7178-3 • Trade Paperback • 288 pages

The Gates of Hell Shall Not Prevail

This hard-hitting book details the modern persecution of the church, giving readers hope for tomorrow and Christlike responses that can help make a difference.

0-7852-7177-5 • Trade Paperback • 304 pages